Whose Holy City?

Whose Holy City?

*Jerusalem and the Future
of Peace in the Middle East*

Colin Chapman

BakerBooks
Grand Rapids, Michigan

Text copyright © 2004 by Colin Chapman
Maps copyright by Tim Williams apart from maps
in chapter 8 copyright by Michael Younan

Published in the USA in 2005 by Baker Books
a division of Baker Publishing Group
P.O. Box 6287, Grand Rapids, MI 49516-6287
www.bakerbooks.com

Original edition published in English under the title *Whose Holy City? Jerusalem and the Israeli-Palestinian Conflict* by Lion Hudson plc, Oxford, England.

Printed in the United States of America

Library of Congress Cataloging-in-Publication Data
Chapman, Colin Gilbert.
Whose Holy City? : Jerusalem and the future of peace in the Middle East / Colin Chapman.
        p.   cm.
    Includes bibliographical references and index.
    ISBN 0-8010-6556-9 (pbk.)
    1. Jerusalem—History. 2. Jerusalem in the Bible. 3. Jerusalem in Judaism. 4. Jerusalem in Christianity. 5. Jerusalem in Islam. 6. Jerusalem—Politics and government—20th century. 7. Arab-Israeli conflict. I. Title.
DS109.9.C453 2005
956.94′42—dc22   2005004582

Introduction and Interview with Ari Shavit on pp. 216–19 by Benny Morris, published in Ha'aretz Daily Newspaper on 9 January 2004. Copyright © 2004 Ha'aretz Daily Newspaper Ltd. Used by permission.

Memorandum of the Patriarchs and Heads of the Christian Communities in Jerusalem on pp. 239–46 is taken from the appendix, pp. 236–40 of *Jerusalem: What Makes for Peace! A Palestinian Christian Contribution to Peacemaking*, edited by Naim Ateek, Cedar Duaybis, and Marla Schrader, Copyright © 1997 Melisende. Used by permission.

Unless otherwise indicated, Scripture is taken from the HOLY BIBLE, NEW INTERNATIONAL VERSION®. NIV®. Copyright © 1973, 1978, 1984 by International Bible Society. Used by permission of Zondervan. All rights reserved.

Contents

Acknowledgments

Since this book started life as a lecture at the Near East School of Theology in Beirut, I want to thank the Academic Dean, Dr George Sabra, for permission to use material from that lecture "Is 'Jerusalem' a Christian Cause?", which appeared in their *Theological Review*, No. XXIV/2, in 2003.

I am grateful to the YWCA in East Jerusalem for hospitality during a visit to Jerusalem in early 2004, and to the staff of World Vision who enabled me to meet people and see the situation on the ground, and in particular several sections of the "Security Wall."

I owe special thanks to Michael Younan of Good Shepherd Engineering in Bethlehem, who provided the maps for chapter 8 to illustrate what's been happening in and around Jerusalem since 1967.

I also would like to thank several friends who have read all or parts of the manuscript and made many valuable comments and criticisms. These include: Salim Munayyir, Peter Walker, Allyn Dhynes, Jonathan Kuttab, Lisa Loden, Phil and Ruth Jenson, Michael Dumper, Jane Clements and Jonathan Gorsky.

I'm specially grateful to my wife, Anne, who has kept the home fires burning and graciously put up with my travels and my preoccupation with writing during the last nine months. Since this book is fruit of our joint involvement in the Middle East over many years, it's a pleasure to be able to dedicate the book to her and to our three grown-up "children."

Introduction

The city of peace becomes a focus of conflict

"The most famous city in the world" is how Jerusalem was described by General Allenby— the general who entered it at the head of the British and Allied forces on 11 December 1917.[1] By liberating it from the Turks, they helped to set in motion the train of events which eventually led to the establishment of the state of Israel in 1948 and the intensification of the conflict between the Zionists and the Palestinians.

The very name "Jerusalem" is usually thought to mean "city of peace," and it is seen as a holy city by Jews, Christians and Muslims alike, who together make up about 55 per cent of the population of the world. It is holy for Jews because its Temple, destroyed in CE 70, was thought to be where the presence of God was located in a special way. It is holy for Christians mainly because this is where they believe Jesus Christ was crucified and raised from the dead. It is holy for Muslims largely because of the Prophet Muhammad's association with the city and because of its role in 1,400 years of Islamic history.

People of all three faiths therefore have their different reasons for regarding Jerusalem as holy and wanting to come from the ends of the earth to worship in their sacred sites. The Church of the Holy Sepulchre, also known as the Church of the Resurrection, has been a magnet drawing Christians ever since it was consecrated in CE 335.

9

Since Jews have prayed facing Jerusalem for at least twenty centuries, there was jubilation in 1967 when Israeli forces gained control of the Old City and access to the Western Wall. Many, however, have felt very uncomfortable with the fact that the most sacred Islamic sites had been built over the ruins of the Jewish Temple. This is what leads Meron Benvenisti, a former deputy mayor of Jerusalem, to say that "The explosive Temple Mount issue bears within it the potential to ignite a worldwide conflagration, and it is, therefore, a conflict of international importance... A bomb is waiting to go off in the heart of Jerusalem, its fuse burning with the fire of the religious fanaticism of Jew, Muslim and Christian."[2]

No one can deny, therefore, that people of all three faiths feel a kind of spiritual attachment to the city, and want to have unrestricted access to it. The really difficult question, however, is about sovereignty: who should control it politically and exercise sovereignty over it—and especially over the Old City where the major sites are situated? Do the Israelis have the sole right to hold on to it for ever? Or is it humanly possible to find a formula that would go some way towards satisfying *both* the nationalist *and* the religious aspirations of the majority of *both* the Israelis *and* the Palestinians, and of Jews, Christians and Muslims?

Conflict of course is not new in this city which, according to Amos Elon, has experienced "twenty ruinous sieges, two intervals of total destruction, eighteen reconstructions, and at least eleven transitions from one religion to another."[3] The most recent warfare was during the Six Day War in June 1967, when Israel captured the whole of Jerusalem and the West Bank. Having won the war, Israel resisted calls from the international community to withdraw from Jerusalem and the West Bank, and instead annexed Jerusalem, making it part of the state of Israel in all but name. In spite of a number of proposals and peace processes, the conflict has dragged on since 1967 and, since the outbreak of the Al-Aqsa Intifada in September 2000 and the building of the Separation Barrier/Security Fence, has seemed to be spiralling out of control.

Jerusalem is regarded by many as *a* key, if not *the* key, to the resolution of the conflict. Naim Ateek, for example, the Director of Sabeel, the Palestinian Liberation Theology Center in Jerusalem, believes that "Jerusalem has become a microcosm of the whole conflict. Both Palestinians and Israelis consider Jerusalem to be the heart of the conflict. . . ."[4] The reason for this claim is that most of the issues in the overall conflict between Israel and the Palestinians are brought clearly and sharply into focus in what has been happening in and around the city. If you understand what has been happening in Jerusalem, you understand what has been happening between Israel and the Palestinians since 1967. If Jerusalem, therefore, perhaps the hardest question of all, could be addressed and resolved in a way that is acceptable to the majority on both sides, it might perhaps point the way to a resolution of the whole conflict. This is one of the biggest nettles that needs to be grasped.

But if the Jerusalem question is so crucial, why hasn't it been addressed more adequately before now? Palestinians have repeatedly pleaded for the subject to be put on the agenda at peace negotiations, but Israel, with support from the USA, has frequently refused to allow it to be discussed. The most generous explanation of this constant postponement is that the issues are so complex and sensitive that they can only be addressed at the end of a long process of negotiation carried on in an atmosphere of peace and co-operation. Another possible explanation is that Israel has the upper hand and has not therefore been in a hurry to make a permanent peace with the Palestinians. It has frequently concentrated on creating facts on the ground in and around Jerusalem, knowing that the longer it can postpone discussion of Jerusalem, the greater the chances of influencing—if not actually prejudging—any agreements about sovereignty and borders that might eventually be made in future negotiations.

What makes the subject so difficult and complex is that politics and religion are very closely intertwined. "In the history of Jerusalem," says Amos Elon, "politics and religion have always overlapped. . . . In Jerusalem, the main issue is religious and political . . . everything ultimately becomes political—that is to say, adversarial."[5] Politicians and historians can often be very impatient with religion and mythology of all kinds, while the religious do not often want to get immersed in the details of history or the grey areas of politics. What is needed therefore is an approach which addresses *both* the history and the politics *and* the religion and theology at the same time.

The historians will want to ask, among other things, who came first, and who are all the different groups and religions that have arrived at a later stage. The political scientists will be concerned about the power equation at the present time, and will want to understand the stages by which Jerusalem has developed and is still developing today. Students of religion will start with the recognition that, in the words of Karen Armstrong, "devotion to a holy place or a holy city is a near universal phenomenon,"[6] and will try to put themselves into the shoes of all the different kinds of Jews, Christians and Muslims who have had such different and conflicting visions of what the city is meant to be. People of faith may even be so bold as to wonder whether, since religion has been a major part of the problem, it might also become part of the solution.

The ten chapters that follow adopt a roughly chronological approach, tracing the history of Jerusalem through the various stages of its history, noting at every stage how politics and religion are inter-related, and how issues that have raised their heads in the past are relevant even today. Thus we begin with the earliest evidence of occupation on the site and trace the history of Jerusalem from the time of Abraham until the end of the Old Testament period. We note in particular the significance of the First Temple built by Solomon and the Second built by Herod, noting how people thought about them and what actually happened to these buildings (Chapter 1).

We then turn to ask how Jesus understood traditional Jewish ideas about Jerusalem and its Temple, and how his death and resurrection in the city affected his disciples" thinking about the city. The writings of the New Testament suggest that the first Christians—both Jewish and Gentile—followed the lead of Jesus in offering a radical re-interpretation of Jewish ideas (Chapter 2).

The fourth century marked the beginning of a completely new phase in Jerusalem's history, when Constantine sought to create a Christian Empire, making Palestine into a "Holy Land" and Jerusalem into a "Holy City." Although this period lasted only about 300 years, these same attitudes have lived on, and there are other examples—notably in the Crusades—of Christians seeking to dominate the city and co-opt it for Christianity (Chapter 3).

While Judaism had its roots in the Old Testament, it began to develop in significantly new directions after the destruction of the

Temple in CE 70 and the banishing of Jews from Jerusalem in CE 135. The Jewish people in exile learned how to adapt to the loss of the Temple; but Jerusalem continued to be a major focus in their prayers and their dreams. Although some of these dreams have been realized since 1948 and 1967, Jews today do not all share the same views about Jerusalem and its Temple (Chapter 4).

The Islamic period begins in CE 638 with the surrender of the city by the Christian patriarch to the caliph Umar. From this time on, Jerusalem plays a significant role in Islamic belief and history, demonstrating the way Islam is believed to have superseded both Judaism and Christianity. This background is important for helping us to understand the Islamic dimension of the Palestinian national movement at the present time (Chapter 5).

Although the roots of Christian Zionism go back many centuries, in its modern form it began to develop soon after the beginning of the nineteenth century, and therefore pre-dates the start of the Zionist movement at the end of the century. How do these Christians interpret the Bible and understand the future? Why do they not only support the state of Israel in all that it does but also believe that Jerusalem will—in the not-too-distant future—play a very significant role in the way the world will end (Chapter 6)?

We then trace the place of Jerusalem in the minds of Zionist Jews from the beginning of the Zionist movement to the establishment of the Jewish state in 1948, and then on to the Six Day War in June 1967. Starting from a situation in which Jerusalem played little or no part in the thinking of Zionists, Jerusalem was declared in 1949 to be Israel's capital, and then in 1967, to the surprise and delight of Jews all over the world, the whole city was taken over and turned into a united city (Chapter 7).

The next chapter traces the various stages by which successive Israeli governments have established their sovereignty in and around Jerusalem, creating new settlements and roads which have transformed the geography and demography of the city and provoked intense opposition from the Palestinians (Chapter 8).

When the subject of Jerusalem has been on the agenda in formal or informal discussions and negotiations, what are the different proposals that have been put forward by the two sides or by outside observers? Should Israel maintain exclusive sovereignty over the city? Could there be any kind of shared sovereignty that enables both sides to feel that their claims and aspirations are respected (Chapter 9)?

There is little hope of negotiations over Jerusalem even being started, however, unless there are some basic changes in the attitudes and policies not only of the two main parties but also of all the outside parties. What are some of the pre-conditions for serious negotiation and peacemaking (Chapter 10)?

This book builds on an earlier book, *Whose Promised Land?*, which was first published in 1983 and had its fourth revision in 2002.[7] That book covers the history of the conflict from the 1880s to 2002 and deals with the biblical arguments about the interpretation of the land and other political and religious issues related to the conflict.

It may seem at times that an outsider is meddling in other people's quarrels and therefore falling into the trap pointed out in the Book of Proverbs: "Like one who seizes a dog by the ears is a passer-by who meddles in a quarrel not his own" (Proverbs 26:17). But because of the nature of Jerusalem—as not just *a* holy city but *the* holy city par excellence—the world can no longer wash its hands as if the quarrel is not its own. If outsiders have contributed so much to the problem, and if the two main protagonists left to themselves are not able to make peace, it may be that, in the words of Kenneth Cragg, "both Israel and the Arabs are in urgent need of perspectives on themselves from outside themselves."[8]

People of all three faiths throughout the world probably want the two main parties to find a way of sharing Jerusalem, a way that enables them to feel that Jerusalem belongs to them and that they belong to Jerusalem. So this contribution to the debate is offered in response to the anguished cry of the Prophet Jeremiah, "Who will have pity on you, O Jerusalem? Who will mourn for you? Who will stop to ask how you are?" (Jeremiah 15:5). Its purpose is to stimulate people of all faiths—and of none—to "pray for the peace of Jerusalem" and to say "peace be within you" (Psalm 122:6–8).

1
Jerusalem in the Old Testament

*A fortress and a pagan shrine
become part of a bigger story*

*"… the Lord, the God of Israel, has granted rest to his people and
has come to dwell in Jerusalem for ever…"*
1 Chronicles 23:25

*"But will God really dwell on earth? The heavens, even the highest
heaven, cannot contain you. How much less this temple I have
built!"*
Solomon's prayer at the dedication of the Temple, 1 Kings 8:27

*"Great is the Lord, and most worthy of praise, in the city of our God,
his holy mountain. It is beautiful in its loftiness, the joy of the whole
earth."*
Psalm 48:1–2

*"You who call on the Lord, give yourselves no rest, and give him
no rest till he establishes Jerusalem and makes her the praise of the
earth."*
Isaiah 62:6–7

*"This is what the Lord says: 'I will return to Zion and dwell in
Jerusalem. Then Jerusalem will be called the City of Truth, and the
mountain of the Lord Almighty will be called the Holy Mountain.'"*
Zechariah 8:3

"… the Lord will rebuild Zion and appear in his glory."
Psalm 102:16

It was not the most obvious place that anyone would choose for a capital city! It was on a land route running north to south in the hill country, but not on a major trade route. It was not on a river or a coast providing a natural harbour, and had limited supplies of water from a spring. Its rocky soil provided little land for agriculture, and it was on the edge of an area of desert. How is it, therefore, that this became the site of Jerusalem?

Earliest evidence of occupation

The earliest evidence of some kind of occupation on Ophel, the name of the ridge to the south of the later Temple area in Jerusalem, comes from around 3200–2800 BCE, while the earliest evidence of permanent settlement comes from around 1900–1800 BCE. The first recorded mention of the place comes in the Egyptian Execration Texts (c. 2000–1800 BCE), where it is mentioned in a list of places in Asia which are enemies of the Egyptian pharaohs.

The name then appears in two of the Amarna letters dated around 1350 BCE, in which the vassal king of Gath on the coast of Palestine accuses another vassal king, the king of Jerusalem, of disloyalty to the Egyptian pharaoh. Five of the other Amarna letters are from the king of Jerusalem, Abdu-Heba, in which he declares his loyalty to the pharaoh, Akhnaton, accuses others of disloyalty and pleads with the pharaoh to send military help. It is interesting that he appeals to Akhnaton by saying, "Behold the king (Akhnaton) has set his name in the land of Jerusalem for ever'—an expression which, as we shall soon see, was later used to speak about Yahweh's relationship to Jerusalem.

In several of these sources the name appears as "Urusalim," probably meaning "Foundation of the god Shalem." The first part of the name, uru, seems to be derived from a Hebrew root, yarah, meaning "to throw" or "to shoot," but when used in another verse in the Old Testament (Job 38:6), it seems to mean "to lay a foundation." Salem is known from texts discovered at Ugarit on the north Syrian coast, where it is the name of a god associated with another god named Shahar, and both are thought to be descended from El, the Canaanite High God. The name "Urusalim" must therefore have meant something like "founded by Salem," indicating that Salem was the main deity recognized there.

The Patriarchs

There is a possible reference to Jerusalem in the book of Genesis in the story of Melchizedek, a mysterious figure who is described as the priest-king of Salem, and who comes to meet Abraham after he has defeated an alliance of kings and rescued his nephew Lot:

> "Then Melchizedek king of Salem brought out bread and wine. He was priest of God Most High, and he blessed Abram, saying, 'Blessed be Abram by God Most High, Creator of heaven and earth. And blessed be God Most High, who delivered your enemies into your hand.' Then Abram gave him a tenth of everything" (Genesis 14:18–20).

Although the identification is not suggested in the text itself, Salem was identified in later Jewish tradition with Jerusalem, indicating the intention, as Naim Ateek suggests, "to cement the association of the holiness of Jerusalem with Abram the patriarch of the people."[1] Unlike the king of Sodom, however, who came out at the same time to meet Abraham but asked to keep all the people whom Abraham had rescued (Genesis 14:17, 22–24), Melchizedek demands nothing and gives Abraham both food and drink. He also gives him a blessing in the name of "God Most High," creator of the universe. Commenting on the attitude towards the Canaanite inhabitants of Salem that is implied in this passage, Karen Armstrong points out that "The story... shows Abraham responding with courtesy to the present incumbents of the city, offering Melchizedek a tithe of his booty as a mark of homage, and accepting the blessing of a foreign god... the story shows respect for the previous inhabitants of Jerusalem and reverence for their traditions."[2]

Another possible reference to the place comes in the story of Abraham being called to offer his son as a sacrifice. Abraham is summoned by God with the words: "Take your son, your only son, Isaac, whom you love, and go to the region of Moriah. Sacrifice him there as a burnt offering on one of the mountains I will tell you about" (Genesis 22:2). Although the text of Genesis itself does not identify Mount Moriah as the site of the later Temple, the connection was made later by the author of 2 Chronicles when he wrote: "Then Solomon began to build the temple of the Lord in Jerusalem on Mount Moriah..." (2 Chronicles 3:1).

Another place that is mentioned in the Genesis account, Hebron, is important for our understanding of the present situation in the country. When Sarah dies, Abraham wants to purchase a piece of land in which to bury her, and enters into negotiation with the Hittites who live there. Although offered the use of the best of the local tombs, Abraham insists on purchasing his own plot of land and paying the full price for it. The chapter ends with what sound like words taken from a written contract: "So Ephron's field in Machpelah near Mamre—both the field and the cave in it, and all the trees within the borders of the field—was legally made over to Abraham as his property in the presence of all the Hittites who had come to the gate of the city... So the field and the cave in it were legally made over to Abraham by the Hittites as a burial site" (Genesis 23:17–20). Abraham buries Sarah in this cave, and when he dies, his sons Ishmael and Isaac are both present when he is buried in the same cave (Genesis 25:7–10). The traditional site of this cave is in Hebron, about forty-five miles south of Jerusalem. Since Abraham plays such an important role both for the Jews and for Muslims, it is understandable that the tombs of Abraham and Sarah have become very important holy sites for people of both faiths.

The conquest

Jerusalem is mentioned as one of the cities that were captured by Joshua during his conquest of the hill country. Its king, Adoni-Zedek, was killed along with four other kings, and their bodies were hung on five trees (Joshua 10:1, 22–26). But later references to Jerusalem in Joshua and the following book, Judges, suggest that the inhabitants of Jerusalem were not completely defeated or banished: "Judah could not dislodge the Jebusites, who were living in Jerusalem; to this day the Jebusites live there with the people of Judah" (Joshua 15:63). In one reference the place is called "the Jebusite city (that

is, Jerusalem)" (Joshua 18:28), and in another "Jebus (that is, Jerusalem)" (Judges 19:10). Judges speaks of another later attack on
Jerusalem: "The men of Judah attacked Jerusalem also and took it.
They put the city to the sword and set it on fire" (Judges 1:8). When
all these references to Jerusalem are put together, it looks as if the
conquest of the land was neither sudden nor complete. It also seems
that the population remained mixed for some time and that it was
not occupied exclusively by the children of Israel.

In view of all the claims that have been made in recent years for
exclusive sovereignty over Jerusalem, it may be important to note
the situation that existed before the conquest. Palestinian Arabs
today ask why Jews in their claims to the city only go back to the
thirteenth century BCE and completely disregard those who lived in
the place for centuries before this. Naim Ateek, for example, wants
people to recognize *all* the different races and religions that have
occupied Jerusalem:

> "A Palestinian theology of Jerusalem must necessarily take into con-
> sideration those salient points that characterised this city, its evolution
> and development since the time of the Canaanites. In other words,
> any theological reflection on the city of Jerusalem must consider a
> cumulative history that spans four millennia. Over this long period of
> time, Jerusalem was impacted by all the civilisations that have come
> to it and gone. . . . They are all equally her children. Jerusalem, at
> the end of the twentieth century, offers us itself as the cumulative
> sum of all its historic past. It presents us with a rich human mosaic
> that has taken thousands of years to create. A theology of Jerusalem,
> therefore, cannot escape taking into consideration all that made Je-
> rusalem what it is today."[3]

David and Solomon

It was not until the time of David that Jerusalem began to play an
important role in the history of the children of Israel, and it did so
initially for political reasons. When David first became king, he was
living in Hebron (2 Samuel 5:1–5), but wanted to move his capital
north to Jerusalem because it had a more central position in the hill
country, and because it was on the border between the two southern

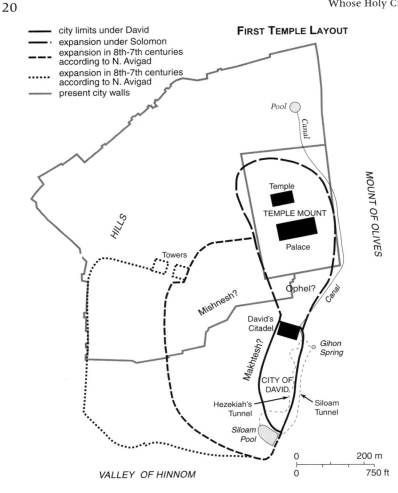

FIRST TEMPLE LAYOUT

- city limits under David
- expansion under Solomon
- expansion in 8th-7th centuries according to N. Avigad
- expansion in 8th-7th centuries according to N. Avigad
- present city walls

tribes of Judah and Benjamin and the northern tribes, and therefore not associated with either of them. Jerusalem was therefore chosen to make a political point and to promote the unification of the tribes, and Jewish and Muslim writers are united in noting the significance of this. Meron Benvenisti, for example, says that "In all likelihood, the very establishment of Jerusalem was itself an act of political planning";[4] and Zaki Badawi writes that because of its location it could "be a place of mediation and peace between the warring factions who had disputed control of the land."[5]

The author of 2 Samuel describes David's capture of Jerusalem, which probably took place around the year 1000 BCE, in this way: "The king and his men marched to Jerusalem to attack the Jebusites, who lived there... David captured the fortress of Zion, the City of David. On that day, David said, 'Anyone who conquers the Jebusites will have to use the water-shaft to reach those "lame and blind" who are David's enemies...'" (2 Samuel 5:6–8). The name "Zion" is related to the word *ziya*, meaning "parched desert," and therefore probably refers to the dryness of the area. It originally referred to the fortress on Mount Ophel to the south of the later Temple, but came to be used as an alternative name for the whole city of Jerusalem.

It seems then that the capture was completed with the minimum of fighting and that there was no slaughter of the Jebusite inhabitants. The story continues: "David then took up residence in the fortress and called it the City of David. He built up the area around it, from the supporting terraces inward. And he became more and more powerful, because the Lord God Almighty was with him" (2 Samuel 5:9–10). David's growing power is demonstrated by the fact that Hiram, king of Tyre, "sent messengers to David, along with cedar logs and carpenters and stonemasons, and they built a palace for David. And David knew that the Lord had established him as king over Israel and had exalted his kingdom for the sake of his people Israel" (2 Samuel 5:11–12).

The following chapter describes David bringing the ark of the covenant to give it a more permanent resting place in Jerusalem (2 Samuel 6:1–23). The ark was a chest that contained the two tablets of the law and other reminders of the period spent in the wilderness, and had first been placed in the Tent of Meeting. Since the ark was a visible reminder of the Exodus and the wilderness period, Jerusalem thus became the natural place in which the people remembered their past history and in particular the covenant that God had made with them at Mount Sinai. From these basic ideas connecting Mount Sinai with Mount Zion, it is possible to see how the idea developed that Zion/Jerusalem had been chosen by God for a special purpose.

After building his palace, David wanted to go on to build a temple. The Chronicler, however, gives a reason why David did not complete the task himself but only made preparations for his son Solomon to build it:

> David said to Solomon: "My son, I had it in my heart to build a house for the Name of the Lord my God. But this word of the Lord came to me: 'You have shed much blood and have fought many wars. You are not to build a house for my Name, because you have shed much blood on the earth in my sight. But you will have a son who will be a man of peace and rest, and I will give him rest from all his enemies on every side. His name will be Solomon, and I will grant Israel peace and quiet during his reign. He is the one who will build a house for my Name. He will be my son, and I will be his father. And I will establish the throne of his kingdom over Israel for ever'" (1 Chronicles 22:7–10).

The fact that the name "Solomon" (*shlomo*) is linked to the word "peace" (*shalom*), draws attention to the feeling often expressed in the Old Testament that Jerusalem (and in particular the Temple) was intended to be a place of peace. While David's wars may have been regarded as necessary, it must have seemed more appropriate that the Temple, a symbol of God's presence among his people, should be built by a man of peace rather than a man of war. Perhaps it is this same instinct that is expressed later in the condemnation of the evil king Manasseh who "filled Jerusalem with innocent blood, and the Lord was not willing to forgive" (2 Kings 24:4).

The rationale for the Temple

The choice of the site for the building of the Temple is traced by the writer of Kings to a prophet named Gad, who, during a time of severe plague, instructs David to "build an altar to the Lord on the threshing-floor of Araunah the Jebusite." When David comes to the threshing-floor just to the north of the royal city, Araunah welcomes him and offers both the animals and the wood for making the sacrifice. Like Abraham over the purchase of the cave in Hebron, however, David insists on buying the threshing-floor and paying the full price for it: "No, I insist on paying you for it. I will not sacrifice to the Lord my God burnt offerings that cost me nothing" (2 Samuel 24:18–25). This story was used after the capture of Jerusalem in 1967 by the

Israeli Minister of Religious Affairs, Zarach Warhaftig, to prove that Jews have had a valid title to the Temple Mount for centuries. When pressed in an interview with the question, "Are you saying that the Temple Mount... is Jewish property even today?," he replied, "Yes, (it was) acquired in more than one sense. Generations have shed blood in order to make the Land of Israel ours; and the full price was paid (by David) in money as well."[6] Many Jews today, it seems, have no hesitation in making such clear connections between the biblical text and the present situation.

Is there any significance in the fact that David offered this sacrifice to Yahweh on a threshing-floor? It has been suggested by many that a prominent rocky place of this kind on the edge of the town could well have been the site of a Canaanite holy place. In more recent centuries, churches have been built all over the Middle East and Europe on hills which must have been sites of pagan worship. If this, therefore, is part of the background to the choice of the Temple site, David may have been wanting to demonstrate that Yahweh, the God of Israel, was more powerful than the traditional Canaanite gods.

It must be reflections of this kind that lead the Israeli Jewish writer Gershom Gorenberg to comment: "If Jerusalem wasn't already holy, it's hard to understand why a city stood there. It's on the edge of a desert; the soil is rocky; the sole spring is grade C; the trade routes cross to the north. You wouldn't come here for gold, wheat or spices. Only to stand at the gate of heaven."[7] Similarly Amos Elon speaks of "the recycling of old holy places for new faiths" and points to the principle that "sanctity is always contagious and is passed on from one creed to the next. New creeds invariably take over the holy places of the old."[8] While this is certainly suggested by the history of religion, for the writers of the Old Testament, holiness is *not* innate in particular places, but is seen as the result of a special act of God.

The pattern of the Temple that Solomon built is very similar to that of Canaanite temples of the same period, with three distinct sections. The cedar wood came from Tyre in Phoenicia, and the builders and craftsmen provided by Hiram, king of Tyre, would have been Phoenicians. But if the construction of the Temple had many similarities to Canaanite temples, there are some significant new ideas that inform the rationale of the Temple in Jerusalem.

So while there is some continuity with traditional religious ideas, the Temple begins to be part of the bigger story that underlies the whole of the Old Testament. Solomon's prayer at the dedication of the Temple introduces some of these new ideas associated with the Temple:

> "But will God really dwell on earth? The heavens, even the highest heaven, cannot contain you. How much less this temple I have built! Yet give attention to your servant's prayer and his plea for mercy, O Lord my God. Hear the cry and the prayer that your servant is praying in your presence this day. May your eyes be open towards this temple night and day, this place of which you said, 'My Name shall be there,' so that you will hear the prayer your servant prays towards this place. Hear the supplication of your servant and of your people Israel when they pray towards this place. Hear from heaven, your dwelling place, and when you hear, forgive" (1 Kings 8:27–30).

The idea of Yahweh, the God of Israel, "putting his Name" in the Temple thus becomes one of the most important ideas associated with the Temple, and is expressed in these words of Moses addressing the people before the conquest of the land:

> "You must not worship the Lord your God in their way. But you are to seek the place the Lord your God will choose from among all your tribes to put his Name there for his dwelling. To that place you must go; there bring your burnt offerings and sacrifices, your tithes and special gifts, what you have vowed to give and your freewill offerings. . . . There, in the presence of the Lord your God, you and your families shall eat and shall rejoice in everything you have put your hand to, because the Lord your God has blessed you. . . . Then to the place the Lord your God will choose as a dwelling for his Name—there you are to bring everything I command you: your burnt offerings and sacrifices..." (Deuteronomy 12:4–11).

With all their attachment to Jerusalem, the people are not to feel that it is they who have chosen this as their capital. Rather it is to be seen as "the place the Lord your God will choose," since he has chosen it "to put his Name there for his dwelling." Because of the Temple, Jerusalem as a whole comes to be thought of as the place where God wants to dwell among his people: "the Lord, the God of Israel, has granted rest to his people and has come to dwell in Jerusalem for ever..." (1 Chronicles 23:25). Jerusalem is "the city the Lord had chosen out of all the tribes of Israel in which to put his Name" (1 Kings 14:21). The root of the word "dwell" in Hebrew is *shakan*, and from it is derived the word *Shekinah*, which was used later by the Jews as a way of speaking about the glory of God and even as a name for God.

The choice of Jerusalem as the site of the Temple is therefore to be seen as something that depends ultimately on the inscrutable will of God working in and through human beings. The idea that Yahweh wants to "put his name there" may have been originally little more than a metaphor about a town and its patron deity. But now it is beginning to be more than a metaphor, and to indicate something about the deeper intentions of God in relation to this people and the world.

Decline leading to destruction

When, after the death of Solomon, the northern kingdom of Israel broke away from the southern kingdom, Jerusalem became the capital of only the southern kingdom of Judah. Peter Walker points out the irony in this change in the status of Jerusalem: "The city designed to bring unity now pointed instead to Israel's division."[9] The godly king Josiah made a deliberate attempt around 622 BCE to discourage worship at local shrines and to make the Temple the centre and focus of all the worship of the southern kingdom. After this, however, came a succession of kings most of whom presided over a sharp decline in the worship and moral standards of the community. From the perspective of the writers of the Old Testament, such radical departure from the ways of Yahweh had to result in judgment. So when in 586 BCE the Babylonians captured Jerusalem, the Temple was destroyed and the ark of the covenant seems to have disappeared, never to be found again. The cream of the population were taken into exile in Babylon, where they remained for the following fifty years. The words of Lamentations, traditionally attributed to Jeremiah, describe the devastation of the

city and came to be used for many centuries by Jews who were
mourning the loss of the Temple:

> "How deserted lies the city, once so full of people!
> How like a widow is she, who once was great among the nations!
> She who was queen among the provinces has now become a slave. . . .
> All who pass your way clap their hands at you;
> They scoff and shake their heads at the Daughter of Jerusalem:
> 'Is this the city that was called the perfection of beauty,
> the joy of the whole earth?'" (Lamentations 1:1; 2:15).

Prophetic interpretations of the fall of Jerusalem

The destruction of the Temple and the exile in Babylon create a
profound crisis of faith for the people. It seems to Israel's enemies
and those who do not understand Yahweh's demands for justice,
that he cannot protect the temple in which he is supposed to live,
and has broken his covenant with his people. The task of explaining
these tragic events falls to the prophets, who explain that God is
judging the people both for the degeneration of their worship and
for the decline of moral standards in society. Other foreign gods are
worshipped alongside Yahweh; the poor are being oppressed; there is
no justice in the courts and the leaders of the community are corrupt.
Since Yahweh has called them to worship in new ways and to follow
higher standards in social life than their neighbours, departing from
these standards has inevitably invited divine judgment.

The three major prophets have a great deal to say about Jerusalem.
Jeremiah, for example, tries to explain in greater detail why the
unthinkable has happened: "Say to them, 'This is what the Lord
says: If you do not listen to me and follow my law, which I have
set before you, and if you do not listen to the words of my servants
the prophets, whom I have sent to you again and again (though
you have not listened), then I will make this house like Shiloh and
this city an object of cursing among all the nations of the earth'"
(Jeremiah 26:4–6).

Their conviction that God has chosen Jerusalem and the Temple
and given them a special status has led them to believe that Jerusalem

and the Temple are inviolable; God is bound to protect the place where he has "put his Name." So when the people protest, "Is the Lord not in Zion? Is her King no longer there?" God's answer through the prophet is: "Why have they provoked me to anger with images, with their worthless foreign idols?" (Jeremiah 8:19). Jeremiah is insistent that the presence of the Temple is no guarantee of its survival and of the protection of Jerusalem:

> "Hear the word of the Lord, all you people of Judah who come through these gates to worship the Lord. This is what the Lord Almighty, the God of Israel, says: Reform your ways and your actions, and I will let you live in this place. Do not trust in deceptive words and say, 'This is the temple of the Lord, the temple of the Lord, the temple of the Lord!' If you really change your ways and your actions and deal with each other justly, if you do not oppress the alien, the fatherless or the widow and do not shed innocent blood in this place, and if you do not follow other gods to your own harm, then I will let you live in this place, in the land I gave to your forefathers for ever and ever. But look, you are trusting in deceptive words that are worthless" (Jeremiah 7:2–8).

His message therefore, in the words of Naim Ateek, is that "the moral and ethical demands of God have priority over the sacredness of the place, even if that place were the temple itself."[10] He has to tell the people that God's anger is directed not against their enemies but against the people and their city:

> "Tell Zedekiah, 'This is what the Lord, the God of Israel, says: I am about to turn against you the weapons of war that are in your hands, which you are using to fight the king of Babylon and the Babylonians who are outside the wall besieging you. And I will gather them inside this city. I myself will fight against you with an outstretched hand and a mighty arm in anger and fury and great wrath. I will strike down those who live in this city—both men and animals—and they will die of a terrible plague..."(Jeremiah 21:3–6).

Jeremiah also, however, has a message of hope, in which he looks forward to a return of exiles to the land and to the spiritual revival of the nation. Chapters 32–33, for example, speak of restoration to the land which will involve forgiveness and inward renewal:

"I will bring Judah and Israel back from captivity and will rebuild them as they were before. I will cleanse them from all the sin they have committed against me and will forgive all their sins of rebellion against me. Then this city will bring me renown, joy, praise and honour before all nations on earth that hear of all the good things I do for it; and they will be in awe and will tremble at the abundant prosperity and peace I provide for it" (Jeremiah 33:7–9).

The prophet Ezekiel, who lived among the exiles in Babylon, has a similar message of judgment and hope. The idolatry that is being practised even in the Temple is so serious that Ezekiel in his vision sees the glory of God, which had earlier been seen over the tabernacle in the wilderness (e.g. Exodus 16:10) and then over the Temple at the time of its dedication by Solomon (1 Kings 8:11), departing from it. He must have shocked his hearers when he compared Jerusalem to an Egyptian prostitute (Ezekiel 23). In spite of the severity of the judgment, however, Ezekiel also holds out the hope of restoration to the land and describes in great detail the spiritual revival that will accompany the return to the land. Eight chapters towards the end of the book describe his vision of a restored temple in Jerusalem, and the book ends with the words: "And the name of the city from that time on will be: THE LORD IS THERE" (Ezekiel 48:35).

The book of Isaiah describes itself as "The vision concerning Judah *and Jerusalem* that Isaiah son of Amoz saw..." (Isaiah 1:1), and the very first chapter introduces the twin themes of judgment and restoration. Jerusalem is compared to the wicked city of Sodom (1:9), and is condemned for its idolatry and its social sins: "See how the faithful city has become a harlot! She once was full of justice; righteousness used to dwell in her—but now murderers!" (1:21). But then there is a message of hope: "I will turn my hand against you; I will thoroughly purge away your dross and remove all your impurities. I will restore your judges... as in days of old. Afterwards you will be called the City of Righteousness, the Faithful City. Zion will be redeemed with justice, her penitent ones with righteousness..." (1:25–27).

Jerusalem remains central in the prophet's visions because of "the Lord Almighty who dwells on Mount Zion" (8:18) and remains central in his vision of the future: "The Lord Almighty will reign on Mount Zion and in Jerusalem..." (24:23). If there is a danger that these hopes will encourage a narrow nationalism, Isaiah seeks to lift their horizons by hinting that what God is going to do *in Jerusalem* will one day have implications *for the whole world*. Thus in an early vision Isaiah sees all peoples coming to Jerusalem because of what God will reveal there (Isaiah 2:1–5). And when he sees a vision of the glory of God filling the Temple, he realizes that the glory of God also fills the whole world as he hears the angels in heaven crying: "Holy, holy, holy is the Lord Almighty; the whole earth is full of his glory" (Isaiah 6:3).

The second part of the book of Isaiah has more to say about the restoration of the people to the land and the redemption of Jerusalem. Several chapters at the end of the book describe the future glory of Zion: "Arise, shine, for your light has come, and the glory of the Lord rises upon you" (60:1). The "wealth of the nations" here has nothing to do with laissez-faire capitalism; rather it is the wealth of the nations that will come to Jerusalem in order to adorn God's "glorious temple" (60:7). The restored Temple thus becomes for Isaiah a symbol of a holistic salvation which includes peace and harmony in society, expressed in terms of a return to the kind of paradise that existed in the Garden of Eden, and of life under an ideal king like David who will rule with perfect justice. It is also closely linked with the idea of "new heavens and a new earth" (65:17–25).

The glorification of Jerusalem, therefore, is not only for the benefit of the children of Israel, but has something to do with the nations. Isaiah's vision is inclusive and universalist in the sense that he sees the Gentiles sharing in the blessings that are showered on Jerusalem. "For my house will be called a house of prayer for all nations" (56:7) and outsiders from other nations will one day join themselves to Yahweh because of the wonderful things that he is going to do in Jerusalem (56:1–8). This is no introverted, nationalistic vision!

Expectations after the exile

These optimistic visions of the prophets were fulfilled only in a very limited way. When Cyrus, king of Persia, conquered Babylon he allowed the Jewish exiles to return to Jerusalem in 538–537 BCE. The main party returned with Zerubbabel in that year, and with encouragement from the prophets Haggai and Zechariah, they eventually rebuilt the altar of the Temple and consecrated it around 515 BCE (Ezra 3–6). A second group returned with Ezra in 458, and a third in 445 with Nehemiah, who set about rebuilding the walls (Nehemiah 1–6).

In the following centuries, however, few of the other great hopes of the prophets seem to have been fulfilled. Apart from the periods under Ezra and Nehemiah there was little evidence of spiritual renewal, and since 586 Jerusalem and the area around the city were under the control of one foreign power after another: the Persians, the Ptolemies, the Seleucids and then the Romans. One major crisis during this period was the desecration of the Temple in 167 BCE by Antiochus Epiphanes, a Seleucid ruler, which was, in the words of F.E. Peters, "an attempt to exterminate the Jewish religion, quite unlike anything Jerusalem had experienced before."[11] In response to this, the Maccabees led the Jewish Revolt, and as a result the Temple was restored and reconsecrated in 164 BCE.

This was the context in which a particular kind of writing known as "Apocalyptic" developed, the clearest example of which is seen in the book of Daniel. Since this book is quoted in the New Testament and has been used at various times in history as a quarry for extracting all sorts of strange apocalyptic ideas about the future, it is worth noting how Mike Butterworth attempts to discuss the dating of the book and the special characteristics of this kind of writing:

"Although according to the text of the book Daniel belongs to the sixth century BC, most scholars do not believe the book was written then. They opt for a second-century BC writer, drawing on well-known stories and adding the visions to bring things up-to-date. His purpose in writing was to give God's people new heart at a time when the nation was under great threat. The issues underlying this are complex. They relate mainly to questions of history (people and events not known from any other source), and the use of two languages. It is possible to argue the early date for Part 1 and a later date (and author) for Part 2. The crunch point is whether the kind of detail in chapter 11 (which seems to relate so clearly to the time of Antiochus IV in the second century) is to be regarded as prophecy, made 400 years in advance. God does not normally work in this way in life or, generally, in the rest of Scripture (though God being God we can hardly deny the possibility!).

"Daniel has a historical setting and is concerned with history, but is not a history in the same way as, for example, the books of Kings. Nor is it quite like the other prophets, who speak to the people in the name of God. It is one of the earliest examples (the only one in the Old Testament), of the genre known as 'apocalyptic' writing, setting out a world-view of history within the great purposes of God... The main thrust of the book is clear: God, the God of Israel, is sovereign ruler of the world, at all times and in all places. For his people this means one thing: total loyalty to him. No matter how powerful the opposing forces, God will in due time (his own time) defeat them all."[12]

If this kind of apocalyptic writing is significantly different from both history and prophecy, it should not be used for writing "history in advance" in the way that many have tried to. Daniel's strange visions were never intended to be interpreted literally. The numbers of days and years are symbolic and need to be de-coded to explain their real meaning. His book has a powerful message for people living in dark days, but should not be used to provide raw material for writing a detailed script for history leading to the end of the world in the way that some Christians have done (see Chapter 6).

Jerusalem in the book of Psalms

If Jerusalem was supposed to be the central shrine for all the tribes, and if the Temple was intended to be the focal point for their worship of Yahweh, it is not surprising that the book of Psalms contains many references to Jerusalem. It is described, for example, as "the hill of the Lord... his holy place" (Psalm 24:3), "your holy hill" (Psalm 15:1), "perfect in beauty" (Psalm 50:2 NRSV), "the city of the Great King" (Psalm 48:8) and "his dwelling place" (132:7 NRSV). "Great is the Lord, and most worthy of praise, in the city of our God, his holy mountain. It is beautiful in its loftiness, the joy of the whole earth" (Psalm 48:1–2). "The Lord," says the Psalmist, "has chosen Zion, he has desired it for his dwelling. 'This is my resting place for ever and ever; here I will sit enthroned, for I have desired it...'" (132:13–14). "Praise be to the Lord from Zion, to him who dwells in Jerusalem" (135:21). Because the king is located in Jerusalem, many psalms speak of the role of the king as the representative of God who is responsible for ordering a just society and caring for the needy.

In Psalm 87 Jerusalem is pictured as the city of God which is open to people from many nations. Some Jewish worshippers might have been shocked to hear that its register of births would include people from Egypt and Babylon, Philistines and Africans from the upper reaches of the Nile. People from all these foreign, pagan nations, for whom the children of Israel had no warm feelings, would one day be included as citizens with full rights in Zion, the city of God. This is a message which must have challenged many nationalistic prejudices!

The parting of the ways

The Temple that was rebuilt in the sixth century BCE stood until the time of Herod, who set about rebuilding it in 19 BCE. Judging by the detailed description given by the historian Josephus and the size of the stones that remain standing today, this rebuilt Temple would have been regarded as one of the wonders of the ancient world. F.E. Peters comments that "the size of the platform upon which the Jerusalem Temple sat far outstripped... every known temple complex in the Greco-Roman world..."[13] The work was not completed until CE 62, and soon after this, in CE 70, it was destroyed by the Romans when they captured the city.

If this then is the story of how Jerusalem became so important for the Jewish people and how its Temple became the central focus for their religion, how did people believe that the glorious hopes about Jerusalem in the prophets would be fulfilled? And how are we to understand later developments in thinking about Jerusalem and its Temple? In Chapter 2 we will trace how the Christian movement emerges within Judaism but eventually branches out on its own, reinterpreting traditional Jewish ideas about Jerusalem and the Temple. In Chapter 4 we will see how the Jewish people adapt to the loss of Jerusalem and the Temple, and how Judaism develops in new directions. Then in Chapter 6 we will find that the movement today known as Christian Zionism has its own distinctive way of interpreting the picture of Jerusalem that we have found in the Old Testament.

From now on, therefore, there is a parting of the ways. But whichever of these different routes we follow, the story that unfolds in the pages of the Old Testament is about how a capital town/city and its Temple seem to become part of a bigger story that has something to do with the whole cosmos.

2
Jerusalem in the New Testament

Jesus of Nazareth challenges and transforms ideas about "the holy city"

"It is Jesus himself… who gives us the warrant to view Jerusalem in an entirely new light…. Jerusalem could never be the same again, now that Jesus had come… Jesus, not Jerusalem, would now become the central 'place' within God's purposes, the place around which God's true people would be gathered."
Peter Walker [1]

"In the last resort this study drives us to one point: the person of a Jew, Jesus of Nazareth, who proclaimed the acceptable year of the Lord only to die accursed on a cross and so to pollute the land, and by that act and its consequences to shatter the geographic dimension of the religion of his fathers. Like everything else, the land also in the New Testament drives us to ponder the mystery of Jesus, the Christ, who by his cross and resurrection broke not only the bonds of death for early Christians but also the bonds of the land."
W.D. Davies [2]

"The coming of Jesus, his death and resurrection in Jerusalem, result in a new theology of Jerusalem, with the city's losing its distinctive theological status as 'the holy city' or 'city of God'."
Peter Walker [3]

If Jesus of Nazareth grew up with traditional Jewish ideas and expectations, fed by centuries of history and reflection, about the significance of Jerusalem and its Temple, did he affirm them or did he challenge them in any way? If his disciples shared the same views as their fellow Jews, what happened when Jesus was no longer with them? Did they continue to think in exactly the same way, holding on to the same hopes about what God would one day do in Jerusalem? Or did they, under the influence of Jesus, rethink their ideas? And if so, did this amount to a slight adjustment or a radical transformation?

The Synoptic Gospels

What is perhaps most significant in all the four Gospels is the obvious fact that the crucifixion and resurrection took place in Jerusalem, and that a large proportion of all the Gospels is devoted to the events of the last week of Jesus" life. The fact that all four Gospels describe the event in which Jesus expels the money-changers from the Temple (Mark 11:15–17; Matthew 21:12–17; Luke 19:45–48; John 2:13–22) suggests that they all saw it as being highly significant. The saying in which Jesus defends what he has done is taken from Isaiah and is related to the Temple: "Is it not written: 'My house will be called a house of prayer for all nations'?" (Mark 11:17; cf. Isaiah 56:7). All four writers seem to have understood the whole event as a prophetic action pointing forward to the destruction of the Temple.

The three synoptic Gospels (Matthew, Mark and Luke) have their own version of a discourse known as the "Eschatological Discourse" or the "Apocalyptic Discourse," in which Jesus speaks about the future— warning in particular of the coming destruction of Jerusalem by the forces of the imperial power of Rome (Mark 13:1–37; Matthew 24:1–51; Luke 21:5–38). This is hardly surprising if, as N.T. Wright suggests, "… it did not take much political wisdom to extrapolate forwards and to suggest that, if Israel continued to provoke the giant (Rome), the giant would eventually awake from slumber and smash her to pieces."[4] Since the destruction of Jerusalem in CE 70 had such far-reaching consequences both for Christians and Jews, it is important to know how Jesus spoke about this catastrophic event which he could foresee and how his disciples understood its meaning. It is helpful to consider each of the Gospels in turn to notice the distinctive ways in which each one treats the subject of Jerusalem and the Temple.

Mark

In this version of the Eschatological Discourse (Mark 13:1–37), Jesus points to the magnificent buildings of Herod's Temple and says, "Do you see all these great buildings? ... Not one stone here will be left on another; every one will be thrown down" (13:2). When pressed by the disciples to explain when this will happen, he speaks in general terms about "wars and rumours of wars," natural disasters and persecution from the authorities, and then goes on to speak about the destruction of the Temple, using the images of "the abomination that causes desolation" and the "coming of the Son of Man" taken from the book of Daniel (12:11 and 7:13–14). When he uses images of cosmic disturbances in Isaiah which are associated with the destruction of Babylon (13:24; cf. Isaiah 13:10; 34:4), he is making a very shocking comparison between God's judgment on Jerusalem and his judgment several centuries before on the city of Babylon (cf. Daniel 9:27; 11:31; 12:11; 7:13–14).

These events then prove to be the occasion for the coming of the Son of Man: "At that time you will see the Son of Man coming in clouds with great power and glory..." (Mark 13:26). Since Jesus uses the term Son of Man, taken partly from Daniel, as his favourite way of referring to himself, the implication seems to be that Jesus is claiming that through the whole series of events between his departure and the destruction of Jerusalem and the Temple, he is going to enter into his kingdom, receiving the authority and dominion that have been given to him by God as the Son of Man.

The parable of the fig tree which follows has been taken by many who follow a Dispensationalist or Restorationist interpretation (see Chapter 6) to be a prediction of the restoration to the land and the establishment of a Jewish state:

> "Now learn this lesson from the fig tree: As soon as its twigs get tender and its leaves come out, you know that summer is near. Even so, when you see these things happening, you know that it is near,

right at the door. I tell you the truth, this generation will certainly not pass away until all these things have happened" (13:28–30; cf. Matthew 24:32–35; Luke 21:29–31).

This parable is seen by these Christians as a prediction of the revival of the Jewish nation in the land. Jesus has already cursed the fig tree on his way to Jerusalem (Mark 11:12–14), acting out the physical destruction of the Temple and, some would say, the nation. Since the fig tree represents Israel, it is argued, the sprouting of the leaves must

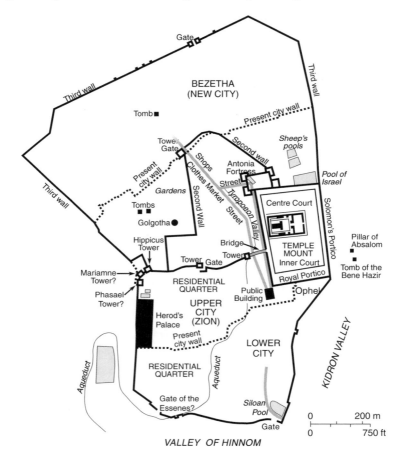

HERODIAN LAYOUT

represent the revival of the nation in the end times. They go on to claim that since the Jewish people did not become a nation until the creation of Israel in 1948, this is the event that Jesus is predicting and claiming to have such significance for the final days of history. This interpretation, however, is rejected by most commentators because it reads ideas into the text which are hardly there. The most natural interpretation is that Jesus is speaking about events that are going to happen *in the near future.* Jesus is simply underlining the point that these catastrophic events will take place during the lifetime of many of his hearers.[5]

In the last part of the discourse Jesus turns to speak about the more distant future and the end of the world, which he refers to as "that day or that hour" (13:32). While he urges his disciples to be awake and watchful, he insists that no one knows when the end is going to be: "No one knows about that day or hour, not even the angels in heaven, nor the Son, but only the Father. Be on guard! Be alert! You do not know when that time will come" (13:32–33). This insistence that no one can know about the timing of events in the distant future ought to discourage all attempts today to write history in advance and construct a timetable of what will happen before the end of the world.

Matthew

We find here some very traditional ways of describing Jerusalem: it is "the holy city" (Matthew 4:5; 27:53), "the city of the Great King" (Matthew 5:35), and it is assumed that God dwells in the Temple (Matthew 23:21). But other ideas are introduced throughout the Gospel which begin to reinterpret these traditional ideas. Jesus claims, for example, to be greater than the Temple: "I tell you that one greater than the temple is here" (Matthew 12:6). He warns that God will judge the Temple by abandoning it: "Look, your house is left to you desolate..." And it can hardly be an accident that in the very next verse we are told: "Jesus left the temple..." (Matthew 23:38–24:1).

While the whole Gospel is about the coming of the kingdom of God, one major theme is that Jesus himself claims to be the real king. Thus Matthew understands the triumphal entry into Jerusalem in terms of the prophecy in Zechariah 9:9: "This took place to fulfil what was spoken through the prophet: 'Say to the Daughter of Zion, "See, your king comes to you, gentle and riding on a donkey, on a colt, the foal of a donkey"'" (Matthew 21:4–5). By entering in this way, Jesus is approaching the city of which he is the rightful king, but is making a point about the kind of king he is. In the words of Peter Walker, "The one who visited the city on a donkey was indeed Zion's true King, the one in whom the city's chequered history was to find resolution, the one who held its destiny in his hand. Truly this was its 'hour of visitation'. It could never be the same again."[6]

In the birth narrative Jesus is identified with Isaiah's prophecy about the virgin: "and they will call him Immanuel—which means, 'God with us'" (Matthew 1:23). But then on two occasions Jesus claims that the divine presence is with his followers *in and through him*: "For where two or three come together in my name, there am I with them" (Matthew 18:20); "and surely I am with you always, to the very end of the age" (Matthew 28:20). These are all further indications of how Matthew understands the relationship between Jesus and the Temple.

Luke

When Jesus is taken as a baby to be presented in the Temple in Jerusalem (Luke 2:21–24), he is met by two people who express the expectations of the Jewish people at the time. The elderly Simeon is described as "righteous and devout" and as one who was "waiting for the consolation of Israel" (Luke 2:25), an expression which sums up all the hopes of many generations about what God was going to do to fulfil the promises in the prophets. Simeon, when he sees Jesus, thanks God that "my eyes have seen your salvation" (2:30), and knows that he can now die in peace. Similarly Anna, an eighty-four-year-old prophetess, has the instinct to believe that the infant Jesus is going to bring about the fulfilment of their dreams, and so begins to speak about him to all who were "looking forward to the redemption of Jerusalem" (Luke 2:38). Both these people therefore come to believe that Jesus will somehow fulfil their hopes for Jerusalem.

When Jesus comes to Jerusalem with his family at the age of twelve to celebrate a festival, he speaks of the Temple as "my Father's house" (Luke 2:49), recognizing a traditional way of describing the Temple and at the same time making a huge claim about his own relationship with God. Less than half way through the Gospel Luke tells us: "As the time approached when he was to be taken up to heaven, he set his face resolutely towards Jerusalem" (9:51 REB). This suggests that from now on everything that Jesus says and does is looking forward to what he knows is going to happen in Jerusalem. The importance of Jerusalem for Jesus is also underlined in a very significant saying concerning the city. When he is told that King Herod wants to kill him, his reply shows that he longs to be received by the people of Jerusalem, but knows that ultimately he will be rejected by them:

> "Go tell that fox, 'I will drive out demons and heal people today and tomorrow, and on the third day I will reach my goal. In any case, I must keep going today and tomorrow and the next day—for surely no prophet can die outside Jerusalem!' O Jerusalem, Jerusalem, you who kill the prophets and stone those sent to you, how often I have longed to gather your children together, as a hen gathers her chicks under her wings, but you were not willing! Look, your house is left to you desolate…" (Luke 13:31–35).

These words contain a strong critique of Jerusalem, which has become a false mother in the possessive way that it holds onto its people. Jesus makes the bold claim that he, like the hen gathering its chicks, is the rightful mother. But his rejection by the people has far-reaching consequences for the city and its Temple, which will shortly be left desolate.

In Luke's version of the Eschatological Discourse there is one important verse about the future of Jerusalem which has been the subject of much controversy: "They will fall by the sword and be taken as prisoners to all the nations. Jerusalem will be trampled on by the Gentiles until the times of the Gentiles are fulfilled" (21:24; "… until their day has run its course" NEB, "… until their time is up" TEV). The discussion here revolves around the question of what, if anything, is implied about the future status of Jerusalem *after* it ceases to be "trampled on by the Gentiles." The Dispensationalists/Restorationists insist that this is a clear prediction that Jerusalem will come once again under the control of the Jews. The fact that this happened in June 1967 indicates for them the profound theological significance of this event and points to the imminence of the Second Coming of Christ.

Most commentators, however, think that these words are far too enigmatic to be taken as a prediction of an event that would take place twenty centuries in the future. The simplest interpretation is that "the times of the Gentiles" means "the time allowed to the Romans." Even if it can be argued that there is a vague hint in these words that Jerusalem may one day revert to Jewish rule, the text gives no indication of the significance of such a development. The emphasis in Jesus' words is on the coming destruction of Jerusalem which will take place *in the lifetime of many of his hearers* rather than on the status of Jerusalem *in the more distant future*. The fall of Jerusalem is to be an act of divine judgment, compared in a shocking way to the judgment on Babylon described by Isaiah. What seems to be most significant, therefore, is that whereas the Old Testament prophets predicted judgment, exile *and* a return to the land, Jesus predicts destruction and exile, *but says nothing about a return to the land*. Instead of predicting the restoration of Israel, he speaks about the coming of the kingdom of God through the coming of the Son of Man.

Another possible clue to the meaning of this saying may lie in the image of "trampling," which is often associated with the trampling of grapes in a wine press. This vivid image is used by Isaiah as a picture of the wrath of God expressed in judgment on his sinful people. In a bold image which links together the themes of judgment and redemption, Yahweh says: "I have trodden the wine press alone; from the nations no one was with me. I *trampled* them in my anger and trod them down in my wrath; their blood spattered my garments, and I stained all my clothing. For the day of vengeance was in my heart, and the year of my redemption has come... I *trampled* the nations in my anger; in my wrath I made them drunk and poured their blood on the ground" (Isaiah 63:3–6). If this is part of the background to the words of Jesus, the "trampling on Jerusalem" becomes another dramatic way of speaking about God's wrath against the city. But this terrible judgment will lead ultimately to "the redemption of Jerusalem."

If this message of judgment is hard for people today to understand or accept, it needs to be noted that in Luke's account it comes from the lips of one who wept over the city: "As he came near and saw the city, he wept over it, saying, 'If you, even you, had only recognized on this day the things that make for peace! But now they are hidden from your eyes. Indeed, the days will come upon you when your enemies will set up ramparts around you and surround you, and hem you in on every side... and they will not leave within you one stone upon another; because you did not recognize the time of your visitation from God'" (Luke 19:41–44 NRSV). It is also clear that judgment is never the last word, for as Peter Walker points out, "Jerusalem's fall serves as an advanced paradigm of God's ultimate judgment upon the world. The predominant note, however, is one of fulfilment in Christ. Jerusalem points to the greatness of Christ."[7]

Acts

If Luke's Gospel is moving steadily towards the crucial events in the last week in Jerusalem, his account of the Christian church in Acts begins with events in the early years in Jerusalem and traces the spread of the message out from there to other parts of the Mediterranean world. In the first chapter the risen Jesus tells his disciples that they are to take the message about him to the ends of the earth: "You will receive power when the Holy Spirit comes on you; and you will be my witnesses in Jerusalem, and in all Judea and Samaria, and to the ends of the earth" (Acts 1:8). N.T. Wright comments: "Jesus' answer is usually taken as 'not yet': 'it is not for you to know times and seasons.' Yet Luke surely intends us to read it as a 'yes, but not in that way': 'you will receive power... and you will be my witness... to the end of the world."[8]

It looks therefore as if this book may have been intended to be a counterpart to the book of Joshua in the Old Testament. Thus just as Joshua describes the conquest of the land in stages, beginning with Jericho and proceeding to the hill country and finally to the north in Galilee, so Acts describes the spread of the Christian message from Jerusalem to other parts of Palestine and Syria, Asia Minor and

Greece and finally to Rome, the capital of the Roman Empire. This then is a totally different kind of conquest from the one carried out by Joshua! The Promised Land has become the earth coming under the rule of Jesus as king.

One of the many speeches in Acts is significant because of its clear critique of traditional Jewish thinking about the centrality of the Land and the Temple. Addressing the Sanhedrin, the supreme Jewish court, Stephen points out that many of the most significant events in the history of the children of Israel took place *outside* the land. By the end of the speech the religious leaders "were furious and gnashed their teeth at him," and the account continues: "But Stephen, full of the Holy Spirit, looked up to heaven and saw the glory of God, and Jesus standing at the right hand of God. ... At this they... dragged him out of the city and began to stone him..." (Acts 7:54–60). Explaining these words against their Old Testament background, Clare Amos points out the special significance of Luke's reference to Stephen seeing "the glory of God":

> "It is a deliberately chosen word. 'Glory' in Biblical terminology stands for the visible presence of God. It is a word that was particularly associated with the temple and its worship, for the very raison d'etre of the temple was to be the physical 'dwelling place' of the deity, the sacramental spot where humanity could encounter the divine presence. So if Stephen introduces this speech in which he gives significant examples of the presence of God far away from Jerusalem, by speaking of these as the actions of the 'Glory of God' (Acts 7:2), he is deliberately stressing that God is more present outside the Promised Land and its temple than within it. Then, as his speech actually draws to its close Stephen gazes (atenisas) into heaven and sees the 'glory' of God—closely linked in his vision to the ascended Christ. Luke is thus implying that now 'glory' has finally disappeared from the temple. Jerusalem, the city where God was (and is!) crucified by the desires and aspirations and passionately held beliefs of men and women is no longer privileged by special presence. It is time for the followers of Jesus to begin to carry out the further stages of the angelic commission of Acts 1:8."[9]

John and Revelation

It is generally believed that this Gospel was written towards the end of the first century, and that it contains eye-witness testimony to the life of Jesus combined with mature reflection of the significance of his life. So it cannot be an accident that approximately 80 per cent of John's narrative is located in Jerusalem. Jesus speaks of the Temple as "my Father's house" (2:16), and there are at least four ideas developed in the Gospel which make a clear connection between Jesus and the Temple.

Jesus is the new Tabernacle. "The Word became flesh and made his dwelling among us. We have seen his glory…" (John 1:14). Since John uses a Greek word (*eskenosen*) which is related to the word "tabernacle" or "tent" (*skene*), what he is saying by implication is this: "In the past the Tabernacle signified God dwelling or living among his people, and the children of Israel saw the glory of God resting on the Tabernacle. But we have now seen the glory of God resting not on the Tabernacle in the wilderness, but on a person—Jesus."

Jesus is the new Temple and has taken the place of the Temple. When Jesus drove the money-changers out of the Temple, he was challenged by the religious leaders who wanted to know what authority he had for doing this. In his reply he hinted that the Temple would later be destroyed. He also spoke about his own body as a temple, the new Temple that would eventually take the place of the Temple building and hinted at his resurrection: "Destroy this temple, and I will raise it again in three days" (John 2:18–22). In identifying Jesus with the Temple in this way, John believes that Jesus sums up and fulfils in himself all that the Temple had stood for. Now that he has come to be the supreme expression of God living among his people, there is no longer any need for the literal, physical Temple.

This is why Jesus explains to the Samaritan woman that before long the presence of God will not be attached either to the Jewish Temple in Jerusalem or to the Samaritan Temple on Mount Gerizim, but that people will be able to worship God in any place: "Believe me, woman, a time is coming when you will worship the Father neither on this mountain nor in Jerusalem… a time is coming and has now come when the true worshippers will worship the Father in spirit and truth, for they are the kind of worshippers the Father seeks. God is spirit, and his worshippers must worship in spirit and in truth" (John 4:21, 23–24).

Jesus fulfils the deeper meaning of the Jewish religious festivals. John says that all of Jesus" visits to Jerusalem took place at the time of a particular festival—especially the Feast of Tabernacles and Passover. These festivals therefore play an important part in John's interpretation of the life of Jesus. So, for example, when Jesus is described as "the Lamb of God, who takes away the sin of the world" (John 1:29), Jesus is compared to the lamb that was always sacrificed during the Feast of Passover, suggesting that Jesus has achieved something much greater than the deliverance from Egypt in the Exodus. When Jesus claims to be the source of life-giving water (John 7:37–38), he is reflecting rituals associated with the Feast of Tabernacles, in which water was poured over the altar. He is also probably referring to the vision in three of the Old Testament prophets of water flowing down from the Temple to the Dead Sea (Ezekiel 47:1–12; Zechariah 14:8–9; Joel 3:18–20. See *Whose Promised Land?*, pp. 324–25). Similarly, against the background of the lighting of the giant candelabra in the Temple, Jesus speaks of himself as "the light of the world" (John 8:12; 9:5). Therefore, by relating the teaching of Jesus to these festivals which were very important in the Jewish understanding of their history and their identity, John is trying to show that Jesus has fulfilled the deeper meaning of these festivals, which were like signs or symbols, pointing beyond themselves to something deeper and more significant.

The Holy Spirit will live within the disciples in order to continue the work of Jesus. If Jesus fulfils the purpose and meaning of the Temple, what happens when Jesus leaves the world? John explains that if the Temple is a symbol of God dwelling among his people, and if Jesus during his lifetime on earth has taken the place of the Temple and embodied the presence of God among his people, the Holy Spirit now comes to make the presence of God real within believers and to continue the work that Jesus had begun. The Discourse in the Upper Room (14–16) and the High Priestly Prayer (17) contain several images drawn from the Temple, suggesting that when Jesus returns to the Father, the disciples can be compared to temples, since the Spirit of God lives within them.

Part of the message of this Gospel, therefore, is that Jesus is the fulfilment of the Temple, and that the building of the Temple is now replaced by a person. There is no longer any need for a "Holy City" or for a Temple as the place where God meets with his people in a special way. N.T. Wright spells out the significance of this claim in these words:

> "It is not enough to say, within a normal Western-Christian mode of thought, that he was 'claiming to be God'. What he was claiming to do was to act as the replacement of the temple, which was of course the dwelling-place of the Shekinah, the tabernacling of God with his people.

> "When Jesus came to Jerusalem he came embodying a counter system. He and the city were both making claims to be the place where the living God was at work to heal, restore and regroup his people. Though many people still say that the Old Testament had no idea of incarnation, this is clearly a mistake: the temple itself, and by extension Jerusalem, was seen as the dwelling-place of the living God. Thus it was the temple that Jesus took as his model, and against whose claim he advanced his own."[10]

In the book of Revelation, attributed traditionally to the writer of the fourth Gospel, Jerusalem is described in one of his visions as "the great city, which is figuratively called Sodom and Egypt, where also their Lord was crucified" (Revelation 11:8). The fact that the Messiah has been crucified in Jerusalem seems to mean that its status has changed; it is no longer "the Holy City," because it is compared in a very daring way to the wicked city of Sodom and to Egypt which had enslaved the children of Israel centuries before. The term "Holy City" is reserved only for "the new Jerusalem" which is part of the "new heaven and new earth" and which comes "down out of heaven from God, prepared as a bride beautifully dressed for her husband":

> "Then I saw a new heaven and a new earth, for the first heaven and the first earth had passed away, and there was no longer any sea. I

saw the Holy City, the new Jerusalem, coming down out of heaven
from God, prepared as a bride beautifully dressed for her husband.
And I heard a loud voice from the throne saying, 'Now the dwelling of
God is with men, and he will live with them. They will be his people,
and God himself will be with them and be their God. He will wipe
every tear from their eyes. There will be no more death or mourning or crying or pain, for the old order of things has passed away'"
(Revelation 21:1–4; cf. 3:12).

In John's vision of this heavenly Jerusalem, there is no need for
any temple: "I did not see a temple in the city, because the Lord
God Almighty and the Lamb are its temple" (Revelation 21:22).
Here then is a powerful vision in which the focus moves away from
the actual city of Jerusalem at John's time, a city with a destroyed
Temple and under foreign rule, to a reality in the eternal world.
"Jerusalem the golden" has become a symbol of creation renewed
and restored. "This," says Peter Walker, "is decidedly not the old,
earthly Jerusalem elevated onto a higher plain, but on the contrary
a quite 'new' city built by God."[11]

There is one further theme in the book of Revelation that needs
to be explored here, because it has played such an important part
in Christian thinking about the end of the world. In one of his
visions John speaks about a period of 1000 years, known as "the
millennium" (Revelation 20:1–6). The passage comes towards the
end of the book and speaks of how the victorious Christ has severely
limited Satan's power, with the result that Christian martyrs are able
to share Christ's victory and his reign. This is how the image of the
millennium is introduced:

"And I saw an angel coming down out of heaven, having the key to
the Abyss and holding in his hand a great chain. He seized the dragon,
that ancient serpent, who is the devil, or Satan, and bound him for
a thousand years... And I saw the souls of those who had been be-
headed... They came to life and reigned with Christ for a thousand
years..." (Revelation 20:1–2, 4).

The debate about the millennium has centred round the following
questions:

1. Is the millennium as described in Revelation 20 to be understood as a literal period of 1000 years which has still to come in the future? Or is it to be understood symbolically in the context of John's highly symbolic descriptions in his visions as a way of describing some other reality?

2. Does the millennium come before or after the Second Coming of Christ? Does the millennium prepare the way for the return of Christ, or does the coming of Christ inaugurate the millennium?

3. How many other passages in the Bible (e.g. in the Old Testament prophets), if any, should be related to the millennial rule of Christ? Is it possible to work out any kind of chronology to enable us to know in advance about the sequence of events leading to the end of the world?

Out of the different answers given to these questions, three main schools of interpretation have been developed concerning the millennium:

1. The pre-millennial position holds that the Second Coming of Christ will take place before the millennium. The return of Christ to this world will usher in a literal period of 1000 years in which Christ will reign over the world from Jerusalem. This is the approach that generally underlies the thinking of Christian Zionists (see Chapter 6).

2. The post-millennial position is that the Second Coming of Christ will take place after the millennium. The 1000 years represents a period in which Christianity spreads throughout the world. At the end of this period of gradual conversion and transformation for the better, Christ will come once again to the world.

3. The a-millennial interpretation is that the 1000 years in the book of Revelation is not to be understood as a literal period of 1000 years in which Christ will reign in the city of Jerusalem, but rather as a symbol describing the period of time in which we now live, following the victory that Christ has won through his death and resurrection. This was John's way of describing what is a present reality—namely the victory of

Christ in which all Christian believers (and especially Christian martyrs) can share. If this, as many Christians believe,
is the most convincing explanation of John's "millennium,"
it cannot possibly be used as the basis for predicting a literal
reign of Christ for 1000 years in Jerusalem or related to many
other passages in the Old and New Testaments which speak
about the future.[12]

Paul

The letters of Paul to a variety of different churches in the Mediterranean
area were written in the two decades before the destruction of the
Temple in Jerusalem. We can assume that Paul was aware of what Jesus
had predicted about the Temple and of how his disciples had come to
think about the city. In one significant passage he describes Christian
believers as "God's temple" (1 Corinthians 3:16–17). N.T. Wright points
out the significance of such a daring claim: "When Paul used such
an image within twenty-five years of the crucifixion (with the actual
Temple still standing), it is a striking index of the immense change
that has taken place in his thought, the Temple has been superseded
by the Church."[13]

For Paul, therefore, there seems to be a "remarkable displacement
of the Jerusalem Temple... well before the events of AD 70."[14] Writing
to the Christians in Galatia, he makes his only clear theological
commentary on Jerusalem through a very shocking comparison: "Now
Hagar stands for Mount Sinai in Arabia and corresponds to the present
city of Jerusalem, because she is in slavery with her children. But
the Jerusalem that is above is free, and she is our mother" (Galatians
4:25–26). De Young comments that this passage "represents, perhaps,
the sharpest polemic against Jerusalem in the New Testament... Far
from being pre-occupied with hopes for a glorification of the earthly
Jerusalem, Paul's thought represents a most emphatic repudiation of
any eschatological hopes concerning the earthly city."[15]

When writing to the young church in Rome, Paul seeks to correct
attitudes that are creeping into the thinking of Gentile Christians.
Because the majority of the Jewish people had not recognized Jesus
as Messiah, some Christians were concluding that God had rejected

them as his people. At the beginning of his response Paul speaks about "my brothers, those of my own race, the people of Israel" and lists their many privileges: "Theirs is the adoption as sons; theirs the divine glory, the covenants, the receiving of the law, the temple worship and the promises. Theirs are the patriarchs, and from them is traced the human ancestry of Christ…" (Romans 9:2–5). He insists that God has not rejected his people who are still "loved on account of the patriarchs" (11:28). Because of their rejection of Jesus as Messiah, however, they are like branches of an olive tree that have been "broken off because of unbelief" (11:20). In spite of this Paul holds out the hope that they can still be grafted back into the olive tree, for "if they do not persist in unbelief, they will be grafted in, for God is able to graft them in again" (11:23). Paul therefore looks forward to a better future for the Jewish people. But since there is no mention of the land or Jerusalem, it seems that for Paul, Jerusalem has lost the centrality that it once had, and that Jesus has replaced Jerusalem as the centre of the Jewish faith.

Hebrews

For the anonymous author of this letter, writing before or after the Fall of Jerusalem in CE 70, the city of Jerusalem has very little significance for disciples of Jesus, even for those who are Jewish. The writer touches on several themes from the Old Testament, but sees them all as having been fulfilled in Jesus the Messiah: the role of Moses (Hebrews 3:1–19); the Promised Land (Hebrews 4:1–13); the priesthood (Hebrews 4:14–5:10); Melchizedek (7:1–28); and the tabernacle and its sacrifices (8:1– 9:18). Then at the climax of the letter we are told, "You have not come to a mountain that can be touched and that is burning with fire (Mount Sinai)… But you have come to Mount Zion, to the heavenly Jerusalem, the city of the living God. You have come to thousands upon thousands of angels in joyful assembly, to the church of the firstborn, whose names are written in heaven. You have come to God, the judge of all men, to the spirits of righteous men made perfect, to Jesus the mediator of a new covenant, and to the sprinkled blood that speaks a better word than the blood of

Abel" (Hebrews 12:18–24). Chris Wright points out the significance
of this radical reinterpretation of Old Testament themes:

> "Hebrews" affirmations of what 'we have' are surprisingly compre-
> hensive. We have the land, described as the 'rest' into which we have
> entered through Christ, in a way which even Joshua did not achieve
> for Israel (3:12–4:11); we have a High Priest (4:14, 8:1, 10:21) and
> an Altar (13:10); we have a hope, which in the context refers to the
> reality of the covenant made with Abraham (6:13–20). We enter
> into the Holy Place, so we have the reality of tabernacle and temple
> (10:19). We have come to Mt. Zion (12:22) and we are receiving a
> kingdom, in line with Haggai 2:6 (12:28). Indeed, according to He-
> brews (13:14), the only thing which we do not have is an earthly,
> territorial city."[16]

In the pages of the New Testament, therefore, a new but consistent
way of thinking about Jerusalem emerges. This is how Peter Walker
attempts to sum it up in his *Jesus and the Holy City: New Testament
Perspectives on Jerusalem*:

> "Jerusalem has lost whatever theological status it previously pos-
> sessed. The way the Old Testament ascribes to Jerusalem a special,
> central and sacred status within the ongoing purposes of God is not
> reaffirmed by the New Testament writers. Instead they see God's pur-
> poses as having moved forward into a new era in which the previous
> emphasis on the city (as well as on the Land and the Temple) is no
> longer appropriate. The coming of Jesus has been its undoing. An
> event, which to outsiders might have appeared so minuscule within
> the long history of this famous city, has had a quite disproportionate
> effect upon the city."[17]

If this then is how Jesus and his followers thought about Jerusalem,
how well did Christians in the following centuries understand the
message, and how did it affect the way they related to the city? In
the next chapter, we shall consider how, after a period of 300 years
in which Jerusalem was very insignificant for the tiny minority of
persecuted Christians in the Roman Empire, Jerusalem began to play
an important role in Constantine's Christian Empire.

It will become very clear in Chapter 4 that the Jewish people
learned to adapt to the loss of the Temple, but continued to think of

it as something fundamental to their faith. In Chapter 5 we shall see how Jerusalem became for Muslims a symbol of the way Islam had superseded both Judaism and Christianity. And in Chapter 6 it will become obvious that the movement known as "Christian Zionism" has a very different way of interpreting the picture of Jerusalem that has emerged in this chapter.

Our survey so far, however, seems to confirm Peter Walker's claim that "It is Jesus himself... who gives us the warrant to view Jerusalem in an entirely new light...."[18]

3
"Christian" Jerusalem

*Triumphant Christianity supersedes
Judaism and Roman paganism*

"So was the New Jerusalem built over against the one so famous of old."
Eusebius, Bishop of Caesarea, fourth century [1]

"The principal motive which draws people to Jerusalem is the desire to see and touch the places where Christ is present in the body."
Paulinus of Nola, fourth century [2]

"The whole world runs to see the tomb which has no body."
John Chrysostom, fifth century [3]

"We, the inhabitants of Jerusalem, as it were, touch with our hands each day the truth through these holy places in which the mystery of our great God and Saviour took place."
Sabas, CE 511 [4]

"Visiting the holy sites helps us to live the holy events of salvation as we see and feel them not only with our eyes and senses but with our hearts and souls."
Anba Abraham, 1996 [5]

If the first Jewish followers of Jesus believed that they had seen the face of God *in a person*, the Word of God "made flesh," it is not surprising that after a time they ceased to feel quite the same attachment *to the city* to which Jews had come for centuries to meet with God. Jesus had foreseen that the confrontation between Rome and the Jewish nation would one day come to a head. He had also warned that the city and the Temple would be destroyed by the Romans and that this catastrophe could only be interpreted as a divine visitation, comparable to the city's destruction at the hands of the Babylonians five centuries before.

Because of the way Jesus reinterpreted traditional ideas about the city, therefore, there must have been something distinctive about the attitudes of the first Jewish Christians to Jerusalem. But as times changed and more and more Gentiles became Christians, there were bound to be further developments in Christian attitudes to Jerusalem. If we want to account for the variety of attitudes that have been taken by Christians at different times, everything seems to depend on their answers to four key questions: (1) How much do they feel the need and the desire to visit the holy sites in Jerusalem? (2) Do they feel the need for Christians to exercise exclusive sovereignty over the city? (3) How do they respond to pagan religion and to Jewish and Muslim claims to Jerusalem? (4) How do they understand the role of Jerusalem at the end of the world? The variety of Christian attitudes to Jerusalem over the centuries can be explained not only by the way they have understood the example set by Jesus but also by the answers they have given to these questions in different contexts.

For the first few years Jerusalem was the centre of the new Christian movement, and an important church council took place here that is recorded in the book of Acts (Acts 15:1–35). Jewish Christians would no doubt have kept alive the memory of what had happened to Jesus in Jerusalem. At the time of the Jewish revolt, Christians who did not feel that they could identify with the aspirations of the revolt took refuge in Pella on the east of the Jordan—no doubt following the instruction of Jesus who had said "... let those who are in Judea flee to the mountains" (Mark 13:14). When the revolt was suppressed and the Temple had been destroyed, they would have returned to the city. But because from CE 70 onwards they could see the Temple in ruins before their eyes, Jerusalem and its Temple no longer played an important role either in the way they worshipped God or in the way they understood their relationship with God. For the next 260 years under Roman rule there was some kind of continuous but low-key Christian presence in Jerusalem. Persecution and the establishment of new churches with their own leadership all round the Mediterranean, however, ensured that it never became the permanent "headquarters" of the church.

When early in the fourth century Constantine began to make Christianity the official religion of the Roman Empire, Jerusalem became an important place for Christians for the next 300 years, and was regarded as "the Mother of all churches." After that, for thirteen centuries Jerusalem was a major city in the Islamic Empire. Islamic rule was interrupted for two separate periods totalling around one hundred years under Crusader rule, and it finally came to an end when a Western imperial power, Britain, captured Jerusalem from the Turks in 1917 and controlled it for thirty-one years. Then, after a period of nineteen years when it was divided between Jewish and Jordanian rule, it came in 1967 under full Jewish control. These then are the different political situations in which Christians have had to work out their attitudes to Jerusalem.

Constantine

When Constantine experienced his conversion to Christianity in CE 312 and became emperor in 324, he no doubt saw the advantages of making Christianity the religion of the Roman Empire. As part of this strategy, therefore, he embarked on an ambitious building programme in Rome and elsewhere to establish Christianity as an official religion. He also moved his capital to Constantinople, determined to make it a thoroughly Christian city. At the Council of Nicea in 325 he agreed to a request from Bishop Makarios of Jerusalem for permission to demolish the temple of Venus/Aphrodite, which the Romans had built over the traditional site of the crucifixion and the empty tomb, and to build a church in its place. It may not be out of place to point out that if Christians today can feel some sympathy with the motives of Bishop Makarios, they ought to be able to understand the feelings

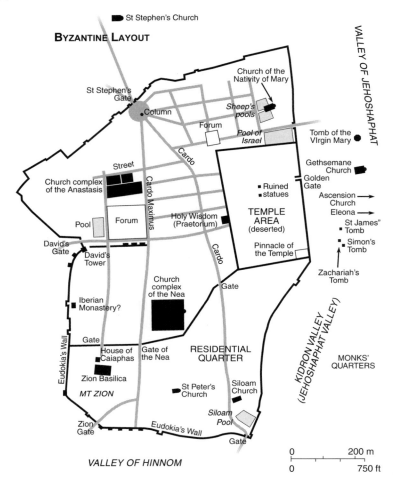

St Stephen's Church

BYZANTINE LAYOUT

VALLEY OF JEHOSHAPHAT

Church of the
Nativity of Mary

St Stephen's
Gate

Column

*Sheep's
pools*

Forum

*Pool of
Israel*

Tomb of the
Virgin Mary

Cardo

Street

Gethsemane
Church

Golden
Gate

Church complex
of the Anastasis

Cardo Maximus

• Ruined
• statues

Ascension →
Church

Eleona →

Pool

Forum

Holy Wisdom
(Praetorium)

**TEMPLE
AREA**
(deserted)

St James"
• Tomb

David's
Gate

David's
Tower

Cardo

Pinnacle of
the Temple

• Simon's
. Tomb

Gate

Zachariah's
Tomb

Church
complex
of the Nea

KIDRON VALLEY

(JEHOSHAPHAT VALLEY)

Iberian
Monastery?

Gate

Eudokia's Wall

House of
Caiaphas

Gate of
the Nea

**RESIDENTIAL
QUARTER**

MONKS'
QUARTERS

Zion Basilica

MT ZION

St Peter's
Church

Siloam
Church

Zion
Gate

Eudokia's Wall

*Siloam
Pool*

Gate

VALLEY OF HINNOM

| 0 | | 200 m |
| 0 | | 750 ft |

of many Jews today who find it very painful to see Islamic holy places (the Dome of the Rock and the Al-Aqsa Mosque) built over the site of the Jewish Temple (see Chapter 5).

The bishop in Jerusalem at that time came under the authority of the famous bishop of Caesarea, Eusebius, and was no doubt anxious to improve the status of Jerusalem over that of Caesarea. Bishop Makarios's personal motives would therefore have coincided with Constantine's ambitions since, in the words of Peter Walker, "the emerging Christian empire needed powerful symbols of the new order, which Jerusalem could provide in a unique way. The 'Jerusalem mystique' was present and powerful, the potential of the city inviting, the presence of the pilgrims demanding and the possible increased status of the Jerusalem Church compelling."[6] At the same time, Christian monks were settling in the wilderness of Judea, making it an important centre for monasticism, with around 400 monasteries by the end of the fourth century. The ecclesiastical position of Jerusalem did not change, however, until 451 when at the Fourth Ecumenical Council the bishopric of Jerusalem was turned into a patriarchate with jurisdiction over the whole of Palestine.

Constantine wanted the new church in Jerusalem, the Anastasis, the Church of the Resurrection (known generally in the West as the Church of the Holy Sepulchre), to be the most splendid church in the world, and to provide evidence of the triumph of Christianity over both Roman paganism and Judaism. Bishop Eusebius clearly understood the mind of the emperor, therefore, when he wrote to him: "It is fitting... that in your wisdom you order and make provision for everything necessary, that not only shall this basilica be the finest in the world, but that the details also shall be such that all the most beautiful structures in every city may be surpassed by it."[7]

Unable to visit Jerusalem himself because of his involvement in the Arian controversy, Constantine sent his mother, Helena, on a pilgrimage to Palestine in 326. Not only did she commission two basilicas to be built to mark the site of the nativity in Bethlehem and the site of the ascension on the Mount of Olives, but during the excavation of the traditional site of Calvary, she is reported to

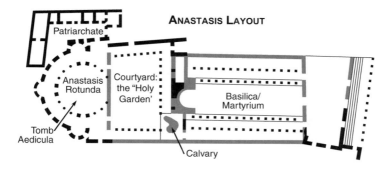

ANASTASIS LAYOUT

Patriarchate

Anastasis Rotunda

Courtyard: the "Holy Garden'

Basilica/ Martyrium

Tomb Aedicula

Calvary

have discovered part of the actual cross on which Jesus had been crucified. The consecration of the new basilica on 17 September 335 made the point that Jerusalem from now on was to be a "Christian Jerusalem" and Palestine a Christian Holy Land, providing public symbols of the new Christian empire. Pilgrimage flourished in a new way, with heightened interest in all the holy places, and more elaborate and colourful rituals in the churches in and around Jerusalem. Unfortunately, one of the consequences of Constantine's policy of Christianizing Jerusalem was that Jews were not allowed even to enter Jerusalem for many centuries.

Submission to Islam

When the Muslim armies besieged Jerusalem in 638, Sophronius, the patriarch of Jerusalem, knew that he would have to surrender, but insisted that the surrender should be made to the most senior figure of the Islamic state. When Umar eventually arrived from Medina, the patriarch rode out of Jerusalem on a horse wearing his full patriarchal robes to meet the caliph Umar, who was wearing "camel-hair garments all soiled and torn"[8] and riding on a white camel. The agreement was signed on the Mount of Olives, and as in other agreements made with Christians, their safety and freedom of worship were guaranteed.

Together they rode back to the city, where Umar declined the patriarch's invitation to say his prayers in the Church of the Holy Sepulchre. The reason he gave was that if he once said his prayers in this church, Muslims would later want to claim it as a place for Islamic worship. We shall see later how the caliph discovered the ruins of the Temple and set about claiming the site for Islam (see Chapter 5).

If these developments represented a triumph for Islam and were seen by some Christians as a welcome release from oppression by Byzantium, others were not so optimistic. This, for example, is how a Christian writer of the ninth century recorded the feelings of the patriarch Sophronius as he escorted Umar round the Temple Mount: "When Sophronius saw this he exclaimed, 'Truly this is the Abomination of Desolation spoken of by Daniel the Prophet, and it now stands in the Holy Place,' and he shed many tears."[9] Sophronius is reported to have died broken-hearted a few weeks after the surrender.

The Crusades

When the Muslim Arabs took control of Jerusalem in 638, they allowed Christians and Jews to remain in the city and to practise their religion, although with certain limitations. But the destruction of the Anastasis in Jerusalem in 1009 on the orders of the caliph in Egypt, al-Hakim, known as "the mad caliph," and the difficulties experienced by many pilgrims from Europe in reaching Jerusalem became the pretext that was used by the Emperor Alexius Comnenus I in Constantinople to appeal for help from Pope Urban II. This is part of one contemporary account of the Pope's sermon at Clermont in France on 27 November 1095, and gives a clear indication of some of the motivation for the Crusades:

"From the confines of Jerusalem and the city of Constantinople a horrible tale has gone forth and very frequently has been brought to our ears; namely, that a race from the kingdom of the Persians, an accursed race, a race utterly alienated from God, a generation indeed which has neither directed its heart nor entrusted its spirit to God, has invaded the lands of those Christians and has depopulated them by the sword, pillage, and fire... it has either entirely destroyed the churches of God or appropriated them for the rites of its own religion... On whom, therefore, is the task of avenging these wrongs and of recovering this territory (lost by the Byzantine Christians) incumbent, if not upon you? ... Enter upon the road to the Holy Sepulchre; wrest that land from the wicked race, and subject it to yourselves... Jerusalem is the navel of the world; the land is fruitful above all others, like another paradise of delights. This the Redeemer of the human race has made illustrious by His coming, has beautified by His presence, has consecrated by suffering, has redeemed by death, has glorified by burial. This royal city, therefore, situated at the centre of the world, is now held captive by His enemies, and is in subjection to those who do not know God, to the worship of the heathen. Therefore she seeks and desires to be liberated and does not

cease to implore you to come to her aid... Accordingly, undertake
this journey for the remission of your sins, with the assurance of the
imperishable glory of the kingdom of heaven."[10]

When the Crusaders captured Jerusalem on 15 July 1099, they
slaughtered almost everyone in sight—Muslims, Jews and even
Christians. The following eyewitness accounts give some impression
of the horror of what happened:

> "If I tell the truth, it will exceed your powers of belief. So let it suffice
> to say this much at least, that in the Temple and Porch of Solomon,
> men rode in blood up to their knees and bridle reins. Indeed, it was
> a just and splendid judgment of God that this place should be filled
> with the blood of unbelievers, since it had suffered so long from their
> blasphemies." (Raymond of Aguiles in Provence)[11]

> "It was impossible to look upon the vast numbers of the slain without
> horror; everywhere lay fragments of human bodies, and the very
> ground was covered with the blood of the slain. It was not alone the
> spectacle of headless bodies and mutilated limbs strewn in all direc-
> tions that roused horror in all who looked upon them. Still more
> dreadful was it to gaze upon the victors themselves, dripping with
> blood from head to foot, an ominous sight that brought terror to all
> who met them. It is reported that within the Temple enclosure alone
> about 10,000 infidels perished, in addition to those who lay slain every-
> where throughout the city in the streets and squares, the number of
> whom was estimated at no less." (William of Tyre)[12]

> "Oh what a stench there was around the walls of the city, both within
> and without, from the rotting bodies of the Saracens slain by our
> comrades at the time of the capture of the city, lying wherever they
> had been hunted down!" (Fulcher of Chartres, writing about a visit
> six months after the event)[13]

The Crusading movement affected the whole of Europe profoundly
for almost 200 years. But as Amos Elon points out, the spirit of the
Crusades lived on for centuries even after the final defeat of the
Crusaders at Acre in 1291: "In 1422, as Henry V of England lay dying
in France, in the middle of the Hundred Years' War, he interrupted
the officiating priest reading him the last rites and declared that 'if it

had pleased God to let him live to old age' he would have marched on Jerusalem after the pacification of France."[14] When Columbus set sail for the new world in 1492, he was hoping, among other things to find new sources of wealth to finance a continuation of the Crusades.

For many Muslims the Crusades have left a legacy which has continued right up to the present time, and in Chapter 5 ("Islamic" Jerusalem) we shall have to note the effects of the Crusades on attitudes of Muslims to Jerusalem. At this stage, however, it may be enough to note the brief comment of the famous historian of the Crusades, Steven Runciman: "It was this blood-thirsty proof of Christian fanaticism that recreated the fanaticism of Islam."[15]

The British Mandate

Saladin recaptured Jerusalem from the Crusaders in 1187, but this did not mark the end of Western/Christian attempts to control Jerusalem. On 11 December 1917 General Sir Edmund Allenby entered the Jaffa Gate on the west of the Old City in Jerusalem at the head of the British and Allied forces. He is reported to have said on this occasion, "Now the Crusades have come to an end."[16] The historian, David Fromkin, explains the significance of Allenby's capture of Jerusalem in these words: "The liberation of what he (Allenby) called 'the most famous city in the world' was what the Prime Minister (Lloyd George) had wanted for Christmas; with it, he later wrote, Christendom had been able to "regain possession of its sacred shrines."[17] Lloyd George also said he believed that General Allenby had "fought and won the last and most triumphant of the Crusades."[18]

Similar attitudes were expressed by General Gouraud, the French commander who took Damascus for the Turks in 1917. In a speech delivered to an invited audience at the grave of Saladin, he is reported to have said: "Saladin, we have returned. My presence here consecrates the victory of the Cross over the Crescent."[19] It is hardly surprising, therefore, that the involvement of Britain and other Western powers in the Middle East in the twentieth and twenty-first centuries and their major role in creating the Middle East as it is today are seen by most Arabs and most Muslims as a continuation of the Crusades, in which the Christian West sought to defeat and control the Muslim and Arab East. So, in the words of James Reston, "The symbolism of the Third Crusade hovers over the modern history and modern politics of the Middle East."[20]

Christian responses to the present situation

Twenty-seven years after Israel took over the whole of Jerusalem, the Patriarchs and Christian heads of the Churches in Jerusalem in November 1994 issued a very significant memorandum with the title "Significance of Jerusalem for Christians" (see full text in Appendix). In a paragraph entitled "Lessons of History" they wrote:

> "The experience of history teaches us that in order for Jerusalem to be a city of peace, no longer lusted after from the outside and thus a bone of contention between warring sides, it cannot belong exclusively to one people or to only one religion. Jerusalem should be open to all, shared by all. Those who govern the city should make it 'the capital of humankind'. This universal vision of Jerusalem would help those who exercise power there to open it to others who also are fondly attached to it and to accept sharing it with them."

This is the conclusion of the memorandum:

> "Jerusalem is a symbol and a promise of the presence of God, of fraternity and peace for humankind, in particular, the children of Abraham: Jews, Christians and Muslims. We call upon all parties concerned to comprehend and accept the nature and deep significance of Jerusalem, City of God. None can appropriate it in exclusivist ways. We invite each party to go beyond all exclusivist visions or actions, and without discrimination, to consider the religious and national aspirations of others, in order to give back to Jerusalem its true universal character and to make of the city a holy place of reconciliation for humankind."[21]

This remarkable Christian statement could never have been written either at the time of Constantine or the Crusades! Christians today are a tiny minority among the Palestinians and number only about 20% of the population of the Old City of Jerusalem. Whatever their views about the aspirations of Israeli Jews or Palestinian Arabs, Christians have clearly abandoned any exclusivist claims and any desire to control the city *for the sake of Christianity*.

A variety of Christian attitudes over the centuries

Having traced the development of Christian attitudes from the first century to the present day, we are now in a position to note the main attitudes that Christians have adopted to Jerusalem at different periods of history, and to see how they arose out of the changing situations in Jerusalem that they have faced at different times.

1. From the first century to Constantine: "Jerusalem has no continuing theological significance"

As long as Christians were a minority and often persecuted, they continued, like the New Testament writers, to focus more on the heavenly Jerusalem than the actual Jerusalem which was in a very sorry state. Thus Melito, the bishop of Sardis, could write in CE 160 that Jerusalem is "worthless now because of the Jerusalem above."[22]

These attitudes to Jerusalem in the first three centuries were reflected in the writing of Eusebius, the bishop of Caesarea and the presiding bishop in Palestine until 339. Although he lived for fourteen years under Constantine, his earlier views did not change considerably. As metropolitan for Caesarea and Palestine he probably did not want to see Jerusalem and its bishop gaining more power and prestige.

He never used the name "Jerusalem," but always referred to the city by its Latin name, "Aelia" (named after the Emperor Aelius Hadrianus). To him Jerusalem symbolized the death of Judaism. God had finally rejected Jerusalem because it rejected the Messiah, and the church had taken the place of Jerusalem. The city no longer had any theological significance, and "it in no way excels the rest [of the earth]."[23] "The Church of God has been raised up in place of Jerusalem that is fallen never to rise again."[24] Karen Armstrong points out that these third-century Christians seem to have "indulged in some rather unholy gloating when they contemplated the fate of the Jews...."[25]

2. The Marcionite approach: "The Christian God has nothing to do with Jerusalem's role in the Old Testament"

This was the approach which made a sharp distinction between Jesus and the God of the Old Testament. Some theologians even questioned whether the Temple and its sacrifices had ever been instituted by God. Although Marcion was condemned as a heretic in Rome in 144, views of this kind have been revived in the twentieth century by Christians—especially by some in the Middle East—for whom the Old Testament is such an acute problem that they want to ignore or reject it completely. The stronger the connection that is made between Israel in the Bible and the state of Israel today, the harder they find it to accept the Old Testament as in any sense a Christian document. They find it hard to reconcile the ethnocentrism and the arrogant nationalism that they see in the Old Testament with the more open and positive attitude to people of other cultures and races in the New Testament.

3. The early millennialist approach: "Christ will reign in Jerusalem in the millennium"

Perhaps as a reaction to the previous approaches which down-play the importance of Jerusalem, this approach gives Jerusalem great significance in the end times after the Second Coming of Christ.[26] Three of the best-known Church Fathers in the second century, Justin Martyr, Tertullian and Irenaeus, all held a form of millennialism, believing that the millennium was a literal period of 1,000 years during which Christ would rule the world from Jerusalem. These ideas need to be distinguished, however, from the modern expressions of millennialism which were developed in the nineteenth century (see page 65 and Chapter 6).

4. After Constantine: "Jerusalem does have theological significance; it needs to be a 'Christian Jerusalem'"

The conversion of Constantine in 313 led quite soon to a significant change in the thinking of Christians about Jerusalem. Having set his mind to establish a Christian Empire, he started from 325 to make Jerusalem thoroughly Christian. These new attitudes to Jerusalem were reflected in the writings of Cyril, who succeeded Eusebius and was bishop of Jerusalem from 348. By emphasizing the incarnation, he developed a more "sacramental" approach to Jerusalem and the holy places, in which the association of Christ with Jerusalem justified the idea that Jerusalem could be thought of as a "holy city."[27] He refused to see it as "the Guilty City," believing that its judgment in the first century was not "final." And rejecting the Roman name of Aelia, he reverted to using the biblical name "Jerusalem," calling it a "holy city." He expressed the contrast between the old Jerusalem and the present Christian Jerusalem by saying: "*that* Jerusalem crucified Christ, but that which now is worships him."[28]

These newer attitudes were summed up by Paulinus of Nola in the fourth century who wrote: "The principal motive which draws people to Jerusalem is the desire to see and touch the places where Christ is present in the body."[29] The incarnational approach developed by Cyril has had a profound effect on Christian thinking for centuries right up to the present day, and provides a large part of the motivation of Christians who visit Jerusalem not just as tourists but as pilgrims.

5. The Crusades: "Christendom must recover the Holy City— whatever the cost"

However much Christians today express a sense of shame about the Crusades, one could argue that they represented the delayed reaction of Western Christendom to the Islamic conquest of lands which in the seventh century were predominantly Christian. They were perhaps a natural response for people who felt that a city which was an important part of their faith had been taken over by an alien power. Philip the French king, one of the main leaders of the Third Crusade, declared: "We came here for the sake of God, to save our souls and to conquer the Kingdom of Jerusalem from the infidels."[30] For Richard the Lionheart, the other leader of the same Crusade, the goals were the recovery of three things—Jerusalem, the holy cross and the kingdom of Jerusalem: "Jerusalem," he said, "is for us an object of worship that we could not give up even if there were only one of us left."[31]

According to this way of thinking, it is not enough for Christians to have access to the holy sites, since it is not acceptable that Christians wanting to go to Jerusalem should be at the mercy of others. Christians must regain exclusive control of the city in order to guarantee free access for pilgrims and to make a political statement about the power of Christendom.

These attitudes have been totally repudiated by the vast majority of Christians in the twentieth and twenty-first centuries because they represent, in the words of Kenneth Cragg, "a terrible aberration disavowing the meaning of the very Cross they carried."[32] Many Christians therefore feel an acute sense of shame and embarrassment over what Christians in previous generations have thought, said and done in relation to Jerusalem. While they can hardly be held responsible for the actions of ancestors many centuries ago, some have wanted to express some kind of "apology," like those who took part in the Reconciliation Walk organized by Youth with a Mission beginning in 1999, the 900th anniversary of the capture of Jerusalem by the Crusaders.[33]

6. Christian Zionism: "Christians should support Jewish claims to Jerusalem"

While the millennialist views of the first centuries looked forward to the special role of Jerusalem in the millennium *after* the Second Coming, the Christian Zionist view believes that Jerusalem plays a special role within history *at the present time* and will do so even more *in the near future*. These Christians believe that the return of Jews to the land since 1880, the establishment of the Jewish state in 1948 and the capture of East Jerusalem in 1967 should be interpreted as the fulfilment of biblical prophecy and as significant events pointing to the fact that the Second Coming will soon take place. We shall later have to note the strange irony in the fact that in the nineteenth century Christian Zionism *pre-dated* the Zionist movement by many decades. There was more support for Zionism from Christians of this kind in Europe and the USA than there was within the Jewish community. This approach, which is adopted today by many millions of Christians all over the world and especially in the USA, is explored and challenged in greater detail in Chapter 6.

7. Christians in the Palestinian national movement: "Christians should identify totally with Muslims in the conflict over Jerusalem"

Lebanese and Syrian Christians today are very aware—and often proud—of the enormous contribution made by Christians in the region to the Arab Renaissance in the nineteenth century.[34] In the Palestinian context as well, Christians have been fully involved in the national movement. Very soon after the Balfour Declaration in 1918, for example, Muslim–Christian associations were formed in Palestine, which represented "the first experience of political and public collaboration between Muslims and Christians."[35] Writing in 1996 Naim Ateek stated that "Palestinian Christians and Muslims stand together in solidarity as one people in the struggle for a just peace in Palestine."[36] The Statement of a conference organized by Sabeel in the same year emphasized Christian–Muslim solidarity on this issue: "... the Palestinian Christians gathered stressed their unity with Palestinian Muslims in striving for peace and the establishment of a sovereign state in their homeland, with Jerusalem as its capital."[37] Other Christians also have been at pains to articulate very positive attitudes towards Muslims: "... had it not been for the resurrection and Christian history, Muslim history would not be as important. In Jerusalem, Christianity was reborn with the entry of Umar ibn al-Khattab and Islam, which manifested its message and its tolerance when Umar met Sophronius with love, approval, respect and covenant, the covenant of God and the covenant of person to person. Ever since that time, it is difficult to separate the two histories. One was embodied in the other, and the two became one. They are of the same essence, with different natures that complement each other, Christian and Muslim."[38]

At the same time it needs to be recognized that at certain times the relationships between Christians and Muslims in the national struggle have not been as positive as these statements would suggest. Anthony

O'Mahoney, for example, points out some of the strains that appeared in the 1930s and 1940s: "Muslim–Christian unity and cooperation in the national movement came under stress as some Muslim leaders sought to stress the predominance of Islam in the formation and development of a Palestinian national identity... Muslim–Christian relations were also strained by some Muslim leaders who considered that Islam, as the religion of the majority which had for centuries dominated and ruled over the *dhimmi,* demanded that Christians should venerate and even embrace Islam as the foundation of the Arab national movement."[39] As a result, he says, "Although the Muslim–Christian association had been established in the form of a partnership between Muslim and Christian leaders and notables, the Christians realized the dominant role of the Muslims over the movement, which forced them into a marginal position."[40]

It seems also that the rise of Islamism since the mid-1980s and the Islamization of the whole conflict have made some Christians feel much less secure within the Palestinian movement. A recent American observer notes tensions that have developed in the Bethlehem and Beit Jala area since the beginning of the Intifada: "Most of the Christian Beit Jalans I interviewed were quite aware of very real divisions between Muslims and Christians that had arisen within their own community... there was something pulling them apart from their Muslim neighbours even if they also knew that the bigger divide was the valley that separated them from where the Israelis lived."[41]

It is not hard, therefore, to understand why Jerusalem played such an important role both for Constantine and his Christian Empire and for the Crusaders who wanted to win back the Holy Land and claim it as their own. They lived with a world view that believed that there should be a close relationship between church and state, and that the Christian faith needs to be commended and upheld by force of arms. Such a world view, however, can never be revived in a situation where Christians are a powerless minority. It is also very clear that this way of thinking is very far removed from the spirit of Jesus who suffered, died and rose again in Jerusalem. It hardly seems to be touched by the writings of the New Testament which show a disinterest in the physical Jerusalem because of the new reality of Christ.

4
Jerusalem in Judaism

The forbidden city lives on in the hopes and prayers
of a scattered people

"Jerusalem is God's eternal capital."
Mayer Gruber [1]

"For the Jewish people Jerusalem is not a city containing holy places
or commemorating holy events. The city as such is holy."
Professor Zwi Werblowsky [2]

"The land of Israel is the centre of the world. Jerusalem is the centre
of the land of Israel. The Temple is the centre of Jerusalem. The ark
is the centre of the Heichal. The rock of foundation is in front of the
ark and on it the whole world rests."
The Talmud [3]

"No serpent or scorpion ever did harm in Jerusalem… nor was
there ever a destructive fire or ruin in Jerusalem.
    "When God created the world, he had ten measures of beauty to
distribute. Nine he gave to Jerusalem, one he gave to the rest of the
world. God also distributed ten measures of sorrow. Nine he gave to
Jerusalem, one he gave to the rest of the world."
Traditional saying about Jerusalem [4]

"The Temple Mount is Israel's eternal holy place…"
Rabbi Avraham Yitzhak Hacohen Kook, 1920 [5]

"Next year in Jerusalem!"
Traditional exhortation at the end of the Passover liturgy

The destruction of Jerusalem and its Temple in CE 70 was a defining moment for the Jewish people. The city that had been the focal point of national unity for nearly eleven centuries was razed to the ground by its Roman conquerors. The Temple that had been the focal point of their religion for almost as long now lay in ruins and there seemed to be no hope of ever rebuilding it. Another defiant revolt in 132 against the imperial power that seemed to be setting out to destroy the Jewish religion was ruthlessly suppressed in 135, and this time the Jews were banned—on pain of death—from even entering Jerusalem.

The Christian movement began as one of a number of distinct, even warring, sects within Judaism in the first century, but gradually parted company from the others. Some Jewish Christians were able to stay within the wider Jewish community, preserving both their Jewishness and their distinctive beliefs about Jesus. The majority, however, felt compelled to separate. And with Gentiles in many countries now joining the movement, Jewish Christians were soon outnumbered and the centre of gravity of the Christian churches moved away from Jerusalem.

Rabbinic Judaism, which became the dominant expression of Judaism in the following centuries, was based on at least two convictions: first, that Jerusalem remained the place where God had chosen to "put his name" for all time; and secondly, that the Jewish people should not give up hope of the restoration of the city and its Temple. Although the Temple was mere rubble for 600 years and the site was then completely taken over by another religion (Islam), Jerusalem continued to generate a powerful spiritual energy for the Jewish people. Today, after twenty centuries of dispossession, dispersion and humiliation, Jerusalem is once again in Jewish hands. What then has Jerusalem meant for the soul of Judaism over these twenty centuries? And what does it mean to Jewish people today?

The Jewish Revolt of ce 66–70

In the early stages of the revolt the Jews were able to dislodge the Romans from Jerusalem. It was not long, however, before reinforcements were sent under the Roman general Titus, and the city was captured. When Roman forces broke into the inner courts of the Temple on 28 August in CE 70, 6000 Jewish Zealots died attempting furiously to defend it. Once it was captured and set alight, the struggle to defend the city was over. The Temple was completely demolished, except perhaps for the western wall of the Sanctuary.

The Jewish historian Josephus in his book *The Jewish War* records in great detail the fighting that took place in various parts of the country and finally in Jerusalem. Having started out as a general in the Jewish forces, he went over to the Roman side because he was convinced that the resistance was futile. He describes his own efforts at various stages to persuade the Jews to give up their senseless opposition and save their lives by surrendering to the Romans. His estimate of the total number of Jews killed in the war is about 700,000. This is part of his graphic account of the systematic destruction of Jerusalem and the Temple:

> "While the Temple blazed, the victors plundered everything that fell in their way and slaughtered wholesale all who were caught. No pity was shown for age, no reverence for rank; children and greybeards, laity and priests alike were massacred. The roar of the flames streaming far and wide mingled with the groans of the falling victims; and owing to the height of the hill and the mass of the burning pile, one would have thought that the whole city was ablaze...

> "The Romans, thinking it useless, now that the Temple was on fire, to spare the surrounding buildings, set them all alight, both the remnants of the porticoes and the gates, excepting two... these also they subsequently razed to the ground. They further burnt the treasury-chambers, in which lay vast sums of money, vast piles of raiment and other valuables; for this, in short, was the general repository of Jewish wealth, to which the rich had consigned the contents of their dismantled houses...

> "The Romans, now that the rebels had fled into the city, and the sanctuary itself and all around it were in flames, carried their standards into the Temple court, and setting them up opposite the eastern gate, they sacrificed to them, and with rousing acclamations hailed Titus as supreme commander. So glutted with plunder were the troops, one

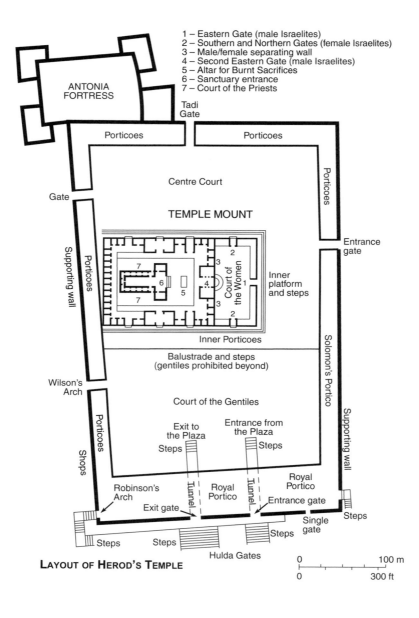

1 – Eastern Gate (male Israelites)
2 – Southern and Northern Gates (female Israelites)
3 – Male/female separating wall
4 – Second Eastern Gate (male Israelites)
5 – Altar for Burnt Sacrifices
6 – Sanctuary entrance
7 – Court of the Priests

ANTONIA FORTRESS

Tadi Gate

Porticoes   Porticoes

Porticoes

Centre Court

Gate

TEMPLE MOUNT

Supporting wall

Porticoes

Entrance gate

7

3
2

6   4   Court of the Women   1

5

Inner platform and steps

7

3
2

Solomon's Portico

Inner Porticoes

Balustrade and steps
(gentiles prohibited beyond)

Wilson's Arch

Supporting wall

Court of the Gentiles

Porticoes

Exit to the Plaza

Entrance from the Plaza

Steps   Steps

Shops

Royal Portico

Robinson's Arch

Tunnel   Royal Portico   Tunnel

Entrance gate

Exit gate

Steps

Single gate

Steps   Steps   Steps

Steps

LAYOUT OF HEROD'S TEMPLE

Hulda Gates

0   100 m

0   300 ft

and all, that throughout the whole of Syria, the standard of gold was depreciated by half its value...

"... He then gave his troops permission to burn and sack the city... Neither its antiquity nor its ample wealth, nor its people spread over the whole habitable world, nor yet the great glory of its religious rites, could aught avail to avert its ruin. Thus ended the siege of Jerusalem....

"The army, now having no victims either for slaughter or plunder, through lack of all objects on which to vent their rage... Caesar ordered the whole city and the Temple to be razed to the ground, leaving only the loftiest of the towers... All the rest of the wall encompassing the city was so completely levelled to the ground as to leave future visitors to the spot no ground for believing that it had ever been inhabited. Such was the end to which the frenzy of revolutionaries brought Jerusalem, that splendid city of world-wide renown...'[6]

It was not only disciples of Jesus who fled from the city when they could see what was going to happen. Rabbi Yohanan ben Zakkai was taken out of Jerusalem by his disciples in a coffin, and later went on to found an academy which played an important role in the compilation of the Mishnah and the development of rabbinic Judaism. Thus Rabbi Yohanan, in the words of F.E. Peters, "escaped like the Christian elders from a Jerusalem destined for ruin and so preserved intact institutions that would return there at a later date and shape the city's spiritual reconstruction."[7] The same writer points out the connection between the city, the Temple and the Mishnah:

"The city and its Temple were permanently and untouchably enshrined in the Mishna more than a century after their destruction, where in the tractate Middoth the Temple's buildings and rituals were as lovingly and as carefully detailed as if there were still Jews passing daily in and out of those precincts. And in Kelim 1:6–9 the holiness of Jerusalem and the Temple are mapped and guaranteed. In both texts the conviction is enormous that in reality neither Jerusalem nor the House of the Lord had been destroyed, as in fact they had not, in the sense that the rabbis intended and that many subsequent generations of Jews understood."[8]

For the next sixty years Jerusalem was in ruins, simply providing a base for the Roman army. Jewish disciples of Jesus returned to Jerusalem, as well as some other Jews, since there was no ban at this stage on Jews living in Jerusalem. One later account speaks of seven synagogues in the area of Sion, south west of the Temple area. Rome tried to make sure that the Jews would learn a lesson and not provoke their rulers again. So, as if to rub salt into the wounds inflicted by defeat, the Romans used taxes levied from adult male Jews as donations to the Temple of Jupiter in Rome.[9] The huge triumphal arch which was built in Rome to celebrate the victory in Judea showed the giant candelabras and other items being taken away from the Temple in Jerusalem and carried by Roman soldiers above their heads. It still stands today at the southern end of the Forum on the Via Sacra. Coins were minted showing a Jewish woman with bound hands and carrying the inscription "Judea captured."[10] This is Amos Elon's summary of how the disaster of CE 70 was perceived by the Jewish people:

"A new Hebrew word was coined to describe the cataclysm—khur-ban—an abstract noun, never before or after used in this sense, to denote a state of transcendental ruination. Time did not soften the sense of loss. The city followed the exiles like a ghost. Wherever they went, they looked back to her. Her ruins continued to rise into view. There was no new land for them anywhere. She became their disembowelled Capital of Memory. Nothing like this ever happened to another vanquished people... The consequences were considerable and are still evident. The loss and destruction of Jerusalem was en-shrined in learned books of speculation written long after the event... Interpretation was piled on interpretation in an endless attempt to come to terms with what seemed a preternatural eclipse."[11]

The Bar Kokhba Revolt, ce 132–35

As far as Rome was concerned, however, the Jewish nation was unwilling to learn its lesson. A visit to Palestine by the emperor Hadrian in CE 130 proved to be a further provocation to the Jews. What sparked the revolt this time was his attempt to wipe out all traces of Jewish Jerusalem and to turn the city into a thoroughly modern Roman city called Aelia Capitolina. He also set about building a temple to Zeus/Jupiter and erecting statues of the emperors Hadrian and Antonius Pius on the Temple Mount. A temple dedicated to Venus/Aphrodite was built on the site of Calvary. Hadrian also issued an edict forbidding circumcision, the ordination of rabbis, the teaching of the law and public meetings. All this amounted to an attempt to suppress the practice of Judaism in Palestine, and this was what provoked the rebellion that was led by Bar Kokhba in 132.

The historian Dio Cassius gives this summary of the causes of the revolt and its devastating consequences for the Jews:

> "But (Hadrian) stirred up a war of no small extent or duration by founding a city at Jerusalem in place of that which had been destroyed, which city he named Aelia Capitolina, and by setting up another temple to Jupiter on the site of the Lord's Temple, for the Jews thought it an outrage that any foreigners should be made citizens of their city and that foreign temples should be set up in it...

> "When the whole of Judea became moved and all the Jews throughout the land were stirred up and gathered together and did the Romans much mischief both by treachery and in open war... then at last Hadrian sent his best generals against them. Of these the first was Julius Severus, who was transferred from his governorship of Britain and sent against the Jews. At first he did not venture to make any direct attack upon them on account of their numbers and their desperation; but he did cut off various groups of them by the numbers of his soldiers and officers, and straitened them for provisions, and shut them up in fortresses. Thus he was able slowly but surely to wear them out and destroy them.

> "Very few Jews survived; Julius Severus took fifty of their most notable forts, 985 of their chiefest villages were laid in ruins, and 580,000 men were slain in skirmishes and battles, while the number of those who perished by starvation, plague, or fire cannot be reckoned. Thus almost the whole of Judea was laid waste..."[12]

One lasting legacy of this war was Hadrian's ban forbidding Jews from entering either Jerusalem or Judea. The text of the decree was: "It is forbidden for all circumcised persons to enter or stay within the territory of Aelia Capitolina; any person contravening this prohibition will be put to death."[13] From now on the two largest Jewish communities in the land were in Tiberias and Sepphoris in Galilee. The severity of the banning of Jews from Jerusalem is conveyed by these words written many years later by Eusebius, the bishop of Caesarea. In spite of the fact that he did not have warm feelings for the Jews and saw the destruction of Jerusalem as a judgment from God, he did at least seem to understand how traumatic this ban was for the Jewish people:

> "From that time onward the entire (Jewish) race has been forbidden to set foot anywhere near Jerusalem, according to the conditions and ordinances of the law of Hadrian which ensured that not even from a distance might Jews have a view of their ancestral soil… When in this way the city was thus interdicted to the Jewish race and suffered the total destruction of its former inhabitants, it was colonized by an alien race, and the Roman city which later rose there changed its name, so that it is now, in honor of the then reigning emperor, Aelius Hadrianus, known as Aelia."[14]

The year 135 therefore marks the end of the military confrontation between Rome and the Jewish nation. If the words of Eusebius sum up part of the legacy of that confrontation for the Jews, these words of F.E. Peters describe how Rome's difficult relationship with a rebellious province and its capital was perceived by the Romans:

> "The Romans had no great interest in Jerusalem: they occupied it because they had to; they incorporated it and surrounding Judea into their empire because they could find no one to rule it; and they destroyed it because rebels chose it as the place of their last stand. They destroyed far more than they built in the city, and when they did choose to rebuild it in AD 135, it was as an object lesson to their defiant Jewish subjects. For the Romans, as for many after them, Jerusalem was a problem. For those who followed them there were at times compensations in their stewardship of the Holy City; but for the Romans there was no profit—material, spiritual, or political—to be had from being masters of that place."[15]

After the Bar Kokhba rebellion there were times when the condition of Jews under Roman rule in Palestine improved. The emperor Antonius

Pius (138–61), for example, allowed Jews to practise their religion. In 141 Rabbi Simon was made patriarch of the Jewish community and was later recognized as head of the Jewish community throughout the empire. His son and successor, Judah I, was a personal friend of Emperor Marcus Aurelius, who had a special interest in Judaism. Around 200, during the reign of Marcus Aurelius, the ban on Jews was not enforced and some returned to Jerusalem. There is evidence that in about 250 Jews were allowed to go to the Mount of Olives on the anniversary of the destruction of Jerusalem on 9 Av to mourn from a distance. A Christian pilgrim visiting Jerusalem in 333 also noted that Jews were allowed to visit Jerusalem on the same date to mourn the destruction of the Temple. In 362 the emperor Julian the Apostate actually gave permission for the Jews to rebuild the Temple, but because of an earthquake and Julian's death in battle, it was never completed.

If we ask how the Jewish people themselves came to interpret the loss of Jerusalem and the Temple, this prayer from the *Authorised Daily Prayer Book* expresses confidence in the sovereignty of God in history, but looks forward in hope to the restoration and rebuilding of Jerusalem:

"Comfort, O Lord our God, the mourners of Zion, the mourners of Jerusalem, and the city that is in mourning, laid waste, despised and desolate; in mourning for the loss of her children, laid waste—with her homes in ruins, despised—all her glory gone, and desolate without inhabitant. She sits with her head covered like a barren childless woman. Legions have devoured her; idolaters have taken possession of her; they have put Your people Israel to the sword, and wantonly have slain the devout followers of the Most High. Therefore Zion weeps bitterly, and Jerusalem raises her voice. My heart grieves for their slain, my soul grieves for their slain. For it was You, O Lord, who consumed her with fire; with fire You will in future restore her, as it is said, I will be to her, declares the Lord, a wall of fire round about, and I will be a glory inside her. Blessed are You—the Lord, who comforts Zion and rebuilds Jerusalem."[16]

Another kind of response is expressed in this tract written by Daniel al-Kumisi at the end of the ninth century, which articulates a kind of "spiritual Zionism" and accepts the challenge of doing something in order to further the ideal of returning to Zion:

> "You should know that it is the villains of Israel who say to one another, 'We are not obliged to go to Jerusalem until He gathers us just as He has scattered us.' These are the words of those who anger (God) and of fools. Even if God had not commanded us to go to Jerusalem from the countries (of the Diaspora) in lamentation and bitterness, we would nevertheless know, by virtue of our own intelligence, that there is an obligation upon all those who suffered from (God's) anger to come to the Gate of the Angry to supplicate Him... You, God-fearers, must therefore come to Jerusalem, dwell there and become its guardians until the rebuilding of Jerusalem...'[17]

Jerusalem in rabbinic, apocalyptic and mystical writings

The starting point for the rabbis in their reflection about Jerusalem and their detailed accounts of everything that used to happen in the Temple was the idea, clearly rooted in Old Testament Scripture, that Jerusalem was God's city, the place that he had specially chosen. Writing in the *Jewish Encyclopedia*, Mayer Gruber suggests that "the later history of Judaism revolves, at least in part, around the unfolding of this idea...'[18] Because of the significance of Jerusalem all prayer should be offered facing Jerusalem. Thus Gruber continues that "this simple regulation... embodies the biblical belief that the Holy City and the Temple are a conduit for prayers of men and women of every nationality to the universal God whom even the heavens cannot contain (1 Kings 8:28–53)."[19]

When they reflected on the special kind of holiness that was attached to Jerusalem, they came to the conclusion that the whole city is holy as God's temple, not just the building of the Temple. The whole land is sacred and different from all other lands, largely because it is far easier to obey all the details of the law in this particular land. As the Mishnah had said, "the Land of Israel is more holy than all lands."[20] Writing in great detail about all the regulations concerning ritual purity and all the different sacrifices that had been offered in the Temple, the rabbis affirmed that the holiness of the Temple and of Jerusalem derived from the real presence of God in the Temple.

As Rabbi Aha is reported to have said in the tenth century, "The Presence of God never leaves the Western Wall."[21] Maimonides in the twelfth century described the area beyond the entrance to the Temple Court as "the camp of the Divine Presence (*Shekinah*)."[22] For this reason, he said, "Even though the Sanctuary is today in ruins because of our iniquities, we are obliged to reverence it in the same manner as when it was standing... for even though it is in ruins, its sanctity endures."[23]

Gruber concludes that for the rabbis "Jerusalem... is not a witness to the past or a future potentiality but an eternal embodiment of varying degrees of hierarchical holiness." He goes on to point out that it is this conviction about the holiness of Jerusalem and particularly about the Temple Mount that "keeps most Jews even today from setting foot on the Temple Mount until God in his own good time will provide in accord with Num. 19 and M Par. the means of purification from corpse uncleanness."[24] Other Jews today are held back from entering the Temple Mount by the conviction that the Third Temple will not be built until after the return of the Messiah or by a desire to avoid offending the sensitivities of Muslims.

This focus on Jerusalem in rabbinic writing was never intended to become an other-worldly escape from this world. Reflecting on God's providence in their exile, some rabbis even suggested that the loss of the Temple had liberated the Shekinah from Jerusalem, and that God might actually have done them a favour by scattering them all over the world.[25] Their exile from the Temple and Jerusalem meant that there was intense interest in how to live wherever they were in obedience to the law of God. Thus, in the words of Gruber, "Rabbinic Judaism has made the holiness embodied in Jerusalem a part of everyday life for Jews around the world."[26] If the Temple had been the centre of their worship, and if a major role of the Temple had been related to the atonement of sin through the sacrificial system, the destruction of the Temple led to a new emphasis on obedience to the commandments and righteous acts in everyday life.

Jewish apocalyptic writers developed the idea of Jerusalem as the centre of the universe, an idea that had earlier been expressed in the second century BCE by Enoch, who described Jerusalem as "the middle of the earth" (Enoch 26:1), and by Jubilees, where Mount

Zion is described as "the centre of the navel of the earth" (8:19). Similarly, developing the idea in Deuteronomy 17:8 (that speaks of "ascending" to the place that God would choose), they thought of Jerusalem as being higher than any other city. Another idea found in these earlier writers and developed further by the apocalyptists is that a heavenly Jerusalem will at some time in the future descend to earth. Sometimes the idea is that the Jerusalem that will one day be built by Jews on earth will reach up to heaven, and that the Temple which is now in heaven will come down to earth. When this idea is developed in the Zohar it reinforces the conviction that the Jews are not to take the initiative to build the Temple, but must wait until God sends it down from heaven. In all these speculations, however, Jerusalem never becomes a heavenly Jerusalem which takes the place of the earthly Jerusalem, as it does in much Christian reflection. Jerusalem remains the real city, firmly fixed *on earth*.

Jerusalem also has a significant place in Jewish mysticism, for, in the words of Amos Elon:

> "Jerusalem—or the disembodied idea of it—remained a compulsion, a ruling passion that gripped Jewish mystics everywhere. The kabbalists were possessed by it. In Jerusalem, they expected to celebrate an occult Sabbath of their history. As city and as symbol, Jerusalem was at the core of their identity as individuals and as a people. Christians and Moslems had other sanctuaries, too—Canterbury, Assisi, Compostela, Mecca, and Medina. Jews had only Jerusalem."[27]

One reason why this mystical tradition is still important is that it continues to inspire much Jewish fundamentalism today. Israel Shahak and Norton Mezvinsky in their *Jewish Fundamentalism in Israel* point out that "Mysticism is still accepted by and constitutes a vital part of Jewish fundamentalism, being especially important in the messianic variety... the ideology of the messianic variety of Jewish fundamentalism is based upon the Cabbala..."[28]

Jerusalem in liturgy

Alongside the writings of rabbis, theologians and mystics, the constant recollection of Jerusalem in liturgy no doubt played a highly significant part in keeping the faith and hope of Judaism alive. The design of every synagogue was seen as a reminder of the Temple, with the front section corresponding to the Sanctuary of the Temple, and the ark containing the Torah taking the place of the Holy of Holies. Amos Elon describes some typical customs and rituals that were developed to keep the memory of Jerusalem alive:

> "Those unable to go on pilgrimage were assured by the Jewish sages that through piety and prayer they were 'building Jerusalem daily'. One adds a row, 'another only a brick. When Jerusalem is completed redemption will come.' The rabbis developed elaborate rules and rituals to keep Jerusalem alive in the memory of her exiles. No home was to be without a zecher lakhurban (reminder of the destruction)—that is, a piece of wall left unfinished or without paint, and a plaque, often with a sketch of the Western Wall, indicating the direction of prayer."[29]

There is a reference to Jerusalem, for example, in a well-known grace said after meals:

> "Have mercy, O Lord our God, upon Israel your people, on Jerusalem your city, on Zion the abode of your glory, on the royal house of David your anointed, and on the great and holy house which bears your name...'[30]

The wedding service contains several references:

> "May the barren one [Zion] greatly rejoice and exult as her children return to her in joy..."

> "Blessed are You—the Lord our God, King of the universe, who created joy and gladness, bridegroom and bride, mirth and song, jubilation and merriment, love, brotherhood, peace and fellowship. Soon, O Lord our God, may there be heard in the cities of Judah, and in the streets of Jerusalem, voices of joy and gladness, voices of bridegroom and bride, the jubilant voices of bridegrooms from their bridal canopy, and of young people feasting and singing. Blessed are You—the Lord, who makes the bridegroom rejoice with the bride."[31]

Jerusalem is mentioned in three of the eighteen Blessings or Benedictions which are recited three times every weekday by many Jews:

> Benediction 14: "Be merciful, O Lord our God, in Thy great mercy, towards Israel Thy people, and towards Jerusalem Thy city, and towards Sion the abiding place of Thy glory, and towards the Temple and Thy habitation, and towards the kingdom of the house of David, Thy righteous anointed one. Blessed art Thou, O Lord God of David, the builder of Jerusalem."

> Benediction 16: "Accept [us], O Lord our God, and dwell in Sion; and may Thy servants serve Thee in Jerusalem. Blessed are Thou, O Lord, who makest peace."

> Benediction 18: "Bestow Thy peace upon Israel Thy people and upon Thy city and upon Thine inheritance, and bless us, all of us together. Blessed art Thou, O Lord, who makest peace."[32]

The cumulative effect of all these references to Jerusalem in liturgy is summed up by Amos Elon in this way:

> "Jerusalem was there every day of the week, every Sabbath, and every holiday, in every religious rite and prayer, morning, noon, and night. No matter where in the world Jews found themselves, they invoked the memory of Jerusalem—when completing a meal, when marrying, when a son was born, when he came of age, when someone died and was buried. No other religion exacted a similar emotional commitment to a specific place… The Jewish dispersion was a spiritual empire with Jerusalem as its capital… Nothing remotely like this sentiment surfaced among any other exiled people or lasted so long."[33]

Jerusalem and the Western Wall today

In June 1967, with Israel's capture of the Old City, Jews obtained unrestricted access to the Western Wall, which had probably been the only remaining part of the containing wall of the area on which Herod's Second Temple had been built. Anyone who has seen Jews of all ages, men and women, coming to pray at the Wall and to celebrate festivals or attend important national occasions on the large courtyard beside the Wall cannot fail to understand the deep significance of this part of the city coming once again under Jewish control. This is the most significant holy site for Jews in Jerusalem and represents the most powerful symbol of their faith and identity. Jerusalem and the Temple Mount thus "retain the mythic place they have held within Judaism for more than two thousand years."[34]

Jews of all kinds today, therefore, both religious and secular, would appreciate the following paragraph which is displayed prominently at all the entrances to the enclosure in front of the Wall, explaining the theological significance of the Western Wall:

THE DIVINE PRESENCE NEVER MOVES FROM THE WESTERN WALL

Jewish tradition teaches that the Temple Mount is the focal point of Creation.

In the center of the mountain lies the "Foundation Stone" of the world.

Here Adam came into being.

Here Abraham, Isaac and Jacob served God.

The First and Second Temples were built upon this mountain.

The Ark of the Covenant was set upon the Foundation Stone itself.

Jerusalem was chosen by God as the dwelling Place of the Shekinah.

David longed to build the Temple, and Solomon his son built the First Temple here about 3000 years ago.

It was destroyed by Nebuchadnezzar of Babylon.

The Second Temple was rebuilt on its ruins seventy years later.

It was razed by the Roman legions over 1900 years ago.

The present Western Wall before you is a Remnant of the Western Temple Mount retaining walls.

Jews have prayed in its shadow for hundreds of years, an expression of their faith in the rebuilding of the Temple.

The sages said about it: "The Divine Presence never moves from the Western Wall."

The Temple Mount continues to be the focus of prayer for Jews from all over the world.

If all Jews can appreciate this statement, they must at the same time be painfully aware that their dreams are only partially realized. The dilemma felt by many devout Jews over their holy sites is spelled out in these words by A.B. Yehoshua, an Israeli novelist and an influential literary figure in Israel today, quoted by Meron Benvenisti:

> "'The problem [of the Western Wall] stems from both its architectural meagreness and the fact of its being a remnant of a marginal part of an ancient structure that was destroyed two thousand years ago, as well as from its absurd juxtaposition with the Temple Mount, of which it once was a part and to which it has now become something supposedly contradictory—in the national sense, above all.' To Yehoshua, the Western Wall embodies 'religious exclusivity' and is 'symbolic of destruction', and the overwhelming impression it makes is of 'Jews standing uncertainly, pessimistically, stranded there before the harsh, bare stone Wall'...

> "The fact that, in this of all places, sovereign and victorious Israel is unable to express its religious and national affinities, and thus actually seems to acquiesce to this allegedly humiliating situation—that of gentiles looking down on Jewish worshippers—has led fanatical elements to unceasingly concoct schemes to blow up the mosques."[35]

Benvenisti also comments on the legal position regarding access to the Temple Mount for Jews that is based on a decision taken by Moshe Dayan soon after the capture of the Temple Mount in 1967 to allow Jews to visit the Temple Mount, but not to pray on it:

> "Dayan's decision was astounding in its daring. The Jews returned after thousands of years of exile and conquered their holy place and symbol of their national independence, and despite this enormous load of emotional baggage, an Israeli leader made a rational decision

in order to prevent a religious war whose consequences were beyond conjecture."[36]

A variety of Jewish attitudes to Jerusalem today

The *Jewish Encyclopedia* sums up a widespread response among Jews to the recovery of Jerusalem in June 1967: "The majority of Israeli Jews and many of their fellow Jewish and gentile sympathizers throughout the word see in these events, both momentous and seemingly miraculous, the harbinger of the messianic era, the veritable reversal of the insult and injury heaped upon God's Holy City by the Romans in the year 70 CE and in the year 135 CE."[37] It has to be recognized, however, that, as Baruch Kimmerling has pointed out, "Israeli Jewish society is far more divided on religious issues than is generally assumed outside of Israel."[38] There seem to be at least five different kinds of Israeli Jews who have different views about the question of the Temple Mount:

1. *Non-religious* or *secular* Jews see the Hebrew scriptures as part of their history and their cultural heritage. While they share the enthusiasm of religious Jews over the restoration of Jerusalem, they refuse to see any profound theological significance in this return. Generally they would totally dissociate themselves from Jews who want to see the rebuilding of the Temple. Israel Shahak and Norton Mezvinsky estimate that 25 to 30 per cent of Israeli Jews are secular.[39]
2. *Traditional* Jews, as described by Shahak and Mezvinsky are those who "keep some of the more important commandments while violating the more inconvenient ones; they do honor the rabbis and the religion."[40] Around 50 to 55 per cent of Israeli Jews come into this category. Some of these would side with the non-religious or secular Jews over the question of the Temple Mount, while others would identify with the more fundamentalist approach of the fourth and fifth groups.
3. The movement known as *Reform Judaism*, beginning in the nineteenth century, has set out to create a new vision of Judaism in which ideas about Jerusalem and the Temple are reinterpreted

in new ways in different contexts. Thus in Charleston, South Carolina, in 1841, for example, Gustavus Pozanski, offered the following prayer at the dedication of a new synagogue in 1841: "This synagogue is our *temple*, this city our *Jerusalem*, this happy land our *Palestine*, and as our fathers defended with their lives *that* temple, *that* city and *that* land, so will their sons defend *this* temple, *this* city, and *this* land." Similarly, *The Union Prayer Book* contains this prayer: "And though we cherish and revere the place where stood the cradle of our people, the land where Israel grew up like a tender plant, and the knowledge of Thee rose like the morning dawn, our longings and aspirations reach outward [towards] a higher goal."[41] The number of Reform Jews in Israel is very small. In the diaspora, however, they are more numerous and influential.

4. The *Haredi, Pre-Modern Orthodox* or *Ultra Orthodox* are strongly opposed to Zionism, and believe that the establishment of Israel with its capital at Jerusalem has no theological significance. They would argue that Jews should *not* take any initiative to change the position of the Temple Mount today, but must wait patiently for the coming of the Messiah. "Some of their leaders," says Amos Elon, "have gone so far as to say that the extermination of six million Jews by the Nazis was divine punishment for the Zionists' efforts to create a secular state."[42]

5. The *Modern Orthodox* or *National Religious* argue that Jews should be allowed to hold religious observances on the Temple Mount. Others have wanted to establish a synagogue or set up a *yeshiva* there. Some of the more extreme groups, like *Atteret Kohanim* (Diadem of the Priests), engage in detailed study of the rituals which they believe will one day be practised in a restored Temple. The following are examples of statements made by people who come into this general category:

"Our sages of blessed memory ruled that pagans were unclean and forbidden entry to the holy place. There is a sacred duty to prevent this sad state of affairs [from continuing] and let no one fear of what [gentiles] might say." (Mordechai Eliahu, shortly before being elected as chief rabbi in 1982)[43]

"I don't want the Wall to be the Third Temple... You will see, the right moment to build it [there] will come. Perhaps there was such a moment in 1967. We missed it... The Almighty will destroy them [the mosques on the Temple Mount]. We will lend him a helping hand... The scenario is clear." (Meir Yehuda Getz, rabbi in charge of the Western Wall, 1983)[44]

"Our reality is inevitably leading us to rebuild the third temple on the Temple Mount. The third temple will stand for ever and ever... The Almighty is at present rebuilding Jerusalem, telling us that from now on it will stand for ever and ever... We are all reborn into a new era. The mountain of the house of the Lord shall be established on the top of the mountains and all nations shall flow unto it." (a Knesset MP, at a seminary convention in the Old City, 1985)[45]

"Determinist believers believe that we have to wait for God. We believe we have to do the maximum that we can do, to see the Dome of the Rock and Al-Aqsa destroyed. This was robbery of the Jewish people at a time when we were so weak... We are not weak any more." (Yehuda Etzion, 1980)[46]

Some who hold beliefs of this kind are prepared to act to further their visions, drawing inspiration, for example, from the Maccabees who in 165 BCE drove the Greeks out of the Temple in Jerusalem and threw out the idols that had been placed in it. In 1982 Alan Harry Goodman, a thirty-eight-year old American Jew, entered the Temple Mount shooting an automatic rifle and entered the Dome of the Rock before surrendering to the police. His motivation was that Jerusalem was not liberated as long as its heart—the Temple Mount—was still under alien Muslim control.[47] Speaking of people of this kind who have from time to time attempted to destroy the Dome of the Rock, Amos Elon says: "All were observant Orthodox Jews. They were convinced that the destruction of the Moslem shrines on the Temple Mount would precipitate the 'religious renaissance' of the Jewish people. They also believed that the 'human' act of destruction would be met by a 'divine' response—the third temple would come down from heaven miraculously intact."[48]

These fourth and fifth groups are the ones that can most clearly be given the label "fundamentalist," and it is estimated that around 20 per cent of Israeli Jews would come into these two groups. Shahak and Mezvinsky also point out that fundamentalist Jews "wield much greater political power in Israel than their percentage of the population might appear to warrant" and that "the number of Jews influenced by Jewish fundamentalism is consistently increasing."[49]

If this is a fair account of the place of Jerusalem in Judaism over the centuries until today, there remain at least four questions which many would want to raise with Jews of all kinds as they face the realities of the situation in and around Jerusalem today:

—If they understand the recovery of Jerusalem today as the fulfilment of the visions of the biblical prophets, how do they understand *other themes* in these same prophets that are associated with the return to Zion—like the spiritual renewal, the just society, God's removal of his presence from a sinful society, and the blessing for all the nations of the world (see Chapter 1)?

—If they have seen *their own dreams* fulfilled, do they recognize *the existence and the dreams of others* in the city? Since Jerusalem today is not what it was in the first or second centuries, and since there are other people there today who make claims to the city, are they willing to find ways to share it with them?

—Do they believe that *the Temple needs to be rebuilt*? If they do, do they believe they should allow the Messiah to rebuild it in his own way and in his own time, or should they take matters into their own hands and work to achieve this themselves—whatever the cost?

—Is it possible to have genuine *dialogue with Jewish fundamentalists*? How do Jews who are *not* fundamentalists engage in dialogue with those who are?

If these questions sound very theological, we shall see in later chapters that they have very immediate political implications.

5
"Islamic" Jerusalem

*Triumphant Islam supersedes
Judaism and Christianity*

*"A prayer in Mecca is equal to two thousand prayers, those in
Medina a thousand, and in Jerusalem five hundred."*
*"A sin committed at Jerusalem is the equivalent of a thousand sins,
and a good work there is the equal to a thousand good works."*
Sayings of the Prophet Muhammad [1]

"Jerusalem is a golden basin filled with scorpions."
Al-Muqaddasi, Arab geographer in Jerusalem, tenth century [2]

*"Happiness is eating a banana in the shade of the Dome of the
Rock."*
Ibn Asakir, twelfth-century Arab historian [3]

*"The original name (Ur-Salem)... for Muslims suggests 'peace'
and corresponds closely to the Muslim concept of the sacred; a place
where peace reigns and conflict is excluded. There is thus a symbolic
psychic linkage between peace and sacredness, between Ur-Salem
and al-Quds or Bait al-Maqdis, the names used by Muslims for the
city."*
Zaki Badawi [4]

*"The question of Palestine, especially after the Israeli Occupation of
Jerusalem, June 1967... is no longer a local one, concerning only
the Arabs of Palestine or the Arab world, but it has also become the
concern of the Islamic world..."*
H.S. Karmi [5]

This is where the third actor arrives on the scene—or is it the fourth? Solomon builds his Temple on what had probably been the site of a pagan Canaanite shrine. Then comes Jesus, who offers a radical reinterpretation of Jerusalem in Judaism. Finally we have Islam, which claims to be the original religion of the human race and to include both Judaism and Christianity within its history, and therefore to supersede them both.

There are two reasons in particular why it is important to understand the background to Islamic claims. First, many in the West and many Israeli Jews are very scornful about these Islamic claims. "It's Mecca and Medina," they say "that are important to them. So what does Jerusalem have to do with Islam?" Secondly, since the Palestinian movement has been weakened by the split between the more secular approach of Arafat and the PLO and the more overtly Islamic approach represented by Hamas, Islamic Jihad and the Lebanese group Hizbullah, it is important to ask how important is the *Islamic* dimension in the Palestinian national movement.

How then does Islam interpret the previous history of Jerusalem? How does it co-opt Jerusalem and all that it had stood for in the past both for Jews and Christians? And why has Jerusalem become such a powerful symbol not only for Palestinian Muslims but for Muslims all over the world?

Muhammad and Jerusalem

According to Islamic tradition, earlier in his life and before his call to be a prophet, Muhammad went with trading caravans to Palestine and Syria, and therefore no doubt visited Jerusalem. When he first received his revelations, he and the Muslim community in Mecca said their prayers facing not in the direction of Mecca, whose shrine at the Ka'aba at the time was full of idols, but in the direction of Jerusalem, in the same way that the Jews did. This was their first *qiblah* until about eighteen months after the Hijrah in 622, when the Prophet received a further revelation, recorded in the Qur'an, instructing them to change the *qiblah* to face Mecca: "The foolish will ask: 'What has made them turn away from their former *qiblah*?' Say: 'The East and the West are God's. He guides whom He will to a straight path'... We decreed your former *qiblah* only in order that we might know the Apostle's true adherents and those who were to disown him... Many a time have we seen you (Muhammad) turn your face towards the sky. We will make you turn towards a *qiblah* that will please you. Turn your face towards the Holy Mosque (*al-masjid al-haram*); wherever you (the faithful) be, turn your faces towards it" (2:142–44). Muslims therefore speak of Jerusalem as the first *qiblah* and the third of the holy places (*ula-lqiblatain wathalith al-haramain*).

During the first stage of Muhammad's ministry in Mecca, soon after the death of his first wife, Khadijah, and his uncle, Abu-Talib, in 619—a time which he himself called "The Year of Sadness'—he experienced what is known as the Night Journey (*isra'*). Muslims believe that, either literally or in a vision, the Prophet Muhammad was transported during the night from the Ka"aba in Mecca to Jerusalem. There he met with Abraham, Moses and Jesus, and together they performed the ritual prayers, with Muhammad taking the lead. "His prayer there as *Imam* (leader) of the Prophets," says Daud A. Abdullah, "indicates that the leadership and ownership of Jerusalem had effectively passed to the *ummah* (community) of Muhammad."[6]

From here Muhammad experienced the Ascent to Heaven (the *mi"raj*), in which he was taken from the first to the seventh heaven, meeting with Adam, Abraham, Moses, Jesus and other prophets. The magic steed which transported Muhammad from Mecca to Medina, known as Buraq, was tied up at the Western Wall, which is therefore known to Muslims as the "Buraq Wall."[7] Amos Elon draws attention to some of the recent discussion about this particular tradition: "It has been claimed, but not proven, that in the Middle Ages Moslems still venerated the Golden Gate as the site where Mohammed entered the sanctuary. According to this theory, the site of al-Buraq was shifted to the Western Wall only after Jewish rights to worship at the wall were informally recognized by the Ottoman sultans."[8]

It is hard to exaggerate the importance of the Night Journey and the Ascent to Heaven in the thinking of Muslims. The event is seen as a commissioning of Muhammad for his ministry as Prophet,[9] and demonstrates the continuity between Islam and the previous religions of Judaism and Christianity. It also indicates a significant change in the role of the Arabs in relation to the Jews in the purposes of God, representing a kind of spiritual conquest of Jerusalem by Muhammad.[10] In Islamic thinking, although God had made a covenant with the Jews giving them the right to the land and to Jerusalem, he ended his covenant with them, and continued it instead with the descendants of Ishmael. Thus, in the words of Zachariah Bashier:

> "Prophethood switched from the Israelites to the Arabs... This change is symbolized in the act in which the Prophet, ushered by Gabriel, led the prayer, in the Aqsa Mosque, with all the Prophets including Adam and Abraham lined up with him... In the history of Islam, this change in the fortunes of the Israelites was also symbolized by the change of the qiblah from Jerusalem to Makkah... According to the Qur'an, the Bani Israe'il are no longer the "chosen people." The Muslims are the best people if they fulfil the conditions of being true to the mission of Islam: You are the best nation (ummah) brought forth to mankind. You enjoin the good and forbid the wrong and you believe in the (One True God)—Allah..." (Al "Imran 3:110).[11]

If this is how the Prophet Muhammad thought about Jerusalem, it is not surprising that a number of sayings attributed to him and recorded in the *Hadith* literature speak of the special sanctity of Jerusalem:

> "Journeys should not be made except to three mosques: this my mosque [in Medina], the sacred mosque [in Mecca], and Al-Aqsa."

> "Go to it and worship in it [the Jerusalem sanctuary], for one act of worship there is like a thousand acts of worship elsewhere."

> "Whoever goes on pilgrimage to the Jerusalem sanctuary and worships there in one and the same year will be cleared of his sins."

> "He who lives in Jerusalem is considered a warrior in the Holy War."

> "He who lives in Jerusalem for one year, despite the inconvenience and adversity, for him God will provide his daily bread in this life and happiness in Paradise."

"Whoever dies in the Jerusalem sanctuary is as if he has died in heaven."[12]

The land and Jerusalem in the Qur'an

There are two clear references to the land in the Qur'an. The first is in a passage which speaks about Moses encouraging the children of Israel to enter the land: "O my people! Go into the holy land (al ard al-muqaddasa) which Allah hath ordained for you..." (Qur'an 5:21, Pickthall).[13] This conveys the idea that this land has been set apart and destined by God for the children of Israel, who are, as it were, Semitic cousins of the Arabs, and related to the Arabs through their ancestor, Ishmael. The second is a verse which speaks about Abraham and Lot in the land, where God says, "We delivered him [Abraham] and Lot, and brought them to the land which We had blessed for all mankind" (Qur'an 21:71, Dawood). These verses provide the basis for the belief that the whole land is holy, a sacred trust (waqf) belonging to God.

There is only one clear reference to Jerusalem—in a verse referring to Muhammad's Night Journey from Mecca to Jerusalem (isra'): "Glory be to him who made His servant go by night from the Sacred Temple [of Mecca] to the Farther Temple (al-masjid al-aqsa, in Jerusalem) whose surroundings We have blessed (alladhi barakna hawlahu), that We might show him some of Our signs" (Qur'an 17:1, Dawood).[14] Commentators have long debated whether this blessing covers Jerusalem or the whole land of Palestine.

There is another passage in the Qur'an, however, which later Islamic tradition has unanimously seen as a reference to the destruction of the Jerusalem Temple first by the Assyrians in 586 BCE and later by the Romans in CE 70: "In the Book We solemnly declared to the Israelites: 'Twice you shall do evil in the land. You shall become great transgressors.' And when the prophecy of your first transgression came to be fulfilled, We sent against you a formidable army which ravaged your land and carried out the punishment you had been promised. Then We granted you victory over them and multiplied your riches and your descendants, so that once again you became more numerous than they. We said: 'If you do good, it shall be to your advantage; but if you do evil, you shall sin against your own souls.' And when the prophecy of your next transgression came to be fulfilled, We sent another army to afflict you and to enter the Temple as the former entered it before, utterly destroying all that they laid their hands on" (17:4–7).

Jerusalem in early Islamic history

In 634, just two years after the death of the Prophet Muhammad, the Muslim Arabs conquered the south of Palestine and began a series of raids in the direction of Jerusalem. In his Christmas sermon that same year, Sophronius, the patriarch of Jerusalem, lamented the fact that it was not possible for Christians to travel from Jerusalem to Bethlehem to celebrate Christmas because of the Arabs who were besieging Bethlehem. Some days later on the Feast of Epiphany, he spoke of the bloodshed, the destruction of monasteries and plundering of towns and villages by the Arabs, who were described as "Saracens" and who "boast that they will conquer the whole world."[15]

When the Muslim armies finally besieged Jerusalem in 638, Sophronius was forced to surrender to the caliph Umar in a meeting, which, as we have already seen, took place on the Mount of Olives (see Chapter 3). The text of the surrender agreement that they signed together has been recorded by the historian Tabari (died 923):

> "In the name of God, the Merciful Benefactor! This is the guarantee granted the inhabitants of Aelia by the servant of God Umar, Commander of the Believers. He grants them the surety of their persons, their goods, their churches, their crosses—whether these are in a good or a bad condition—and the cult in general. Their churches will not be expropriated for residences or destroyed... No constraint will be imposed upon them in the matter of religion and no one of them will be annoyed. No Jew will be authorized to live in Jerusalem with them...'[16]

This last clause represented a continuation of the Christian ban on Jews living in the city, but does not seem to have been observed, since Jews were in fact allowed to live in Jerusalem and were in certain respects favoured by the Muslims. When Sophronius and Umar had ridden back into Jerusalem after signing the surrender, and Umar had declined the invitation to pray in the Church of the Holy Sepulchre, they went together to the Temple Mount, where, with the help of a Jewish convert to Islam, Ka'b al-Ahbar, they were shown the site of the Jewish Temple Mount. The caliph was shocked to find it a heap of ruins and a rubbish heap. He then gave orders that a place of worship should be built here, believing that this was the site of Muhammad's Ascent to Heaven, the place where Abraham was going to offer his son as a sacrifice, and the site of the previous Jewish temples of Solomon and Herod. A fourteenth century Muslim history entitled *Muthir al-Ghiram* describes this visit:

> "It is related as coming from Shadad ibn Aws, who accompanied Umar when he entered the Noble Sanctuary of the Holy City on the day when God caused it to be reduced by capitulation, that Umar entered by the Gate of Muhammad, crawling on his hands and his knees, he and all those who were with him, until he came up to the court of the Sanctuary. Then looking around to the right and the left and glorifying God, he said: 'By God, in whose hand is my soul, this must be the sanctuary of David of which the Apostle spoke to us when he said, "I was conducted there in the Night Journey."' Then Umar advancing to the front (or southern) part of the Haram area and to the western part thereof, said: 'Let us make this the place for the sanctuary [masjid].'...
>
> "Now when Umar came to the Holy City... and saw how there was a dungheap over the Rock, he regarded it as horrible and ordered that the place be entirely cleaned... When Umar first exposed the Rock to view by removing the dungheap, he commanded them not to pray there until three showers of heavy rain should have fallen...'[17]

Fifty-three years after the conquest, the Umayyad caliph Abd al-Malik built the Dome of the Rock (*qubbat al-sakhra*) in CE 691. This shrine was designed not as an ordinary mosque for prayer, but as a shrine that provided Muslims with a place of pilgrimage similar to the Church of the Holy Sepulchre a few hundred metres to the west. While this was "the earliest major example of Islamic sacred architecture,"[18] the architectural style of the building is Byzantine, similar to that of other churches in Jerusalem and elsewhere, and it is very probable that both the designers and the builders were Christians from Palestine and Syria. Al-Muqaddasi, an Arab historian who was a citizen of Jerusalem, clearly understood that it was meant to rival the splendour of the Church of the Resurrection:

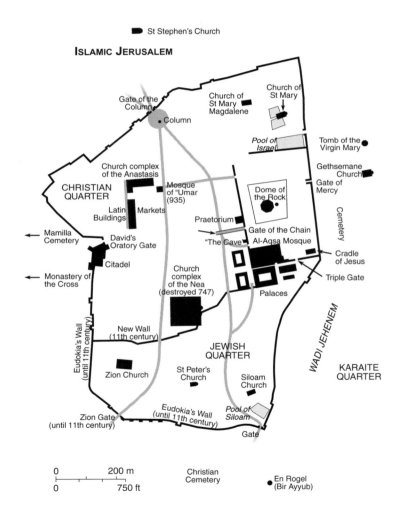

"He [Abd al-Malik] beheld Syria to be a country that had long been occupied by the Christians, and he noted herein the beautiful churches still belonging to them, so enchantingly fair and so renowned for their splendor... So he sought to build for the Muslims a mosque that should prevent their admiring these and should be unique and a wonder to the world. And in like manner, is it not evident how Caliph Abd al-Malik, noting the greatness of the Dome of the Holy Sepulchre and its magnificence, was moved lest it should dazzle the minds of the Muslims, and so erected, above the Rock, the Dome which is now seen there."[19]

Some minor changes and restoration have been carried out over the centuries—with Persian tiles, for example, replacing the original façade—but in other respects it remains basically the same building that was erected in 691.

One of the main inscriptions round the base of the dome is taken from the well-known Qur'anic verse in 4:171, which is addressed to Christians:

"People of the book, do not go to unwarranted lengths in your religion and get involved in false utterances relating to God. Truly Jesus, Mary's son, was the messenger of God and His word—the word which He imparted to Mary—and a spirit from Him. Believe, then, in God and His messengers and do not talk of three gods. You are well advised to abandon such ideas. Truly God is one God. Glory be to Him and no "son" to Him whose are all things in the heavens and the earth, their one and only guardian."[20]

The Dome of the Rock therefore represents the clearest possible statement of how Islam understands its relationship both with Judaism and Christianity. In the words of Karen Armstrong, "The Dome of the Rock... was a dramatic assertion that Islam had arrived and was here to stay. It issued an imperious call to the Christians to revise their beliefs and return to the pure monotheism of Abraham."[21] Amos Elon is more blunt in his description of these texts as "straightforward missionary propaganda coupled with threats to Jews and Christians to submit."[22] These attitudes towards Christian beliefs were also reflected in the fact that from an early period Muslims, including scholars, would refer to the Church of the Resurrection/Holy Sepulchre as *kanisat al-qumama* (Church of the Dung-heap), which was a deliberate corruption of *kanisat al-qiyama* (Church of the Resurrection).[23]

The Al-Aqsa Mosque was built a few hundred metres to the south of the Dome of the Rock in around CE 810 to replace the original mosque that had been built there by the caliph al-Wakil soon after 700. According to some Christian sources it was built on the site of a Christian shrine, the Basilica of the Virgin Mary, built by the Emperor Justinian. Al-Muqaddasi understood that the same motive was at work as with the Dome of the Rock: "This mosque is even more beautiful than that of Damascus, for during the building of it they had for a rival and as a comparison the great church [of the Holy Sepulchre] belonging to the Christians of Jerusalem, and they built this [Al-Aqsa] to be even more beautiful than that other."[24]

During the Umayyad period (661–750) Jerusalem became established as the third most holy site for Muslims after Mecca and Medina and was regularly called *beit al-maqdis* "the holy house." Pilgrims would even circumambulate round the Dome of the Rock in the same way that Muslims performing *hajj* circumambulate round the Ka'ba in Mecca. Many mosques, hospices, schools, libraries and hospitals were built for the increasing number of pilgrims who were visiting the city. In spite of its growing importance as an Islamic city, however, Muslims were still a minority for about 300 years. For as al-Muqaddasi noted, "everywhere the Christians and Jews have the upper hand."[25] Many other important names in Islamic history were associated with Jerusalem, including Bilal, the first *muezzin*, the Umayyad caliph Mu'awiya, Rabi"a the mystic, the legal scholar al-Shafi"i, and the theologian al-Ghazali. From about 1000, as a result of gradual conversion to Islam, Muslims constituted the majority of the population.

Jerusalem and the Crusades

If relations between Muslims and Christians were reasonably harmonious for the first 370 years, they deteriorated in 1009 during the time of the caliph al-Hakim bi-Amr Allah in Egypt, who ordered the Church of the Holy Sepulchre to be destroyed. The church was rebuilt and restored by the Byzantine Emperor between 1030 and 1048. Reports of the capture of Jerusalem by the Seljuk Turks in 1071 spread alarm and panic in Europe. And it was the appeal of the Emperor Alexius to the Pope which provoked the call to Christian Europe to undertake the Crusades.

Christians will never be allowed to forget that when the Crusaders entered Jerusalem on 15 July 1099, they killed almost every person in sight (Jews, Christians and Muslims alike), making the streets run with blood. The Islamic historian Ibn al-Athir (died 1233) gives this matter-of-fact account of the atrocities and plunder that took place:

"In the Masjid al-Aqsa the Franks slaughtered more than 70,000 people, including a few imams and Islamic scholars, devout and ascetic men, who had abandoned their homeland to live in pious isolation in the holy place. The Franks stripped the Dome of the Rock of more than forty silver candelabras, each weighing 3600 drachmas, and a large silver lamp, weighing 44 Syrian pounds, as well as 150 small silver and more than 20 gold candlesticks, and much more booty."[26]

The Al-Aqsa Mosque was turned into barracks for the Knights Templar, with the *mihrab* (the prayer niche pointing to Mecca) turned into a toilet and the basement used for stables. A number of mosques were turned into churches and minarets were silenced for the eighty-eight years that the Crusaders ruled.

Then, in 1187, Saladin (Salah al-Din) reconquered Jerusalem, delaying his entry into Jerusalem in order to make it coincide with the anniversary of the Prophet Muhammad's Night Journey and Ascent to Heaven. He gave orders that the Church of the Holy Sepulchre should not be damaged, and after closing it for three days allowed Christians to enter on payment of a small fee. His forces regained the Dome of the Rock, which had been transformed into a church by the Crusaders, and pulled down the golden cross which had been erected over it. The Al-Aqsa Mosque was also restored and purified, and an ornate wooden pulpit was made by a craftsman from Aleppo and installed in it. Saladin started calling the city al-Quds once again. This is how James Reston sums up Saladin's recapture of Jerusalem:

"By the exemplary behaviour of his soldiers as they took charge of Jerusalem in 1187, Saladin did himself great credit as a wise leader, especially by contrast to the havoc of the first Crusaders in their conquest of the city in 1099. By his protection of the Holy Sepulchre and the other Christian holy sites, his tolerance of other faiths would be long remembered. His actions seemed to define what it meant to be a good Muslim. By his amnesties and various charities toward his enemies he secured forever his reputation for gentility and wisdom."[27]

There is one particular incident during the Crusades which gives a special insight into the thinking of Muslims concerning Jerusalem. At the time when the Crusaders had lost Jerusalem to Saladin and were trying to re-establish their control over the whole country, Richard the Lionheart wrote to Saladin making the bold suggestion that Richard's sister, Joanna, should marry Saladin's brother, Malik al-Adil; they should reign together as king and queen of Jerusalem, and all Palestine should come under Christian rule. Saladin in his reply explained how unthinkable it was for him as a Muslim to surrender Jerusalem to Christian rule:

"Jerusalem is ours as much as yours. Indeed it is even more sacred to us than it is to you, for it is the place from which our Prophet accomplished his nocturnal journey and the place where our community will gather on the Day of Judgement. Do not imagine that we can renounce it or vacillate on this point. The land was also originally ours, whereas you have only just arrived and have taken it over only because of the weakness of the Muslims living there at the time. God will not allow you to rebuild a single stone as long as the war lasts. As for the Cross, its possession is a good card in our hand. That Jesus died on the Cross is a falsehood for us. The Cross cannot be surrendered except in exchange for something of outstanding value to all Islam."[28]

Steven Runciman's verdict on the Crusades from a Western viewpoint is very simple: "Seen in the perspective of history, the whole Crusading movement was a vast fiasco."[29] Muslims at the time perceived the Crusades simply as an invasion by people whom they called "Franks," and had little conception of the Christian motivation behind the conquest. Jeremy Johns sums up the Crusades as "a minor event which occurred on the periphery of the Muslim world and constituted little more than a nuisance to Islam."[30] The contemporary Arab historians never used the word "Crusades," and the Arabic expression that is used today (*al-hurub al-salibiyya*, literally "the wars of the cross') was not coined until many centuries later. According to Antonie Wessels, "Only in the time of the Turkish Ottomans did this appear to become common currency and only for the first time under the influence of French culture in Christian circles."[31]

There can be no doubt, however, about the lasting legacy of the Crusades on Christian–Muslim relations and on the future of Jerusalem. "What had been begun in order to help the Christians," says A.S. Atiya, "ended in inciting the Muslims to a counter-crusade against the whole of Christendom."[32] For Zaki Badawi, "It was the Crusaders who transformed Jerusalem into a potent symbol of Islam once again."[33] Felix Fabri, a pilgrim from Europe in 1480, understood something of the legacy of the Crusades and expressed his foreboding of continuing conflict in the future:

"At this present day the Christians would care little about the Saracens" bearing rule in Jerusalem, provided only that we were allowed freedom to pass in and out of our temple of the Lord's sepulchre without fear and without vexations and extortions. Neither would the Saracens mind if the Christians were lords of the Holy City, if we would render up their Temple to them. But since Christians and Saracens cannot agree about this matter, unhappy Jerusalem has suffered, doth now suffer, and will hereafter suffer sieges, castings down, destructions, and terrors beyond any other city in the world."[34]

H.S. Karmi, like many Muslims today, sees in the Crusades a pattern that has been repeated in more recent history:

"The Crusades... gave Jerusalem a new significance in the eyes of the Muslims. The Crusaders were not regarded as Christians, impelled only by religious zeal, but were found to be Europeans who were desirous of expansion and conquest—an adumbration of European colonialism and imperialism later on. This blend of Christianity and imperialism was counteracted by a blend of Arabism and Islamism. It sharpened the Arab–Muslim interest in Jerusalem, and the proof of it is the lavish care bestowed upon Jerusalem by the Ayyubid and the Mamluk Sultans... The position of Palestine as a holy country for Muslims derives very strongly from the Crusades...."[35]

Jerusalem in Islamic eschatology

Jerusalem came to play an important role in Muslim stories about the Day of Judgment that developed over the centuries—particularly from the time of the Crusades onwards. One widely accepted idea was that when Jesus comes again to the earth, he will kill the Anti-Christ and return to Jerusalem, where he will pray in the mosque, kill all the pigs, break all the crosses, and destroy the synagogues and churches, thus vindicating Islam as the one true religion. He will reign in Jerusalem for fifty years, then die and be buried in Medina beside the Prophet Muhammad.[36]

The historian al-Muqaddasi explained the role of Jerusalem on the Day of Judgment:

> "As to the excellence of the city, why is this not to be the plain of marshalling on the Day of Judgment, where the Gathering Together and the Appointment will take place? Truly Mecca and Medina have their superiority by reason of the Ka'ba and the Prophet... but truly on the Day of Judgment they will both come to Jerusalem and the excellence of them all will be united there."[37]

Some Shi'ite Muslims today make a clear link between the appearance of the Mahdi and the liberation of Jerusalem.[38] Bassam Jirar sums up the role of Jerusalem by saying that "Islam began in Mecca and Medina and will end in Jerusalem."[39] One *hadith* that has been quoted frequently in recent years (and in particular by Osama bin Laden in an interview in 1998[40]) contains a prediction made by the Prophet Muhammad concerning conflict that would one day develop in Jerusalem between Muslims and Jews. Although the authority of this saying is regarded by many Muslim scholars as "weak," it is significant that it is quoted by Muslims in the context of the modern conflict:

> "Abu Hurairah said, 'The Messenger of Allah, peace be upon him, said, "The Last Hour will not come until the Muslims fight against

the Jews, and the Muslims kill them until the Jews hide themselves behind a stone or a tree and the stone or tree will say: 'O Muslim, or slave of Allah, there is a Jew behind me; come and kill him'; but the gharqad tree will not say that, for it is the tree of the Jews."[41]

Many of these traditional ideas have been developed in recent years into a kind of apocalyptic writing that has become very popular and which has strong similarities to Christian writing about the end times (see Chapter 6). Gershom Gorenberg describes an example of this kind of writing in his *The End of Days: Fundamentalism and the Struggle for the Temple Mount*:

> "There was Egyptian writer Sa'id Ayyub's Al-Masih al-Dajjal—that is, The Antichrist—which expands radically on the old Islamic idea that at history's finale a Jewish Antichrist will rule until Jesus, as Muslim prophet, returns to defeat him. The cover shows a hook-nosed man wearing a Star of David on his neck, an army coat with a U.S. flag and a hammer and sickle on the shoulders, and missiles on his back. Published in 1987, Al-Masih al-Dajjal spawned an entire genre of Islamic books on the End."[42]

Islamic views today

There are three areas where the vast majority of Muslims—whether they are Palestinians or not—are in agreement over the claims they make for Jerusalem:

1. The claim of Palestinians to Jerusalem is *based primarily on the length of time that Jerusalem has been in Muslim hands*. This is how H.S. Karmi, for example, states the claim: "The Arab rule for 900 years, and the subsequent Muslim rule for nearly 400 years, during which the Jews, not to mention the Zionists, had almost no religious or secular existence, cannot be expunged at will and denied capriciously."[43] Muslims frequently contrast these periods not so much with the number of years of Jewish occupation of Jerusalem from its capture by David in 1000 BCE to the banishment in 135 CE but to the number of years when Jerusalem was the capital of a united and genuinely indepen-

dent kingdom. In Karmi's reckoning this amounts to a very limited period: "This long period of about 1,300 years of continuous and integrated rule [under Islam] should be contrasted with only about 73 years of an united truly independent Jewish rule in the country, after which the Hebrew monarchy broke up into two quarrelling and fighting kingdoms...'[44]

2. They are at pains to emphasize that *Muslim rule has been far more tolerant than Christian rule*. Their conquests of the city under Umar and Saladin were much less bloody than the capture under the Crusaders, and whereas the Romans and the Christians forbade Jews from entering Jerusalem, Muslims not only gave them access to their holy sites but allowed them to live in the city. Thus Karmi emphasizes the record of Muslims in protecting the holy places: "With the exception of two isolated incidents, notably under the Fatimid Caliph Al-Hakim, the holy places in Jerusalem have been well protected and respected under the Muslims...'[45] Zaki Badawi points out some of the implications of Muslim attitudes to Judaism and Christianity:

> "... it is thanks to Muslims and their recognition of Christianity and Judaism, that the spiritual significance of Jerusalem has been absorbed by all three religions... The Dome of the Rock itself symbolises in concrete form the Muslim concept of Islam as the ultimate and complete revelation of Allah, in that it is located in the city which is at the heart of Christian doctrine and close to the site of the Temple of Judaic tradition... To us, Muslims, it is the purity of that city which makes it a House of God, a house that must be open to everyone."[46]

3. Many Muslims go one step further and argue that because of their record in the past *they are better qualified than either Jews or Christians to rule the city today*. This frequently amounts to a claim to some kind of exclusive sovereignty. Muhammad Al-Khateeb, for example, ends his book *Al-Quds: The Place of Jerusalem in Classical Judaic and Islamic Traditions* with these words: "Ultimately if the entire world truly strives for peace in the city of al-Quds, Muslims must retake the upper-hand

and regain its rule, as they alone would provide continuously the guarantee of freedom of worship and safety for the citizens of the city and they will re-implement Umar's Covenant for a third time. Only then will al-Quds be, as it is meant to be, a City of Peace."[47] A similar claim is made in the statement of the Islamic Summit which met in Lahore in February 1974: "Jerusalem is the unique symbol of the encounter of Islam with other divine religions... [for this reason] Muslims alone can be the impartial and loyal guardians of Jerusalem: they are the only ones who believe, at the same time, in the three revealed religions who have their roots in Jerusalem."[48]

In spite of the near consensus on these points amongst Muslims today, they are not all agreed about the extent to which the *Islamic* claims to Jerusalem should be pressed. The approach of the PLO and the Palestine Authority, for example, has appealed more to principles of human rights and international law than to Islamic ideology. Movements like Hamas, Islamic Jihad and Hizbullah, on the other hand, are uncompromising in arguing their claims on an Islamic basis. One of the articles of Hamas's Charter (1988), for example, includes the following:

"We must not fail to remind every Muslim that when the Jews conquered Noble Jerusalem in 1967, they stood on the doorstep of the blessed al-Aqsa Mosque and shouted with joy: 'Muhammad has died, and left girls behind.' Israel, by virtue of its being Jewish, and its Jews challenge Islam and the Muslims. 'So the eyes of the cowards do not sleep.'[49]

Peter Riddell sums up this approach as it has been articulated by the leaders of Hamas in recent years:

"Quite simply, because of Qur'anic imperatives, land that has once been part of the Islamic domain, and especially holy sites such as Jerusalem, can never be allowed to pass under non-Muslim—in this case Jewish—authority. It was in this context that Jerusalem Mufti Sheikh Ekrima Sabri issued a fatwa (an authoritative ruling on a religious matter) in January 2001 declaring the entire Temple Mount area of Jerusalem as the property of God, in trust to the Muslim waqf authority, and thus unable to be transferred to other sovereignty. The area encompassed by the Sheikh's declaration even extended to the Western Wall, the most sacred site of Judaism. M.A. Rauf articulates such a view concisely in relation to Jerusalem, echoing Hamas views, as follows: 'any property belonging to a Muslim has sanctity. When that property is the "house of God," it becomes a permanent, inalienable property, with sanctity that is incalculable, and the violation of such sanctity is a severe offence to Muslim sensibility."[50]

The ideas of the Lebanese party Hizbullah about the liberation of Jerusalem are explained as follows by Amal Saad-Ghorayeb:

"As a direct consequence of Hizbu'llah's deligitimisation of the Israeli state, the party's long cherished aim of liberating Jerusalem—and by extension, Palestine—from Israeli occupation, constitutes the most rudimentary existential foundation of its struggle with Israel and the underlying theme of the aforementioned existential dimensions.

"According to the party, this aspiration to return 'every grain of Palestinian soil' to its rightful owners necessitates Israel's 'obliteration from existence'. Put simply, the reconstitution of one state is contingent upon the annihilation of another. The only way that the Palestinians can return to Jerusalem, and the 'original Palestine of 1948' generally, is for all Jews, with the exception of those native to Palestine, to 'leave this region and return to the countries from whence they came'."[51]

At the end of this survey four questions remain which many will want to put to Muslims—some of which are very similar to the questions raised about Jerusalem and Judaism:

1. Are Muslims willing to *recognize the claims of others* to Jerusalem? Some of the statements of Muslim religious and political leaders reveal an unwillingness even at times to admit that Jews might have claims to the same sites which are based on history and religion in the same way that Islamic claims are. While they are not being asked to agree with these claims or support them, there often seems a deep-seated reluctance to express any kind of sympathy or empathy with them.
2. Are they willing to *share Jerusalem with others*? Do their Islamic history and theology demand exclusive sovereignty?

3. What happens when there is a *clash of fundamentalisms* —Islamic and Jewish? What if the fundamentalisms within the two faiths look rather like carbon copies of each other?

4. What kind of *debate goes on among Muslims*, especially between those who are Islamist or fundamentalist and those who are not? At what stage, if ever, are Islamists/fundamentalists willing to accept the possibility of compromise, and become less idealistic and more pragmatic in facing the situation that exists today?

6
Jerusalem in Christian Zionism

A dream of victory for some turns into a nightmare for others

"What's happening in Jerusalem today? Jerusalem the Golden is caught in a supernatural crossfire... We are racing toward the end of time, and Israel lies in the eye of the storm."
John Hagee [1]

"In a view of Jerusalem we uncover more than the history *of the world; we also discover the* forecast. *In Jerusalem we can find the key to the future of the universe and the hope of all mankind."*
John Hagee [2]

"In the end, we win, and we will be with Jesus."
Tim LaHaye and Jerry B. Jenkins [3]

"Dispensationalism is one of the most influential theological systems within the universal church today. Largely unrecognized and subliminal, it has increasingly shaped the presuppositions of fundamentalist, evangelical, Pentecostal and charismatic thinking concerning Israel and Palestine over the past one hundred and fifty years."
Stephen R. Sizer [4]

Somewhere between 25 and 70 million Christians in the USA—and no doubt many more in the rest of the world—hold very definite views about the future of Jerusalem, which are based on the way they interpret the Bible. The leaders of this movement claim that they can reach an even larger audience of over 100 million Americans every week through their radio and television programmes, and see them as potential voters.[5] According to Stephen Sizer, "Conservative estimates would suggest that the Christian Zionist movement is at least ten times larger than the Jewish Zionist movement and has become the dominant lobby within contemporary American politics."[6]

These "Christian Zionists" are *Christians* who strongly support *Zionism*, but do so for *Christian* reasons. Their understanding of the future, which is based on a very literal interpretation of the Bible, leads them to believe that the creation of the state of Israel in 1948 and the capture of East Jerusalem in 1967 were highly significant events which provide vital clues to God's plan for the future of the world. This interpretation of history provides great comfort for those who believe it, for "in the end, we win, and we will be with Jesus."[7] But the prospects for those who do not believe it, as we shall see, are not so encouraging.

The origins of Christian Zionism

These ideas have been developed comparatively recently in the history of the Christian church. Although they draw on ideas that have been held in the past, as a complete system they represent a very modern phenomenon which departs significantly from traditional Christian teaching. Several theologians in the first few centuries believed that the millennium referred to in Revelation 20:1–10 would be a literal period of 1000 years in which peace and prosperity would prevail over the whole world. Many Christians in the Middle Ages were fascinated by vivid apocalyptic visions about the end of the world.[8] Thomas Brightman, writing in 1585, was probably the first Christian writer in English who called for the creation of a Jewish state in Palestine as a fulfilment of biblical prophecy.[9] Don Wagner speaks of him as "the British forerunner of Christian Zionism, a type of John the Baptist in this field."[10]

The Puritans in the seventeenth and eighteenth centuries, with their love for the Old Testament, believed that its many prophecies about the Jewish people would one day be fulfilled in a return to their ancient homeland. Then in the nineteenth century a number of Christian teachers and politicians in Britain developed ideas about the future of the Jewish people that were very close to the later Zionist vision and which were eventually adopted as the policy of the British government. Benjamin Disraeli's novel *Tancred* and George Eliot's *Daniel Deronda* popularized the dream of Jewish restoration for many Victorians. Stephen Sizer's recent study of the origins of Christian Zionism points out that one of the most significant people in this process was Lord Shaftesbury who "became convinced that the restoration of the Jews to Palestine was not only predicted in the Bible, but also coincided with the strategic interests of British foreign policy. Others who shared this perspective, in varying degrees and for different reasons, included Lord Palmerston, David Lloyd George and Lord Balfour."[11] This estimate is confirmed by an American writer, Don Wagner, who goes on to say:

"One cannot overstate the influence of Lord Shaftesbury on the British political elite, church leaders, and the average Christian layperson. His efforts and religious-political thought may have set the tone for England's colonial approach to the Near East and in particular to the 'holy' land during the next one hundred years. He single-handedly translated the theological positions of Brightman, Henry Finch, and John Nelson Darby into a political strategy. His high political connections, matched by his uncanny instincts, combined to advance the Christian Zionist vision…

"A final (albeit unknown) contribution of Shaftesbury, was his formulation of a form of the phrase that became the slogan of the Zionist movement: 'A land of no people for a people with no land.' Zionist leaders Israel Zangwell and Theodor Herzl are credited with this slogan, but it is likely that they borrowed it from Lord Shaftesbury, who first cast the idea somewhat differently a generation before them: 'A country without a nation for a nation without a country.' He advanced the theme during the 1840s, more than fifty years before the Zionist movement held its first Congress."[12]

The most significant development in the nineteenth century came through John Nelson Darby (1880–1955), an Irish clergyman who came out of the Church of Ireland and travelled extensively in Europe and the USA, founding around 1500 churches of the "Christian Brethren." Darby brought many of these ideas about the Jews together and added new ones to create a complete system called "Dispensationalism," which described in considerable detail a scenario of how the history of the world would develop through a series of events that would unfold in and around Jerusalem. According to this system the whole of history is divided into a series of "dispensations" or periods of time, the last of which is "the millennium" referred to in chapter 20 of the book of Revelation (see Chapter 2).

These ideas were later popularized by preachers like D.L. Moody in the USA and by Charles Haddon Spurgeon in Britain. Thus, as Don Wagner points out, "By the time Theodor Herzl and the early Jewish Zionist fathers began to lobby British politicians on behalf of the Zionist dream, they found a ready audience."[13] It also needs to be recognized that, in the words of Stephen Sizer, "Christian Zionism, through its active and public support for Jewish restoration to Palestine, predated the rise of Jewish Zionism by at least 60 years."[14] In the twentieth century these ideas were disseminated even more widely through Cyrus I. Schofield, who worked them into detailed notes in what became known as the *Schofield Reference Bible*, published by the Oxford University Press in 1909. This edition of the Bible is described by Sizer as "the most influential book among evangelicals during the first half of the twentieth century."[15]

The distinctive ideas of Christian Zionism

One of the best ways to understand the world view of Christian Zionists is to be exposed to their ideas as expressed in their own words. Three well-known writers of this kind reveal very clearly their understanding of how the conflict over Jerusalem will develop in the near future. *Final Dawn Over Jerusalem* was written in 1998 by John Hagee, a prominent biblical teacher in the USA.[16] *Armageddon* is the eleventh and latest in a series of novels known as the *Left*

Behind series, by Tim LaHaye and Jerry B. Jenkins.[17] They present a fictionalized account of the Rapture (the sudden disappearance of millions of Christian believers who are all suddenly taken up to heaven at the same time) and the Tribulation (a period of severe persecution in which others have the opportunity to become followers of Jesus but are under constant attack from the forces of evil). These books have frequently been on the best-seller list of Christian publishers and of well-known newspapers like the *New York Times* and *USA Today*. By October 2003 they had sold over 50 million copies. The third writer is Hal Lindsey, who has written more than twenty books and been described as "the best known prophecy teacher in the world."[18] His most widely known book, *The Late Great Planet Earth* (1970) has become one of the best-selling books in the world.[19]

In all these books there are six basic convictions which relate to the future of Jerusalem:

1. The Jewish people have a divine right to the whole land of Israel/Palestine and to Jerusalem

Hagee sums up his belief in this way:

> "God established Israel's national geographic boundaries. The exact borders of Israel are detailed in Scripture just as our heavenly Father dictated them. The divine Surveyor drove the original stakes into Judean soil and decreed that no one should ever change these property lines. The real estate contract and land covenants were signed in blood and stand to this very hour. Jews have the absolute right as mandated by God to the land of Israel and, more specifically, to the city of Jerusalem."[20]

2. Jerusalem has a specially significant role as the "city of God," "God's city"

In *Armageddon* we are told that "The so-called Messiah loves the city of Jerusalem above all cities in the world. He even calls it the Eternal City."[21] While some of what the biblical prophets wrote about Jerusalem has been fulfilled, much still remains to be fulfilled.

When all these passages are put together, according to Hagee, "The people of Israel and their Holy City will soon fill the major role in a coming world drama."[22] In the millennium "Jerusalem, that blessed city, will be the capital of Jesus Christ... Jerusalem, the apple of God's eye, will become the joy of the world."[23] "Israel and its Holy City, Jerusalem, holds the keys to the future. What happens in the Jewish state affects what God is doing with the rest of the world, so the better we understand Israel, the more comprehensive will be our grasp of things to come."[24] "The future of the Holy City is the centrepiece of God's blueprint for history. God will reorder, restore, redouble, redistribute, reclaim, remove, renovate, recycle, recommit and redeem until Jerusalem has become the crowning gem of all the cities on earth."[25] Since God views Jerusalem in this way, he is bound to defend it against all attack: "God will preserve Jerusalem. It is *His* Holy City."[26] "If God created Israel by His spoken word, has sworn to defend Israel, and has chosen Jerusalem as His habitation on earth, then will He not fight against those who come against the apple of His eye?'[27]

3. The modern state of Israel is continuous with biblical Israel

There is a direct connection between the people of "Israel" in the Bible and the modern state of Israel, and the really important event since the first century was the establishment of the state in 1948. Thus for Hagee, "The resurrection of God's chosen people is living prophetic proof that Israel has not been replaced. They were reborn in a day (Isaiah 66:8) to form the State of Israel that shall endure until the coming of Messiah."[28] And in *Armageddon* Jesus of Nazareth the Messiah "is the one who is coming to fight for Israel. He will avenge all the wrongs that have been perpetrated upon us over the centuries."[29]

4. The world as we know it will come to an end in the near future

In *Armageddon* we are told that "God has a master plan. It is the culmination of the battle between good and evil that has spanned millennia."[30] "The battle of the ages that has raged since the beginning of time is about to reach its climax."[31] Hal Lindsey, writing in 1981, was confident that "We are the generation that will see the end times... and the return of Jesus."[32] Later, in 1995, in *The Final Battle*, he claims to describe "in more detail and explicitness than any other just what will happen to humanity and to the Earth, not a thousand years from now, but in our lifetime—indeed in this very generation."[33] Lindsey was so convinced about the imminence of the climax that he interpreted the words of Jesus about the coming of the Son of Man in Mark 9:1 to mean that the Second Coming of Christ would take place in the year 1988.[34]

5. The Bible gives detailed predictions about the future

If the Bible is seen as "history written in advance,"[35] it becomes a kind of handbook from which we can read the future. Hagee, for example, explains how he sees the Bible: "God has made it possible to know the future through Bible prophecy. My years of studying the writings of the ancient Bible prophets have given me a panoramic view, not only of what is ahead, but how it will all unfold. The guidelines for tomorrow are available to us today."[36] Similarly, in *Armageddon*, the Antichrist boasts that he knows the future because the Bible gives a detailed plan of what will happen: "Father and son thought they were doing the world a favour by putting their intentions in writing. The whole plan is there, from sending the son to die and resurrect, to foretelling this entire period... I read their book! I know what they are up to! I know what happens next, and I even know where! ... I will win in the end because I have read their battle plan."[37]

These are some of the major events that are predicted with certainty:

—The Rapture, in which millions all over the world who are the "real Christians" will be removed and taken up to heaven in an instant. This event, which inevitably causes chaos when pilots of planes and drivers of cars are spirited away, is based on a literal interpretation of the words of Jesus: "two men will be in the field; one will be taken and the other left behind" (Matthew 24:40), and the words of Paul, "We who are still alive and are left will be caught up... in the clouds to meet the Lord in the air" (1 Thessalonians 4:15–16).

—The Arabs join forces with other Islamic nations and with Russia to attack Israel. "The prophet Ezekiel," says Hagee, "saw a vast Arab coalition of nations coming against Israel (Ezekiel 38–39). These armies will cover the land like a cloud."[38] In *Armageddon*, as they advance, the river Euphrates is dried up, enabling the kings of the East to bring their armaments to Megiddo in Israel on dry land. "Great columns of soldiers, tanks, trucks, and armaments... rolling west from as far away as Japan and China and India."[39]

—In most of the Dispensationalist schemes, predictions in the Old and New Testaments about a desecration of the Temple (e.g. Daniel 9:27; Matthew 24:15; 2 Thessalonians 2:3–4) are taken to mean that there has to be a restored Jewish Temple in Jerusalem at the time of the Second Coming. Hal Lindsey therefore states dogmatically:

> "Obstacle or no obstacle, it is certain that the Temple will be rebuilt. Prophecy demands it... With the Jewish nation reborn in the land of Palestine, ancient Jerusalem once again under total Jewish control for the first time in 2,600 years, and talk of rebuilding the great Temple, the most important sign of Jesus Christ's soon coming is before us... It is like the key pieces of a jigsaw puzzle being found... For all those who trust in Jesus Christ, it is a time of electrifying excitement."[40]

In case we wonder what happens to the present Dome of the Rock to enable the Temple to be rebuilt, in the *Left Behind* series the Antichrist makes a peace treaty with Israel in which the Muslims agree to move the Dome of the Rock to New Babylon and the Jews are thus able to rebuild the Temple.[41] Another explanation that has been offered is that Orthodox Jews will blow up the mosque and this will provoke the Muslim world. It will lead to a cataclysmic holy war with Israel. This will force the Messiah to intervene.[42] It was ideas of this kind which motivated an Australian Christian, Denis Michael Rohan, in 1969 to attempt to set fire to the Al-Aqsa Mosque. The fire was put out, but it completely destroyed the famous Aleppo pulpit that had been put there by Saladin (see Chapter 5). At his trial Rohan explained that he wanted to see the Jewish Temple rebuilt "for sweet Jesus to return and pray in it."[43]

—In the conflict between Israel and these enemies, God will intervene to defend the Jews, using nuclear weapons. According to Hagee:

> "In the latter days, just prior to the Second Coming, the nations of the world will gather to fight against Jerusalem, and God will defend His habitation on earth... I believe this (Zechariah 14:12) is Zechariah's description of a nuclear blast, which can generate 150 million degrees Fahrenheit in one millionth of a second... God will allow the use of nuclear weapons in this great battle against Israel, but then He will step into the fray... God will open fire with His divine artillery and rain down on Israel's offenders 'great hailstones, fire, and brimstone' (Ezekiel 38:22). The battle casualties will be staggering. Five out of six enemy troops that attack Israel in this Russian-led pan-Islamic force will die. It will take seven months to bury the dead (Ezekiel 39:12). It will take seven years to burn the implements of war (Ezekiel 39:9)."[44]

—The capture of Jerusalem proves to be the final trigger for the Second Coming of Christ. According to Hal Lindsey, "The Bible also makes clear that Jerusalem—the focal point of the end times fighting—will be vanquished by Israel's enemies in the hours just before the Lord comes. In fact, it seems that the destruction of the holy city is the final straw that angers God and provokes Jesus" return."[45] When this happens Christ appears "on a white horse with ten thousand of his saintly army,"[46] who are described as "the Calvary cavalry,"[47] and Jesus returns in triumph to the Mount of Olives where he initiates a literal period of 1000 years in which he rules the world in peace.[48]

6. The Bible provides a basis for specific political policies today

If this is what Christians Zionists believe about the future of Jerusalem, it is not surprising that these ideas are translated into very clear views about the present conflict in Israel. For Hagee, for example, Israel is "America's only true friend in the Middle East,"[49] and "God blesses the man or nation that blesses Israel or the Jewish people."[50] Israel therefore becomes the key to America's survival: "Why is it so important for America to lock arms with the nation of Israel? The reasons are revealed in the biblical history of the Jewish people. America's fate depends upon our treatment of the nation of Israel."[51]

Christian Zionists therefore support Jewish claims to Jerusalem as the undivided and eternal capital of Israel.[52] As a result, Hagee is extremely critical of the Oslo Accord that was signed between Israel and the Palestinians in 1993: "What happened in the Rose Garden in 1993 was the first major birth pang of World War III. The peace process leads Israel down the road to disaster."[53] Moreover, he explicitly rules out the possibility of shared sovereignty with the Palestinians:

> "A shared Jerusalem? Never! A 'shared Jerusalem' means control of the Holy City would be wrested away from the Jewish people and given, at least in part, to the Palestine Liberation Organization. I say 'never,' not because I dislike Arab people or Palestinians, but because the Word of God says it is God's will for Jerusalem to be under the exclusive control of the Jewish people until the Messiah comes. According to Genesis chapters 12, 13, 15, 17, 26 and 28, only the Jewish people have a legitimate claim to the city. That's not my viewpoint, that's God's opinion! God doesn't care what the United Nations thinks or what the NCC (National Council of Churches) believes. He gave Jerusalem to the nation of Israel, and it is theirs."[54]

If these ideas were simply believed privately by individuals and taught in the churches for the edification and encouragement of Christians, the rest of the world might have little cause for concern. But when they are turned into arguments in support of particular policies, the rest of the world is forced to sit up and take notice. There is plenty of evidence, for example, to show that two American presidents in particular have not only talked about their convictions on these subjects but admitted that they have influenced their policies regarding the Middle East. Jimmy Carter in recent years has adopted a more even-handed approach to the conflict and in December 2003 supported the Geneva Accord. In 1978, however, he described the state of Israel as "a return at last to the biblical land from which the Jews were driven so many hundreds of years ago... The establishment of the nation of Israel is the fulfilment of biblical prophecy and the very essence of its fulfilment." But when he was critical of Israel's settlement policy on the West Bank and proposed the creation of a Palestinian homeland, he lost the support of many Jews and Christians, who gave their support in the 1980 election to Ronald Reagan.[55]

Some of Reagan's statements show the extent to which his political views were influenced by his biblical interpretation: "We have a pledge to Israel to the preservation of that nation... we have an obligation, a responsibility, and a destiny." "We could be the generation that sees Armageddon." "Israel is the only stable democracy we can rely on as a spot where Armageddon could come."[56] Speaking to Tom Dine, the Director of AIPAC, an Israeli lobby group in the USA, he said: "You know, I turn back to your ancient prophets in the Old Testament and the signs foretelling Armageddon, and I find myself wondering if we're the generation that is going to see that come about."[57]

Ideas of this kind continue to influence government policy. For, as Paul Vallely of the *Independent* suggests in relation to the *Left Behind* series, "The trouble is that these books are seriously influencing the foreign policies of the United States, and the approach of President George Bush to life-and-death issues involving Israel and Iraq, and America's semi-detached attitude to the United Nations."[58] Perhaps we are beginning to understand, therefore, why the White House continues to receive so many thousands of emails from Christians urging George Bush to reject the "Road Map for Peace" and to support the policies of recent Israeli governments over Jerusalem. It seems that, as Jerry Falwell has said, "The Bible Belt is Israel's safety net in the US."[59]

The assumptions of Christian Zionism

All these beliefs of Christian Zionists can be traced back to two fundamental assumptions. The first is that the Bible must always be interpreted literally; when it speaks about the future, we have to understand that its predictions have to be fulfilled in a very precise and literal way. Little allowance is made for the fact that some of the prophetic writings in the Bible are visions which are described in vivid and highly symbolic language. Schofield, for example, was insistent that "Not one instance exists of a 'spiritual' or figurative fulfilment of prophecy... Jerusalem is always Jerusalem, Israel is always Israel, Zion is always Zion... Prophecies may never be spiritualised, but are always literal."[60] And Hal Lindsey says, "If you take the Bible literally, then you come up with the premillennial point of view... I *hate* those who read their ideas into the scripture by using allegory."[61]

This means that the millennium described in the visions of John (see Chapter 2) has to be interpreted as a literal period of 1000 years. Thus in *Armageddon,* when Jesus comes back to this world, he will come "to set up his millennial kingdom, re-establishing Israel and making Jerusalem the capital forever!... Jerusalem will be made more beautiful, more efficient. It will be prepared for its role as the new capital in the Messiah's thousand-year kingdom."[62] Descriptions in Revelation of a great, final battle at Armageddon are combined with passages in the prophet Zechariah describing enemies who attack the city of Jerusalem. Armageddon therefore becomes the staging area of the world's armies, and "The actual conflicts will take place... at Petra... and at Jerusalem... the One World Unity Army consists of all the soldiers, livestock, rolling stock, and munitions available anywhere. The fighting force of untold millions covers the plains of Israel from the Plain of Megiddo in the north to Bozrah in Edom in the south and stretches east to west almost the entire breadth of what was once known as the Holy Land."[63]

The second assumption is that the church is totally distinct from the Jewish people. These writers are insistent that "Scripture plainly indicates that the church and national Israel exist side by side and that neither replaces the other—not yesterday, not today, not tomorrow."[64] "... Scripture describes and defines two Israels: one is a physical Israel, with an indigenous people, a capital city called Jerusalem and geographic borders plainly defined in scripture. Yet there is also a spiritual Israel, with a spiritual people and a spiritual New Jerusalem. Spiritual Israel, the church, may enjoy the blessings of physical Israel, but it does not replace physical Israel in God's plan for the ages."[65] One consequence of this approach, as Don Wagner points out, is that the nation of Israel will become "God's primary instrument" to carry out His will... "In this way, the Christian Church becomes a non-factor in the premillennial approach, for it has been removed from history and replaced with the nation of Israel."[66]

If it is not already obvious why these ideas are radically different from the more traditional ways of interpreting the Bible that have been explored in Chapters 1 and 2, the following observations may point out some of the far-reaching—and dangerous—implications of Christian Zionist ideas about Jerusalem.

1. This approach represents a very confusing mixture of theology and fiction, of Bible and pure fantasy

Paul Vallely describes the process by which all the novels in the *Left Behind* series have been written: "LaHaye prepares thirty- to fifty-page summaries for each book, which turn biblical references to plagues, famines, wars and storms into succinct modern plot points. He suggests a few characters, and then Jenkins, who has written more than eighty novels, churns out the fictional prose and dialogue."[67] It seems therefore as if there is no need for the study of history or political science; the writers move straight from the text of the Bible to construct their fantasy about the future.

In *Armageddon* there are references to several places in Jerusalem today like the Yad Vashem Historical Museum, the Rockefeller Museum, the Jaffa Road, the Bethesda Pool and several of the Gates like the Damascus Gate and the Dung Gate. The "garden where the traditional site of Jesus' tomb lay" is probably a reference not to the churches that mark the traditional sites of the crucifixion and the empty tomb but to Gordon's Calvary, a site that was discovered in the nineteenth century and has become popular with Christians from the West. But at many points we enter a world of fantasy that bears little relationship to the realities on the ground. Those who have seen the River Jordan, for example, will be surprised to read that it is deep and wide enough to have many touring boats sailing on it. When a helicopter carrying forces of believers lands on the Temple Mount, we read of "hundreds of angry people scattering and raising their fists... It was amazing to see the zeal in their eyes when their ancient holy sites were threatened."[68] It seems that there are no Palestinians in Israel but only Jews, and of course no suggestion that there might be some genuine, believing Christians among the Palestinians. There is absolutely nothing in the books which relates to the actual history of what has happened in the region in the last hundred years—let alone the last twenty centuries. One is left wondering how, in the authors" minds, they imagine that the situation on the ground today is supposed to develop into the fantastic scenario that they describe.

Because the ancient city of Babylon is located in the modern Iraq, and because in the book of Revelation Babylon is used as a symbol of an evil state, Iraq becomes the headquarters of the Antichrist's government which plans a meeting for all the leaders of the world in a building in Baghdad "where the Iraq Museum used to be before the war."[69] Ninety per cent of the weaponry of all the nations of the world—"enough firepower to destroy the planet'[70]—is collected at Al Hillah, south of Baghdad. Nicolae Carpathia, the leader of all the forces arrayed against God, is described as "former president of Romania; former secretary-general, United Nations; self-appointed Global Community Potentate...'[71] It hardly needs to be pointed out that in this way Romania, Iraq and the United Nations are inevitably cast in a very bad light.

2. If these novels provide comfort and encouragement to believers, there is no incentive to deal with the realities that exist today

Some Christian readers of the *Left Behind* series will no doubt enjoy being caught up in the adventures of all the characters who dash round the world in planes, helicopter and cars. One character seems to enjoy using deadly weapons: "That missile was God's protection, but wasn't it fun to attack with the directed energy weapon?'[72] Those who already believe will certainly feel secure in the knowledge that they are on the winning side, because everything is "in the believers' favor."[73] One of the heroes in *Armageddon* learns "that God was real, he was in control, he was the archenemy of Antichrist, and in the end God would win... She was too polite to gloat, but she couldn't deny some private satisfaction in knowing that one day she would be proved right."[74]

If there is no attempt by any of these writers to understand what the present conflict between Israel and the Palestinians over Jerusalem is all about, there is also no suggestion that Christians (or anyone else for that matter) should want to find peaceful solutions to the conflict. Since the script describes a final conflict which is inevitable and will shortly come to its dreadful climax, all that matters is that people are encouraged to decide to be on the winning side and therefore put their trust in Christ. Any attempt to resolve the conflict would simply result in delaying the Second Coming of Christ. The logic here is that "We're not going to try to stop prophesied events, of course, but it'll be good to know exactly what's happening."[75] Human activity helps to usher in the coming of Christ: "... if that's what it took to usher in Jesus, well, bring it on."[76]

These ideas have been explained by televangelist Pat Robertson in this way: "The next event on the clock is the return of Christ. Things in society should get worse rather than better. If Christians worked to turn our nation around, that would delay Christ's return." Vallely comments: "Peace is not only impossible, it's not even desirable, since wars are what will usher in the end times. Which is why another televangelist, Jim Robinson, was able to deliver the opening prayer at a Republican National convention with the words, 'There will be no peace until Jesus comes. Any preaching of peace prior to his return is heresy. It is against the word of God. It is anti-Christ."[77]

3. Some of the predictions seem less likely today than they were when they were written

It is not difficult to imagine how American Christians during the period of the Cold War could think of Russia as an evil empire because of its atheistic ideology, its suppression of the Christian faith and its warlike rhetoric against the West. It is understandable therefore that during that period of stand-off between the USA and Russia, Hagee could imagine this kind of scenario: "The Scud missiles Saddam Hussein launched from Iraq could next be launched from the Golan Heights. Or the attack could come from the Mediterranean Sea via missiles launched from Russian submarines sold to wealthy Arab nations...'[78] Since Russia has at various times had very close political relationships with Syria and Egypt, it is not surprising that Hagee could make predictions like this in the 1980s: "... a reborn Russia seeking to again become a military superpower will in the near future lead a massive pan-Islamic military expedition in an attempt to conquer Israel... Russia will say to the Islamic nations, 'You want Jerusalem and the temple mount as a holy site. We want the Persian Gulf oil. Let's join forces to rule the world!' Watch as in the future Russia becomes extremely congenial to all Islamic states."[79]

But what happens when Russia ceases to be the great superpower that is locked in battle with the USA? What happens when the Berlin Wall comes down, when Russia's military and political power is severely weakened, when it is driven out of Afghanistan, and when the southern republics gain a large measure of independence? When predictions begin to seem less likely, they have to be quietly withdrawn or rewritten. When Egypt and Syria, for example, came together in 1959 to form the United Arab Republic, many students of prophecy pointed to this as the fulfilment of Isaiah's prophecy about a highway linking Egypt and Assyria (Isaiah 19:23). Did they then reject the idea when they found that the union lasted for only two years? On the basis of Jesus" parable of the fig tree in Mark 13:28–31, Hal Lindsey confidently predicted that the Second Coming would be in or around the year 1988 (i.e. forty years, the length of one generation, after 1948). Writing in 1970 in *The Late Great Planet Earth*, he spoke of the army attacking Israel as "The

Russian Force," which also included Chinese and African armies. But in 1997 he spoke about "The Russian–Muslim force," and by 1999 it had become a "Muslim–Russian alliance."[80] The script, in other words, has to be constantly rewritten.

4. The full Dispensationalist scenario involves intense suffering for millions

In *Armageddon* the city of Babylon is destroyed in one hour; every building is levelled, every resident is slaughtered, the entire metropolis is aflame, and all that is left is ash and smoke.[81] The slaughter in the battle of Armageddon is so great that it creates rivers of blood over four feet or more deep.[82] It is the fate of the Jewish people, however, that cannot easily be passed over. One dispensationalist writer, Charles Ryrie, describes the battle as "the time of Israel's greatest bloodbath," and another scholar, Walvoord, similarly predicts "a holocaust in which at least 750 million people will perish..."[83] The alternative to destruction for the Jews is conversion to Christianity. In *Armageddon*, therefore, we are told that, on the basis of Zechariah 13, "The Bible teaches that a third of the remaining Jews will turn to Messiah before the end."[84] Charles M. Sennott sums up bluntly the alternatives for Jews in this scenario: "They will either have to embrace Jesus as Lord or perish in the final battle."[85]

An American journalist, Grace Halsell, in *Prophecy and Politics: Militant Evangelists on the Road to Nuclear War*, spells out the implications of this vision of the future for the Jewish people as it is painted by Christian Zionists of different kinds: "Convinced that a nuclear Armageddon is an inevitable event within the divine scheme of things, many evangelical dispensationalists have committed themselves to a course for Israel that, by their own admission, will lead directly to a holocaust indescribably more savage and widespread than any vision of carnage that could have generated in Adolf Hitler's criminal mind."[86] Gershom Gorenberg, an Israeli Jew, writing in *The End of Days: Fundamentalism and the Struggle for the Temple Mount*, sums up the likely reaction of many Jews to this vision of the future of Jerusalem and the Jews: "The ultimate goal was Israel's good only if you consider the slaughter or conversion of Jews to be in their own interest."[87]

5. If Jews welcome the support of Christian Zionists who have these hopes and expectations about the future of the Jewish people, they do so for political rather than religious reasons

Prime Minister Ariel Sharon, addressing a Christian Zionist rally in Jerusalem in October 2002, said, "You are the best friends Israel has."[88] When Charles M. Sennott asked David Bar-Illan, one of Netanyahu's chief advisers, about what seemed to be a cynical alliance, the reply was: "We worry much less about what goes on in their minds, and focus on what they do on the ground to support us."[89] "Professor Wistrich," according to Richard Harries, the Bishop of Oxford, "suggests that most Jews probably take a fairly cynical view, namely that 'These guys are nuts, but we want all the votes we can get for Israel, and we can't afford to worry about the theological niceties' or, as he himself puts it more soberly, 'From the Jewish point of view, it has not always been easy to balance the advantage of such support against the disadvantage of its linkage with a programme or at least a hope for conversion.'"[90]

Some Jews, however, have strongly criticized Israeli reliance on Christian fundamentalism. Leonard Fein, for example, writes: "Have we no shame? When we make common cause, however limited, with these people, we add to their strength—and we diminish this nation [Israel]... The evangelicals are doubtless warmed by our embrace. When they are warmed, I am chilled."[91]

Some readers will no doubt be appalled to find that these are the ideas that, along with other interests, are influencing the policy of the one superpower in the world towards Jerusalem and the Israeli–Palestinian conflict. If at least three presidents in recent times have held views of this kind, many in their administrations have probably shared the same views. And governments that want to stay in power have to listen to this large Christian lobby, whose interests seem to coincide with those of many Jews in the USA and with right-wing governments in Israel.

Christians who *do not* share these views are equally appalled—and ashamed—to find that the Bible and beliefs of this kind are being exploited for political ends and have such enormous and immediate consequences. Peter Walker, whose work underlies the approach developed in Chapters 2 and 3 (Jerusalem in the New Testament and "Christian" Jerusalem) shows how reading from the same hymn sheet, it is possible to sing a very different tune. This is how he spells out why the beliefs of Christian Zionists are rejected so vehemently by other Christians:

"Although they were faced with the very same Old Testament passages as we are today, the New Testament writers did not reach a 'Zionist' conclusion. Instead they reached a distinctively Christian conclusion which affirmed the faithfulness of God to his ancient promises and saw these as now fulfilled, even if in an unexpected way, in the coming of Jesus. Biblical Christians today need to follow their lead. To do otherwise, either denying this fulfilment in Jesus, or seeking for a further, more literalistic fulfilment belittles and misconstrues the greatness of what God has done in Jesus and is ultimately derogatory to the person of Jesus and his uniqueness.

"… the future expectation of the New Testament writers did not include some end-times rebuilding of the Temple or a 'restoration' of Jerusalem, precisely because in Jesus that Temple has been revealed and that restoration accomplished.

"… the appeal to Jerusalem's uniqueness does not become the basis for some 'special pleading' in which God's universal concerns for righteousness, mercy, love and promotion of his Gospel are somehow swept aside as though here God has some quite different agenda. This is important, since belief in the 'sacred' nature of Jerusalem can fuel the conviction that God's purposes here might somehow be different elsewhere. There are no 'special rules' for Jerusalem. The supposed 'sacredness' of Jerusalem may blind people to their ethical responsibilities; by contrast, acknowledging Jerusalem's specialness (its centrality in biblical history) should have the opposite effect. Here, above all, it would be ironic if the biblical message went unheeded, but so appropriate if it was obeyed."[92]

Christian Zionism is a novelty that goes against the mainstream of twenty centuries of Christian tradition, and is increasingly being labelled by other Christians as a heresy.[93] Starting from the same—or similar—views about the *authority* and *inspiration* of the Bible that are held by Christian Zionists, but with a different approach to its *interpretation*, this whole book points to other ways of using the Bible in relation to the questions surrounding Jerusalem—ways that might be more genuinely Christian and at the same time more appropriate to the realities on the ground. It is to these realities that we now turn.

7

Jerusalem and Zionism up to 1967

A pious dream is turned into a reality

"I believe that when the guns stop firing you may get your Jerusalem."
Lord Balfour, speaking to Chaim Weizmann [1]

"Tel Aviv was the real capital of Zionism until the foundation of the state of Israel—and, in all but name, for some time thereafter."
Bernard Wasserstein [2]

"Jerusalem was and will for ever be our capital. Eretz Israel will be restored to the people of Israel. All of it. And for ever."
Menachem Begin [3]

"We have united Jerusalem, the divided capital of Israel. We have returned to the holiest of our Holy Places, never to part from it again."
Moshe Dayan, 7 June 1967 [4]

"Jerusalem is one city, indivisible, the Capital of the State of Israel."
Israeli Knesset, 28 June 1967 [5]

Jerusalem was very insignificant for the first Zionists and hardly entered into their thinking about the new homeland they wanted to create in Palestine. Jews had been praying for the restoration of Zion for centuries, and rabbis and spiritually- minded individuals had been coming to settle in Jerusalem for generations. Those involved in movements of "spiritual Zionism," like the "Lovers of Zion," had strong religious motivation for returning to Jerusalem. But the first real Zionists were interested in the coastal plains and avoided Jerusalem, despising it for its backwardness. How did it come about then that Jerusalem gradually became more and more important for the Zionist movement? If the first Zionists regarded it as provincial and backward, why did their successors fifty years later want to make it the capital of the Jewish state?

Jerusalem in the nineteenth century

A Frenchman, Constantin Volney, visiting Jerusalem in 1784 was shocked by the state of the city after 270 years of Ottoman rule. "We scarcely can believe we view that celebrated metropolis," he wrote, "which, formerly, withstood the efforts of the most powerful empires... in a word, we with difficulty recognize Jerusalem."[6] Karen Armstrong paints a depressing picture of Jerusalem at the beginning of the new century:

> "The nineteenth century began badly in Jerusalem. There was poverty and tension in the city. The Ottoman system was still in disarray, and the people suffered from bad government... There was also friction between the different communities... The different Christian denomi-nations coexisted in a state of poisonous animosity that could flare into physical violence at the smallest provocation... The city of peace was seething with frustration and resentment, and the old ideal of integration seemed a vanished dream. The anger frequently erupted in riots and uprisings."[7]

The first major catalyst for change came during the period of about ten years when the city was taken over and ruled by Ibrahim Pasha, the son of Muhammad Ali in Egypt (1832–40). There was a deliberate attempt to modernize the city, and the introduction of a secular judicial system improved the status of both the Christian and Jewish minorities. Europeans were encouraged to settle and to bring their skills, and they inevitably saw this as an opportunity to increase their influence in the country. In 1839 the first consulate of a European power was established when William Young arrived as British vice-consul, and France, Prussia and Austria followed this example by opening consulates during the next fifteen years.

Although Egyptian rule ended in 1840, the process of modernization could not now be stopped. Greater religious freedom was allowed by the Ottoman sultan and this helped both Christians and Jews to strengthen their positions. Western churches and mission agencies, both Protestant and Catholic, established schools and hospitals, and these initiatives encouraged Jews to start their own philanthropic work. Archaeologists and other scholars began to visit the country, followed by more and more visitors—early examples of today's tourists. The population increased steadily throughout the century: in 1850 the Jews of Jerusalem were 6000 (40%) out of a total population of 15000; by 1880 they had increased to 17000 (55%) out of 31000; and by 1900 they were 35000 (64%) out of 55000. When the rising population could no longer be contained within the Old City, new Jewish suburbs were built to the west and Arab suburbs to the north and east. In 1863 a municipal council was set up with nine members—six Muslims, two Christians and one Jew, with an additional Jew being added in 1908.

The new interest shown in Jerusalem by European powers encouraged the Ottoman authorities to take a greater interest in the city themselves. As a result of all these developments, Jerusalem came to be recognized as the main city in Palestine. Thus, in the words of Karen Armstrong, "From being a deserted, desperate city, Jerusalem was being transformed by modernity into a thriving metropolis, and for the first time since the destruction of the Temple, Jews were once again gaining an ascendancy."[8]

Jerusalem in early Zionism

We have already seen that earlier in the nineteenth century the vision of Jews returning to Palestine was far more widely accepted in certain Christian circles than it was among Jews (see Chapter 6). There were far more Christians than Jews who sincerely believed that such a restoration could—and would—actually come about. While Jews dreamed and prayed about a return to Zion, it was only a very small minority who took any practical steps from the 1880s onwards to realize these dreams, and most of these were not pious, practising Jews. "Theologically," says Amos Elon, "Zionism was the great Jewish heresy of the nineteenth century."[9]

For the first Zionists who built their settlements on the coastal plains and in Galilee in the 1880s, Jerusalem simply was not very important. Many of the new settlers did not even come to Jerusalem, or else were in no hurry to visit the place. In 1882 Moshe Leib Lilienblum, for example, when describing his vision for the Jewish state could write, "We do not need the walls of Jerusalem, nor the Jerusalem temple, nor Jerusalem itself."[10] When Theodor Herzl wrote *Der Judenstaat* (*"The Jewish State"*) in 1897, he did not even mention Jerusalem. On a visit to Palestine in 1898 he imagined that the capital of the state he dreamed of would be on the slopes of Mount Carmel in Haifa. "When I remember thee in days to come, O Jerusalem," he wrote, "it will not be with pleasure. The musty deposits of two thousand years of inhumanity, intolerance, and uncleanliness lie in the foul-smelling alleys... What superstition and fanaticism on every side!"[11] Similarly when Chaim Weizmann visited the Jewish quarter of Jerusalem in 1918, he described it as "nothing but filth and infection. The indescribable poverty, stubborn ignorance and fanaticism—the heart aches when one looks at it all."[12] Later, in 1937, he said concerning the Old City, "I would not take the Old City [even] as a gift. There are too many complications and difficulties associated with it."[13]

The reasons for these negative attitudes towards Jerusalem in the minds of the first Zionists were related to the nature of Zionism itself and the nature of Jerusalem. "Zionism," says Bernard Wasserstein in his *Divided Jerusalem: The Struggle for the Holy City*, "until long after the establishment of the state of Israel in 1948, remained predominantly and often aggressively secular."[14] "Jerusalem," on the other hand, "... was regarded as the home of all that was primitive and backward-looking in Judaism. Far from viewing Jerusalem with affection, they despised it and all that it stood for, particularly the traditional dependence of Jews on *halukah* (charitable dole)."[15] Wasserstein explains the variety of views about Jerusalem among the first Zionists as follows:

> "Early Zionist thinkers generally avoided attributing special importance to Jerusalem. The exponent of 'spiritual' Zionism, Ahad Ha-am, was repelled by his first encounter with the Jews of Jerusalem in 1891; when he later moved to Palestine, he chose rather to settle in Tel Aviv. The founder of political Zionism, Theodor Herzl, was shocked by Jerusalem's filth and stench when he first visited it in 1898... The early Zionist settlers in Palestine from the 1880s onwards, and particularly the socialist Zionists, who arrived in large numbers after 1904, looked down on Jerusalem and all it stood for in their eyes by way of obscurantism, religiosity and squalor... David Ben-Gurion... did not bother to visit it until three years after his immigration to Palestine...
>
> "Modern Hebrew literature too contained deeply contradictory tendencies regarding Jerusalem... In the first half of the twentieth century, a stream of writing hostile to Jerusalem, loathing it, demystifying it, even stressing its irrelevance... shaped a profoundly negative view of Jerusalem in the Hebrew literary imagination. Of course, this was only one stream of thought—but in its time perhaps the most influential and truly expressive of the Zionist revolution against Jewish traditionalism.
>
> "Thus spiritual values exalting Jerusalem competed with, and were overshadowed by, other religious, social, political and intellectual forces in forming the ambivalent modern Jewish view of Jerusalem."[16]

It is hardly surprising, therefore, that for the first fifty years or so Jerusalem hardly featured in the Zionist vision or in their plans for a Jewish homeland or state.

Preparation for independence (1948)

After Allenby entered Jerusalem in December 1917 at the head of the Allied forces it was natural that the city became their main base in Palestine and then the headquarters of the British Mandate authorities from 1920 onwards. Following the commitment made by the British government in the Balfour Declaration to support the Jewish National Home, the British authorities created the context in which the Jewish community could grow in numbers through steady immigration and become more firmly established. Benny Morris writes that "during the period between the two world wars, the enterprise unfolded under the protective carapace of British rifles and under a beneficent and efficient administration that made the tasks of the settlers and their Jewish Agency infinitely easier."[17] According to Tom Segev, another of the new Israeli historians, "Contrary to the widely held belief of Britain's pro-Arabism, British actions considerably favored the Zionist enterprise."[18]

Arab resentment against the increasing numbers and power of the Jewish community led to violent confrontations, and serious riots took place in Jerusalem in 1920 and 1929, and then again during the Arab Revolt in 1936. As a result of these conflicts a certain measure of voluntary segregation began to take place, with Arabs moving out of Jewish areas and Jews moving out of Arab areas. When, therefore, a Jerusalem committee of the Zionist Executive put forward a plan in 1937 for the partition of Jerusalem, they naturally wanted to keep the largest possible Jewish population within the Jewish areas of the city. In addition to the western suburbs they also wanted to retain Mount Scopus, but there was no suggestion that they should attempt to control the Old City.

In February 1947 the British government finally had to admit defeat in resolving the conflict and decided to hand the problem over to the United Nations, which immediately set up the United Nations Special Commission on Palestine (UNSCOP). After a visit to Palestine and weeks of deliberation, the majority of this commission recommended the creation of two states, Jewish and Arab. They also recommended that Jerusalem should be enlarged to include Bethlehem and that the whole area should become a *corpus separatum*, a separate entity that would be demilitarized and come under international rule. The partition plan was adopted by the General Assembly by thirty-three votes to thirteen, with ten abstentions, on 29 November 1947.

The Palestinian Arabs were bitterly resentful about the partition plan, partly because they believed that the allocation of land to the Jewish areas was grossly unfair, and partly because they felt that the plan was imposed on them without adequate consultation and therefore ignored the principle of self-determination. Instead of making plans to establish a Palestinian Arab state, therefore— which they *could* have done at the same time as the Jewish state was established—they responded by trying, with the help of neighbouring Arab states, to destroy the new Jewish state.

In preparing for the time when the Jews would gain their independence after the end of the British Mandate in 1948, David Ben-Gurion, who was at that time head of the Jewish Agency Executive in Palestine, spoke of a plan "to increase Jewish settlement in Jerusalem and its environs… and to ensure that the capital of our country will have a Jewish majority."[19] In spite of this the Zionist leadership did not make any special claims for Jerusalem. The reason for this was that, in Wasserstein's words:

> "They did not wish, by vainly demanding sovereignty over west Jerusalem, to risk losing international support for the creation of a Jewish state. Their diplomatic strategy was based on a resigned acceptance of the likelihood of internationalization of the city. With that in mind, they focussed their attention on the proposed borders for such an international zone in order to secure two objectives: a Jewish majority in the area and territorial connection to the Jewish state, if necessary in the form of a corridor. Why were the Zionists ready to sacrifice Jerusalem? David Ben-Gurion summed the matter up with stark simplicity. This, he said, was 'the price to be paid for statehood'."[20]

Between the passing of the UN Resolution on partition on 27 November 1947 and the end of the Mandate in May 1948, tension between the two communities resulted in violent clashes in different parts of the country and further segregation in Jerusalem. The British authorities felt powerless to contain the violence, but made matters worse by not allowing the UN even to enter the country until two weeks before the end of the Mandate.

Another important factor that militated against the interests of the Palestinian Arabs was that the Jewish leadership had already reached a secret understanding with the Jordanians. They had made it clear that when they established their state they would not be opposed to Jordan annexing the whole of the West Bank, including East Jerusalem. This crucial agreement was reached at a meeting between Golda Meir and King Abdullah on 17 November 1947. Both sides preferred this arrangement to the possibility of Palestinian Muslim leaders taking control in Jerusalem. This is how Benny Morris explains the understanding between the Jewish and the Jordanian leaders:

> "The key to understanding what was happening, and Arab disunity, lay in Amman. For two years Abdullah had been locked in intermittent, secret negotiations with the Jewish Agency with the aim of annexing eastern Palestine. He favoured partition, but between himself and the Jews... Meir in effect agreed to the proposed Jordanian takeover of the West Bank... Abdullah was far from confident of Arab victory and preferred a Jewish state as his neighbour to one run by the ex-mufti... A key feature of the Arabs" plans was the complete marginalization of the Palestinians."[21]

Britain must have been fully aware of this understanding between the two parties and given its approval. Its responsibility, therefore, both for enabling the Jewish state to come into being and for preventing the creation of a Palestinian state at this stage is summed up by Avi Shlaim in this way:

> "Many Arabs still view Israel as a bridgehead planted in their midst by Western powers determined to keep Arabs divided and to frustrate their national ambitions. As the power that issued the Balfour Declaration, Britain bears the brunt of these accusations despite its repeated claim that support for a Jewish National Home in Palestine did not imply support for turning Palestine into a Jewish state. In fact, the one thing Britain did not do during the twilight of its rule in Palestine was to act as midwife in the birth of Israel. Britain simply accepted the emergence as inevitable. If Britain was guilty of anything, it was of helping King Abdullah frustrate the establishment of a Palestinian state."[22]

This, therefore, is how Shlaim sums up the result of the first war of 1948–49 between Arabs and Israel:

"The winners were the Israelis, who extended their borders beyond the UN lines, and Abdullah, who captured the West Bank and later annexed it to Transjordan. The losers were the Palestinians, who have been without a homeland ever since… 1948… was a year of Jewish triumph and Palestinian tragedy."[23]

Independence (1948) and the declaration of Jerusalem as capital (1949)

In the Declaration of Independence establishing the state of Israel that was signed in Tel Aviv on 14 May 1948, there was no reference to Jerusalem or of any capital for the new state.[24] The new government operated from Tel Aviv and had to strengthen its hold on the Jewish majority areas of Jerusalem in order to counteract the influence of the more extreme Jewish paramilitary organizations and the ultra-orthodox and anti-Zionist groups which were strong in the city at the time.

Although the UN partition plan had called for the internationalizing of Jerusalem, this part of the plan was not actually voted on until December 1949. During this period, therefore, the new Jewish state faced an awkward dilemma over Jerusalem: they wanted to hold on to the Jewish areas of the city but resisted the idea of internationalization and, in spite of the agreement between Meir and Abdullah, did not really want King Abdullah of Jordan to take over control of East Jerusalem. The ambiguity of Israel's position during this time was clearly expressed in these words of Walter Eytan, Director General of the Foreign Ministry:

"It is certainly true that we are trying to have our cake and eat it too, in other words, to maintain our hold on the New City while at the same time trying to keep the Old City from falling into Abdullah's hands. The reason for this is that we are caught in a trap which presents us with only two logical choices: either we agree to the internationalization of the entire city, which we do not want, or else we agree to Arab rule in those parts of the city which are not in our possession—which we also do not want. Under these circumstances we are forced to take a stand lacking all logic…"[25]

In the months following the declaration of the state, the process of voluntary segregation continued until, on 6 March 1949, a British newspaper could report: "Nowhere are the results of spontaneous partition more clear-cut than in Jerusalem. Here, through intimidation, through open or surreptitious fighting, and sometimes by sensible exchange of houses, Arab and Jewish residents have sorted themselves out into separate blocks with partially derelict 'no-man's-lands' between."[26] As fighting continued, the Belgian chairman of the Truce Commission negotiated an agreement with both sides on 16 June, under which "each of the opposing parties withdrew its forces to an agreed line, and a no-man's land was established between the two lines, the houses and buildings in the no-man's land being evacuated."[27] Sporadic fighting continued for some weeks and finally came to an end after a UN Security Council Resolution on 15 July.

Only a few days before this, on 28 June, Count Bernadotte, President of the Swedish Red Cross, who had been appointed by the UN as the official mediator between the two sides, made his own proposal for the future of Jerusalem. He suggested that the idea of internationalization should be dropped, and proposed instead "inclusion of the City of Jerusalem in Arab territory, with municipal autonomy for the Jewish community and special arrangements for the protection of the Holy Places." In defending his proposals against fierce attacks from the Jewish side, he explained why he was proposing a change to the original UN plan: "Jerusalem stands at the heart of what must be Arab territory in any partition of Palestine. To attempt to isolate this area politically and otherwise from surrounding territory presents enormous difficulties..."[28]

Some weeks later, on 16 September, he withdrew these suggestions and recommended to the UN that Jerusalem "should be placed under effective United Nations control with maximum feasible local autonomy for its Arab and Jewish communities, with full safeguards for the protection of the Holy Places and free access to them, and for religious freedom."[29] The following day, however, 17 September, he was assassinated by a group of three men from the Lehi paramilitary organization, one of whose leaders was Yitzhak Shamir, who later became Prime Minister. Count Bernadotte's role as mediator and his personal views about Jerusalem must have been perceived as a threat to the more hard-line Jewish groups which had more ambitious visions for the borders of the Jewish state and the future of Jerusalem.

The final armistice agreement between the two sides came into effect in Jerusalem on 30 November 1949. By this time Arabs had left several mixed or mainly Arab areas in West Jerusalem as well as most of the Arab villages to the west of the city, and Jews had evacuated parts of the Old City where they were living. Wasserstein sums up in one sentence the reasons for the departure of the Arabs: "In some cases the Arabs were expelled or intimidated into leaving; in others they fled for fear of massacre."[30]

Very soon after this, on 9 December 1949, eighteen months after the state of Israel had come into being, the UN General Assembly voted on the proposal for the internationalizing of Jerusalem, which had been part of the partition plan accepted in 1947. The resolution that was finally passed on this occasion reaffirmed that "the City of Jerusalem shall be established as a *corpus separatum* under a special international regime and shall be administered by the United Nations."[31]

The day after the vote at the UN, Menachem Begin, at that time commander of the underground group Irgun, expressed the convictions of Irgun and of many Jews who were totally opposed to the idea of internationalizing Jerusalem: "The partition of Palestine is illegal. It will never be recognized... Jerusalem was and will for ever be our capital. Eretz Israel will be restored to the people of Israel. All of it. And for ever."[32] This view was no doubt shared by the Prime Minister Ben-Gurion, since it was in response to this UN resolution that he made the bold proposal that Jerusalem should be made the capital of the new state. In a statement to the Knesset on 5 December he said that Israel would never accept foreign rule over Jerusalem: "We see it as our duty to declare that Jewish Jerusalem is an organic and inseparable part of the State of Israel—as it is an inseparable part from Israel's history, Israel's faith and the soul of our people. Jerusalem is the heart of the hearts of the State of Israel."[33]

When, therefore, Ben-Gurion announced on 13 December in the Knesset that the Knesset and government would be moved from Tel Aviv to Jerusalem, this decision was not the result of a long process of debate and consultation—either public or private—but very much a decision made by Ben-Gurion himself in a short period of time. According to Wasserstein, his proposal was "a characteristically headstrong reaction to the UN General Assembly resolution of 9 December."[34] He later explained why he had taken such a risky gamble: "I knew we had an ally—Transjordan. If they were permitted to hold on to Jerusalem, why weren't we? Transjordan would permit no one to get them out of Jerusalem; consequently no one would dare remove us."[35] Avi Shlaim gives his understanding of the enormous significance of Ben-Gurion's decision:

> "It was not apparent at the time even to Ben-Gurion's close party col-
> leagues that his assertive public posture concealed deep inner doubts
> and anxieties. To his diary he confided that the decision over Jeru-
> salem was one of the most difficult and fateful decisions he had ever
> been called upon to make, for it involved not just defiance of the UN
> but a confrontation with the Muslim, Catholic, and Soviet worlds.
> It was a campaign in which Israel, for the first time in its short his-
> tory, was pitted against the entire world. If the world had its way,
> reasoned Ben-Gurion, 100,000 Jews would have been placed outside
> the boundaries of the State of Israel. Moreover, the loss of Jerusalem
> would only be a beginning. It would be followed by international
> pressure to take back the refugees and to place other religious places
> under international supervision; the end result would be loss of in-
> dependence and anarchy. Jerusalem was thus the all-important test
> case. If Israel defeated the UN resolution, the question of borders
> would be solved and the pressure to repatriate the refugees would
> cease: 'Our success in Jerusalem solves all the international problems
> around the State of Israel.'"[36]

The Six Day War and the capture of Jerusalem (1967)

Jerusalem remained divided along the armistice line for seventeen years. The only point at which it was possible to cross from one side to the other was at the Mandelbaum Gate, a quarter of a mile north of the Damascus Gate. This situation changed dramatically as a result of the Six Day War, a war that is described by Avi Shlaim as "the only one that neither side wanted."[37] As a result of Nasser's brinkmanship, hostilities began on 5 June 1967 with a massive

Israeli air attack destroying the Egyptian air force while it was still on the ground. Jordan found itself drawn into the war partly through Nasser's misinformation about the extent of his own losses, and Jordan's involvement brought both Syria and Iraq into the war. The Israeli government no doubt expected and hoped that Jordanian forces would not attack Israeli positions in Jerusalem and the West Bank. But when the Jordanian army began shelling Jewish areas of Jerusalem, some in the Israeli government believed that these attacks provided adequate justification for capturing the whole of East Jerusalem. Both within the government and the army, however, opinions at this stage were still divided, with some rejecting the idea of capturing the Old City and some seeing it as an opportunity to complete the unfinished business of 1948. Michael Oren describes the debate that went on within the Israeli cabinet:

> "Emotions… flared as the ministers… spoke their minds. 'This is the hour of our political test,' Begin opened. 'We must attack the Old City in response both to the unheeded warnings we sent Hussein as well as to the Jordanian shelling.' Allon concurred: 'We all want to see the Old City as an indivisible part of Israel—or that Israelis at least have access to the Holy Places.' But Eshkol advised caution. 'We have to weight the diplomatic ramifications of conquering the Old City,' he said. 'Even if we take the West Bank and the Old City, we will eventually be forced to leave them.'… In the end, the ministers agreed not to agree, accepting a compromise formula proposed by Eshkol: 'In view of the situation created in Jerusalem by the Jordanian bombardment, and after warnings were sent to Hussein, an opportunity has perhaps been created to capture the Old City.'"[38]

On the third day of the war, 7 June, when Jordan refused to withdraw its forces from Jerusalem, the Israeli army proceeded with its plan to take East Jerusalem. They first captured Mount Scopus and then moved south along the Mount of Olives, thus completely surrounding the Old City. Even at this point there was a possibility that the Old City might not be taken, since the Jordanian authorities were given one further opportunity to withdraw their forces. When this offer was refused, the Israeli forces quickly entered the Old City through the Lion Gate under the leadership of Moshe Dayan, Yitzhak Rabin

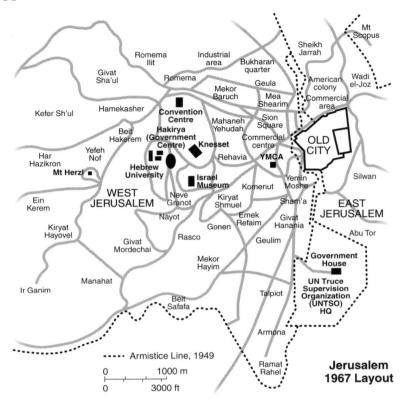

Jerusalem
1967 Layout

and Uzi Narkiss, the officer in charge of Central Command, and
before long had fanned out in the direction of the Temple Mount, the
Western Wall and the Damascus Gate. Motta Gur, the commander of
the paratroop brigade which captured the Old City sent this message
by radio to General Narkiss: "The Temple Mount is in our hands
(*Har ha-Bayit be-Yadenu*)."[39]

An Israeli officer later described his feelings as he entered the
Temple Mount: "There you are on a half-track after two days of
fighting, with shots filling the air, and suddenly you enter this wide
open space that everyone has seen before in pictures, and though I'm
not religious, I don't think there was a man who wasn't overwhelmed
with emotion. Something special had happened."[40] Rabin, the Chief
of Staff, later recalled his emotions as he watched hundreds of soldiers
and orthodox Jews dancing in front of the Western Wall: "This was

the peak of my life. For years I had secretly harbored the dream that I might play a role... in restoring the Western Wall to the Jewish people... Now that dream had come true, and suddenly I wondered why I, of all men, should be so privileged..."[41]

Two incidents took place on the Temple Mount that same day which give some indication of the different views that were held by Israeli Jews concerning the future of this area. When Israeli forces entered the Temple Mount, an Israeli flag was flown from the top of the Dome of the Rock. Moshe Dayan, however, who commanded the Israeli forces in the whole of the Jerusalem area, gave orders for it to be removed. While standing on the Temple Mount, Shlomo Goren, the chief Rabbi of the Israeli Army, said to General Uzi Narkiss, the officer commanding Central Command in the army, "Uzi, this is the time to put a hundred kilograms of explosives in the Mosque of Omar [the Dome of the Rock]—and that's it, we'll get rid of it once and for all." Narkiss's reply was: "Rabbi, stop it!" According to Narkiss, Goren walked away without any further comment.[42]

Three days after the capture of the Old City, on 10 June, the Israeli government gave orders for the Mughrabi Quarter immediately adjacent to the Western Wall to be destroyed. This work was completed by 10 October, creating the large, open plaza to the west of the Wall. The government lost no time in making other decisions which had long-term consequences for Jerusalem. "On June 14," says Benny Morris, "Allon proposed to the cabinet that Israel immediately begin to reconstruct and settle the Jewish Quarter of the Old City, and to surround Arab East Jerusalem with a ring of new Jewish neighborhoods. The aim was to turn all of Jerusalem into an inalienable part of Israel. 'If we don't [start doing] it in a day or two, we never will,' he said."[43] On 18 June the decision was taken to annex East Jerusalem and the Arab areas around it. Then, on 28 June, the Knesset passed legislation declaring that "Jerusalem is one city, indivisible, the Capital of the State of Israel."[44] The significance of these decisions is spelled out by Avi Shlaim in this way:

"The annexation of East Jerusalem was the first and most dramatic assertion of Israel's claim to sovereignty over its ancient homeland. Zion, one of the ancient names for Jerusalem, was at the heart of the

Zionist dream for the restoration of a Jewish kingdom in Palestine. The members of the Knesset who voted for the annexation of East Jerusalem had no doubt about Israel's moral claim to the whole of Jerusalem. As for peace, they believed that it could be attained only from a position of strength—by demonstrating to the Arabs that Israel could not be defeated. Ze'ev Jabotinsky, the founder of Revisionist Zionism, had made the case for the creation of such an iron wall against Arab rejection forty years earlier. In this context the annexation of Jerusalem was seen as an act of peace insofar as it demonstrated to the Arabs the unflinching resolve and the power of the Jewish state. But in another sense the annexation of East Jerusalem represented an abrupt reversal of the policy of the Zionist movement over the preceding three decades. From 1937 until 1967 the Zionist movement was resigned to the partition of Jerusalem, and in 1947 it even accepted the UN plan for the internationalization of the city. But from 1967 on there was broad bipartisan support for the policy that claimed the whole of Jerusalem as the eternal capital of the State of Israel."[45]

Who was to blame for 1967?

One widely held opinion is that the Palestinian Arabs had only themselves to blame for losing East Jerusalem and the Old City in the Six Day War. It was Nasser, it is argued, who provoked Israel by ordering the UN forces to evacuate Sinai and by closing the Straits of Tiran to Israeli shipping. It was Nasser and other Arab leaders in Syria, Jordan and Iraq whose warlike rhetoric gave Israel reason to fear for its survival. The Arabs brought defeat on their own heads through their brinkmanship and their disastrous miscalculation of Israel's response. Michael Oren, for example, points out that Israel had no plans for taking the West Bank or capturing East Jerusalem:

> "Beyond the goals of eliminating the Egyptian threat and destroying Nasser's army, no other stage of the conflict was planned or even contemplated, not the seizure of the entire Sinai Peninsula, not the conquest of the West Bank, nor the scaling of the Golan Heights. Even the 'liberation' of Jerusalem, as Israelis call it, regarding the event as the most significant of the war and assigning it almost messianic ramifications, came about largely through chance. The vagaries

and momentum of war, far more than rational decision making, had shaped the fighting's results. Had Egypt accepted the cease-fire after the first day's fighting, had the Jordanians refrained from seizing Government Hill or had Dayan stuck to his opposition to conquering the Golan (to cite only a few 'if's), the region would have looked much different..."[46]

Another view—also put forward by some Israeli historians—is that while the Arabs certainly did provoke Israel into a pre-emptive attack, Israel had probably been looking for a pretext to attack the Arabs. Avi Shlaim, for example, believes that Israel was far from blameless in the process. "Israel's strategy of escalation on the Syrian front," he says, "was probably the single most important factor in dragging the Middle East to war in June 1967... Many of the firefights were deliberately provoked by Israel..."[47] Wasserstein's view is that "Even had Hussein not opened hostilities, Israel would probably have been unable to resist the temptation to take Jerusalem in 1967."[48] And Benny Morris is very frank about those in Israel who had territorial ambitions:

> "Israel's leaders understood Hussein's predicament. But there were those among them who were eager to 'exploit to the full' any rash actions by him. After all, since 1949 Ben-Gurion had been calling Israel's failure to conquer East Jerusalem and, by extension, the whole of the West Bank 'a lamentation for generations'—a phrase that was in continuous use among Herut and Ahdut Ha'Avoda politicians between 1949 and 1967. In an article published shortly before the outbreak of the war, Allon wrote: 'In... a new war, we must avoid the historic mistake of the War of Independence [1948]... and must not cease fighting until we achieve total victory, the territorial fulfilment of the Land of Israel."[49]

Israel's conquest of the West Bank and East Jerusalem in 1967 opened a Pandora's box, creating cruel dilemmas with which it has been living ever since. Were they to hold on to all the territory they conquered or give it back? Were they to trade land for peace—to withdraw from occupied land and make peace with all the neighbouring countries? The alternative was to annex the whole of the West Bank and make it part of Israel. But if all the Palestinians on the West Bank and Gaza thereby became citizens of Israel with a right to vote in elections, it would only be a matter of time before Arabs would outnumber Jews and take over power through the democratic processes. This would mean the end of Israel as a Jewish state.

In the following chapter we shall see how the creation of facts on the ground in and around Jerusalem showed Israel's dominant response to this dilemma. For as far as Jerusalem was concerned, Israelis quickly made up their minds that the "liberation" of Jerusalem was "irreversible." "As a Jew and as a citizen of Israel," declared Israel's ambassador to Rome, "it is clear to me that Jerusalem belongs entirely to Israel. That fact was determined 1000 years before Christianity and 2000 before Islam, and the Vatican had better find a way of reconciling itself to it."[50] "It was inevitable," says Meron Benvenisti, "that the reunification legislation—smelted in the furnace of such a profound spiritual experience—would be regarded as eternal and irreversible from the moment of its enactment."[51]

8
Jerusalem since 1967

*An unexpected conquest encourages
dreams of "the Greater Israel"*

"Israel eventually found that, by taking east Jerusalem, it had
opened a veritable Pandora's box."
Bernard Wasserstein [1]

"The lack of reference for Palestinian residents of Jerusalem is one of
the most difficult aspects of our lives. We are neither fully Israeli, nor
are we allowed to be fully Palestinian, and so we live in a sort of no
man's land. It is intolerable."
Zakaria al-Quq [2]

"In 1967, with the conquest of the West Bank and Gaza Strip (and
Sinai and the Golan Heights), the original, full dream of Zionism—
of Jewish statehood in the whole of Palestine—once again burst
forth, to inflame and complicate the conflict."
Benny Morris [3]

"Israel's position was expressed in practical terms by the
establishment of demographic and physical 'facts' in East
Jerusalem… The Israelis had faith that in this way, physical facts
would create political facts."
Meron Benvenisti [4]

"The 'eternally unified capital' of the state of Israel is the most
deeply divided capital in the world."
Bernard Wasserstein [5]

"The victory in the 1967 war," says Amos Elon, "… had come to most Israelis as a surprise. Many seemed to feel something miraculous had been involved. Rabbis spoke of messianic stirrings. Politicians referred to the finger of God. Jerusalem—until 1967, a sleepy little town at the far end of a narrow corridor in the hills—came to personify a new element in the consciousness of the nation… The most emotionally charged gains were in Jerusalem…"[6]

Having now gained control of the whole of East Jerusalem on 7 June, the Israeli government proceeded on 28 June to pass legislation extending the area of the Jerusalem municipality to the north, east and south, and making them all part of the state of Israel. Effectively this amounted to the annexation of Jerusalem and large areas around it and sent a clear message that they would never give up Jerusalem. They were separating Jerusalem from the West Bank, but still had to face up to the question of what to do with the rest of the occupied territories in the West Bank, Gaza and the Golan Heights.

We turn now to dwell for a moment on the significance of 1967 for Jerusalem and for Israel, to note the response of the international community to the war and the subsequent occupation as expressed in Resolution 242, and then to highlight the changes that have been made on the ground in and around Jerusalem since 1967.

The significance of 1967 for Jerusalem and Israel

The conquest of 1967 proved to be a highly significant watershed in five ways.

It gave Israel access to the Wall. Elon speaks of the liberation of the Western Wall as the highest point in the victory, and describes the effect of their new access to the Wall in these terms:

> "The Western Wall was both trophy and myth… The Wall was a monument in the domain of memory and of faith. At this moment, it symbolized a widespread urge to transform the political into the religious… The 1967 war abruptly confronted modern Israelis with the geography of their remote history. Its cradle was not Tel Aviv, an ultramodern city on the sea, but the walled Old City of Jerusalem,

where the ancient Jewish temple had stood. In the words of one prominent witness: 'We felt we were joining hands with history.'[7]

Access to the Wall had profound significance even for Jews who were far from religious: "The Western Wall has become, in effect, a temple where people venerate not God so much as the people he is said to have chosen, and their nation-state."[8]

It gave them a thirst for more. Many Jews were satisfied that they could now reach the Wall. Some of the first troops who entered the Temple Mount, however, were given a taste of something that still lay beyond their grasp. So, for example, Colonel Mordechai Gur explained why, having set foot on the Temple Mount, he decided not to visit the Western Wall: "I had achieved my aim. The Temple Mount *is* the Western Wall, too. On the Temple Mount, I am in the drawing room. I am not attracted by the exterior walls. Here I feel at home. The farthest frontiers of longing. Temple Mount. Mount Moriah! Abraham and Isaac. The zealots. The Maccabees. Bar Kokhba. Romans and Greeks. All converge in one's thoughts."[9] Many Israeli Jews today still feel the frustration of knowing that the ultimate prize still eludes them. The site of the Temple is beyond their grasp because it lies under the Dome of the Rock.

It produced a new fusion of nationalism and religion. By coming in contact with all that Jerusalem had stood for, the Zionist movement, which had until now been very secular, began to develop some very religious tendencies. When Rabin was given the honour of giving a name to the war that had just been won, some of the suggestions included "The War of Daring," "The War of Salvation" and "The War of the Sons of Light." His choice of "The Six Day War," according to Michael Oren, was not simply "the least ostentatious" but was intended to evoke the idea of the six days of creation.[10] Menachem Begin was before long referring to the West Bank by the biblical terms "Judea and Samaria" and always spoke of their "liberation" rather than their "conquest" or "occupation." One of the effects of the conquest, therefore, according to Elon, was that it "fused in some hearts the intransigence of aroused nationalism with the archaisms of religious fundamentalism..."[11] Benny Morris makes the same point when he says:

"This largely secular group was almost immediately overshadowed by
religious nationalists who declared that the 'miraculous' conquests
were at'halta dege'ula, the start of divine redemption, and that the
settlement and annexation of the conquered territories were a divine
command, in accordance with the teaching of the historic sage of their
movement, Rabbi Avraham Yitzhak Hacohen Kook… the admixture
of messianism and nationalism proved heady and powerful."[12]

It proved to be a turning point for the Arabs. The crushing defeat in the
war was a profound humiliation not only to the Palestinians but to all
the Arabs and the Muslim world in general. This was the third major
defeat by Israel, and this time they lost control of four significant
pieces of land—the West Bank (including East Jerusalem), Gaza, Sinai
and the Golan Heights. If this humiliation drove some to despair, it
galvanized others in a way that the previous defeats had not done.
"The Jewish community's 1967 victory," says Meron Benvenisti,
"supposedly should have dictated the unconditional surrender of
the defeated community, but this did not take place, much to the
surprise of the victors."[13] A resurgence of religious zeal among Jews
and the aggressive programmes of the settlers stimulated a similar
religious zeal, fused with nationalism, among many Palestinian Arabs.
This is how Amos Elon sums up the special significance of the loss
of East Jerusalem:

"The fall of Jerusalem to the Jews aroused and fanaticized the Arab
world as had no other event since the Crusades. Among Palestinians,
a new kind of awareness grew, a mirror image of Zionism, a zeal, a
violent passion highlighted by indiscriminate terror. 'If I forget thee,
O Jerusalem' now became the war cry of Arabs and Moslems from
Syria to Saudi Arabia and from Morocco to Iran."[14]

It engendered a new defiance among Israeli Jews. Victory in the war gave
Israelis a new confidence in themselves and a new determination
to stand up for themselves, not only against Arabs in the region,
but against hostility and criticism from the rest of the world. It led
to a policy of creeping annexation, based on the conviction that by
creating more and more facts on the ground in occupied territory, they
were consolidating their control over Jerusalem and the Palestinians,
and getting nearer to their dream of "the Greater Israel." "The war…

unleashed currents," says Benny Morris, "within Israeli society that militated against yielding occupied territory and against compromise. Expansionism, fuelled by fundamentalist messianism and primal nationalistic greed, took hold of a growing minority, both religious and secular, getting its cue, and eventually creeping support, from the government itself."[15] Amos Elon similarly says that "... in the testy atmosphere of pressure, counterpressure, and heavy theological argument after a costly war, a new, defiant mood was growing in Israel, along with a strong resolve concerning Jerusalem."[16] And Abba Eban writes, "We interpreted the War not just as a victory, but as a kind of providential messianic event that changed history permanently and gave Israel the power to dictate the future."[17]

World reaction to 1967

A resolution declaring Israel's annexation invalid was passed by the United Nations General Assembly on 4 July 1967 by 99 votes to none with 20 abstentions (including the USA). After a mild response in the early days, the American administration's official position was that East Jerusalem was occupied territory. Thus, in the words of Avi Shlaim, "America supported the exchange of land for peace, refused to acknowledge the Israeli annexation of East Jerusalem, and considered the building of Jewish settlements in the occupied territories illegal and an obstacle to peace."[18]

Several weeks of discussion and debate in the UN led to the passing of Resolution 242 on 22 November 1967, which was sponsored by Britain and adopted unanimously. Although it does not mention Jerusalem by name, it is still very significant. It has been universally recognized as providing *the agreed legal basis* for any settlement of the wider conflict. The first part of the resolution reads as follows:

"The Security Council,

Expressing its continuing concern with the grave situation in the Middle East,

Emphasizing the inadmissibility of the acquisition of territory by war
and the need to work for a just and lasting peace in which every state
in the area can live in security,

Emphasizing further that all member states in their acceptance of the
Charter of the United Nations have undertaken a commitment to act
in accordance with Article 2 of the Charter,

1. Affirms that the fulfilment of charter principles requires the establishment of a just and lasting peace in the Middle East which
should include the application of both the following principles: (i)
Withdrawal of Israeli armed forces from territories of recent conflict;
(ii) Termination of all claims or states of belligerency and respect for
and acknowledgement of the sovereignty, territorial integrity and
political independence of every state in the area and their right to live
in peace within secure and recognized boundaries free from threats
or acts of force...."

Israeli governments have argued that the assumption has always
been that withdrawal would take place only in the context of a final
negotiated settlement with all the surrounding Arab states. It also
needs to be pointed out that while the resolution calls on Israel to
withdraw from occupied territories, it also requires Arab states to
recognize the existence of Israel and cease hostilities against it.

Changes on the ground in and around Jerusalem since 1967

In the following pages we trace the changes that have been made
by Israel in five distinct stages, beginning with the situation that
existed between 1949 and the war in 1967.

Stage 1: Divided Jerusalem (from 1948 to 1967)

Jerusalem is divided along the armistice line that was agreed after
the end of hostilities between Jewish forces and the Jordanian army.
The only crossing point between East and West Jerusalem is at the
Mandelbaum Gate situated a quarter of a mile north of the Old
City.

The Palestinian area around Jerusalem runs from Bethlehem to Ramallah as "a contiguous urban/suburban complex" with "a single urban identity." Jerusalem is seen by the Palestinians as "the centre of their lives in all aspects of social, economic, religious and cultural matters."[19]

East Jerusalem and the West Bank are incorporated into Jordan from 1950 and ruled from Amman.

Stage 2: The Annexation of East Jerusalem (1967)

On 28 June 1967, seventy square kilometres of East Jerusalem, including 28 surrounding villages in the West Bank, are annexed to West Jerusalem, which already covers thirty-eight square kilometres. The annexation extends the jurisdiction of the Jewish municipality over the whole of the annexed area, and Israeli law and civil administration are imposed within this area.

The Palestinians of East Jerusalem are classified as "Permanent Residents of Israel." Those not recorded as such are classified as absentees and therefore forced to leave.

The Mughrabi Quarter in the Old City is destroyed to make space for an enlarged plaza to the west of the Western Wall. Development begins to rebuild and resettle the Jewish Quarter.

Although given the opportunity to take part in elections for the Jerusalem Municipality, Palestinians in East Jerusalem have generally refused to do so, on the grounds that casting their vote would amount to recognition of the Israeli annexation, which they have consistently regarded as illegal.

Palestinians point out that the Municipality spends far less per capita on Arab areas than it spends on Jewish areas. The Israeli response is that Palestinians have only themselves to blame, and that if they were willing to take part in elections, they would be able to influence decisions of this kind.

Between 35 and 40 per cent of the land annexed to the Jerusalem Municipality is private Palestinian land. At first it is designated as "green areas" or "open areas," which means that building is prohibited. But the land is later used to establish more than fifteen settlements. This leaves 11 per cent of East Jerusalem (i.e. 7 per cent of the total

Stage 1: Divided Jerusalem (from 1948–67)

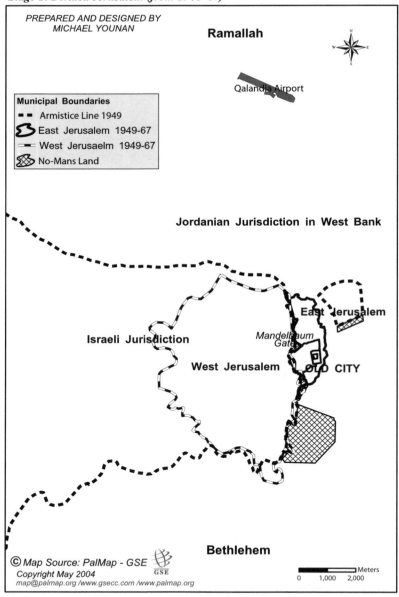

Stage 2: The annexation of East Jerusalem (1967)

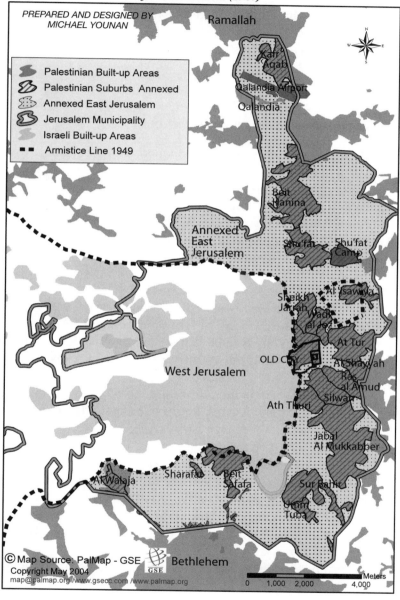

PREPARED AND DESIGNED BY
MICHAEL YOUNAN

Palestinian Built-up Areas
Palestinian Suburbs Annexed
Annexed East Jerusalem
Jerusalem Municipality
Israeli Built-up Areas
Armistice Line 1949

Ramallah

Kafr
Aqab

Qalandia Airport

Qalandia

Beit
Hanina

Annexed
East
Jerusalem

Shu'fat

Shu'fat
Camp

Sheikh
Jarrah

Al Isawiya

Wadi
al Joz

At Tur

OLD CITY

West Jerusalem

At Shayyah

Ras
al Amud

Ath Thuri

Silwan

Jabal
Al Mukkabber

Ar Walaja

Sharafat

Beit
Safafa

Sur Bahir

Umm
Tuba

© Map Source: PalMap - GSE
Copyright May 2004
map@palmap.org /www.gsecc.com /www.palmap.org

GSE

Bethlehem

Meters

0   1,000   2,000   4,000

area of the city) available for housing and community development for the Palestinians.[20] Palestinians claim that there are restrictions on the granting of building permits for Palestinian construction and development. The Israeli response is that the same criteria are applied to both sides, and that Arabs have engaged in a great deal of illegal building.[21]

Stage 3: Declaration of Jerusalem as "a Unified City" and the Building of Settlements (beginning 1980)

In 1980 Jerusalem within the municipal borders is declared "the eternal capital of Israel." Palestinians in East Jerusalem are given new IDs. As a result there is now a clear distinction between Palestinians from East Jerusalem (who have blue IDs) and Palestinians from the West Bank (whose IDs are orange).

The Israeli government initiates and finances building programmes within the Municipality of Jerusalem which include:

1. Settlements forming two circular belts round Jerusalem whose object is, in the words of Teddy Kollek, the Mayor of Jerusalem, "to ensure that all of Jerusalem remains forever a part of Israel. If this city is to be our capital, then we have to make it an integral part of our country and we need Jewish inhabitants to do that."[22] These belts include:

   (a) an inner circle including Gilo, East Talpiot, Ramot, the French Hill, Ramat Eshkol, Rekhes Shu'afat, Pisgat Ze'ev and Neveh Ya'aqov.

   (b) an outer circle including Ma'aleh Adummim, Avir Ya'acov, Giv'at Ze'ev, and Har Adar. This circle also includes a scheme known as E-1 Plan or "the East Gate Plan," which seeks to connect these settlements with West Jerusalem. Also included in this circle are the settlements of Efrat, the Etzion Block and Betar Illit, which are part of the Districts of Bethlehem and Ramallah.

   (c) ten settlement points in the heart of Palestinian neighbourhoods, inhabited by around 2000 Jewish settlers (e.g. Salwan, Rasal'Amud, Sheikh Jarrah and the Old City).

Stage 3: The declaration of Jerusalem as a "unified city" and the building of settlements (beginning 1980)

PREPARED AND DESIGNED BY MICHAEL YOUNAN

Ramallah

Pesagot

Migron

Tal Tsion

Kokhav Ya'acov

Ma'ale Mikhmas

Beit Horon

Ofer

Sha'ar Benyamin

Neve Erez

Giv'at Ze'ev

Ataro

Geva Binyamin

Giv'on Hahadasha

Neve Ya'aqov

Har Shmuel

Pisgat Ze'ev

Almon Ein Prat

Har Adar

Pisgat Omer

Kefar?

Ramot

Rekhes Shu'afat

Anatot

Ke

Ramat Eshkol

French Hill

E1

Mishor

OLD CITY

Mount Scopus

Ma'ale Adummim

West Jerusalem

Jewish Quarter

Annexed East Jerusalem

Kedar

East Talpiot

Giv'at HaMatos

Gilo

Har Gilo

Har Homa

Bethlehem

Meters
0   4,000

Betar Illit

a'ot   Neve Daniel

Rosh Tzurim

El'azar   Efrat

Kefar Etzion

Migdal Oz

Te

© Map Source: PalMap - GSE
Copyright May 2004
map@palmap.org /www.gsecc.com /www.palmap.org

- -	Armistice Line 1949
	Palestinian Built-up Areas
	Palestinian Suburbs Annexed
	Israeli Settlements
	IS Settlements in E Jerusalem
	E1 Settlement Plan
	Annexed East Jerusalem
	Jerusalem Municipality
	Israeli Built-up Areas

2. A network of roads and highways which can be used only by Israelis or Palestinians with special permission. These roads are bypass networks for the Israeli settlements, and have the effect of isolating Palestinian built-up areas. Most are built on confiscated land.

This programme involves the confiscation of 30000 dunams (1 dunam = 1000 square metres) for settlements and for roads (equal to 34 per cent of Jerusalem's Palestinian land). There are special incentives for Israeli Jews to move to East Jerusalem. Restrictions are placed on the development of Palestinian areas.

Stage 4: The closure of the West Bank and the setting up of permanent check-points (since 1993)

A network of check-points is established—some permanent and other impromptu check-points or barricades. A special permit is required for individuals to enter Jerusalem, and West Bank vehicles cannot enter Jerusalem. Palestinians wishing to travel from Bethlehem to the north of Jerusalem without a special permit need to travel on the road via Wadi al-Nar, a rough, circuitous and difficult route.

Since the start of the second Intifada, all roads connecting Palestinian villages surrounding Jerusalem have been blocked, so that no movement of vehicles from these places to Jerusalem is possible.

A policy of Jewish infiltration into Arab areas is implemented by individuals and groups, often with government backing. Thus in 1987 Ariel Sharon moved into an apartment in the Muslim quarter of East Jerusalem, and was followed by a number of Yeshiva students. In 1992 Sharon explained his motives: "We have set a goal for ourselves of not leaving one neighbourhood in East Jerusalem without Jews, not even one."[23] Arabs, of course, are not allowed to settle in Jewish areas of the city.

The following chart details the numbers of Jews, Muslims and Christians in Jerusalem at different stages since 1922: [24]

Year	Total	Jews	Muslims	Christians	Others
1922	62,700	34,100	13,400	14,700	500
1931	93,100	53,800	19,900	19,300	100

Stage 4: 1993–2004 Jerusalem and West Bank closure

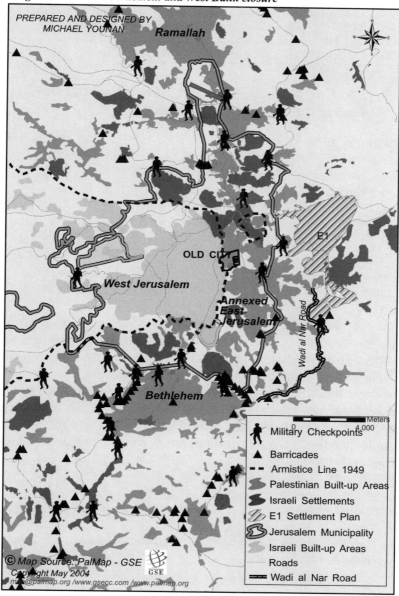

PREPARED AND DESIGNED BY
MICHAEL YOUNAN   Ramallah

E1

OLD CITY

West Jerusalem

Annexed East Jerusalem

Wadi al Nar Road

Bethlehem

Meters
0   4,000

Military Checkpoints
Barricades
Armistice Line 1949
Palestinian Built-up Areas
Israeli Settlements
E1 Settlement Plan
Jerusalem Municipality
Israeli Built-up Areas
Roads
Wadi al Nar Road

© Map Source: PalMap - GSE
Copyright May 2004
GSE
mail@palmap.org /www.gsecc.com /www.palmap.org

Year	Total	Jews	Muslims	Christians	Others
1946	164,400	99,300	33,700	31,300	100
1967	263,300	195,700	55,000	12,700	
2002	680,400	447,900	209,900	14,400	

Stage 5: The "Separation Barrier" around Jerusalem—the "Jerusalem Envelope" (since June 2002)

By January 2004, 188 kilometres of the so-called "separation barrier" have been built to the north and north-west of Jerusalem. The section around Jerusalem is likely to be around 80 kilometres long.

The separation barrier is generally at least thirty metres wide. In Abu Dis, south-east of the Old City, the barrier is no more than one metre wide, with a swath of cleared land that is about five metres wide. It consists of *either* electrified metal fence at least 3 metres high, with buffer zones on both sides and a trench two metres deep filled with barbed wire; *or* a solid concrete wall between three and ten metres high. At every stage it is built on confiscated Palestinian land.

As a result of this process, Bethlehem, Beit Jala and Beit Sahour are separated from Jerusalem in the south, and Ramallah, Beitunya and Al-Bireh from Jerusalem in the north. The Palestinian community thus becomes fragmented, "a patchwork of separation, segregation and the differentiation of people and land." The separation barrier creates "a Jerusalem enclave totally separate from the West Bank, a political, economic, social, cultural and religious capital divorced from its people."[25] "East Jerusalem has become an isolated, almost peripheral city."[26]

Some observations

As a result of changes on the ground made since 1967, the following observations can be made:

1. *Jerusalem and the surrounding area have been annexed to Israel.* The motive for the annexation and the subsequent building

Stage 5: Separation Barrier around Jerusalem— "The Jerusalem Envelope" (since June 2002)

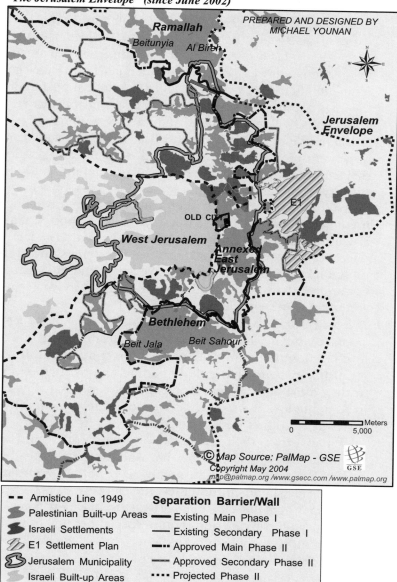

Legend:

- - Armistice Line 1949	**Separation Barrier/Wall**
Palestinian Built-up Areas	**——** Existing Main Phase I
Israeli Settlements	**——** Existing Secondary Phase I
E1 Settlement Plan	**-■-** Approved Main Phase II
Jerusalem Municipality	**——** Approved Secondary Phase II
Israeli Built-up Areas	**····** Projected Phase II
	···· Main Projected Phase III
	-···· Road Connectors

of settlements has been articulated by many Israelis. In 1997, referring to plans for the building of Har Homa, Benyamin Netanyahu said, "The battle for Jerusalem has begun." In the words of the Israeli writer Avi Shlaim, "It was a blatant example of the Zionist tactic of creating facts on the ground to preempt negotiations… It was part of a policy pursued by all Israeli governments after 1967, whether Labour or Likud, of surrounding the huge Greater Jerusalem area with two concentric circles of settlements, with access roads, and military positions."[27]

2. *Palestinians in East Jerusalem are under Israeli law, but are not citizens of Israel.* They are considered residents and can lose their status as residents after seven years if not present in the country. They cannot vote in national elections, only in municipal ones, and travel between countries on a travel document called a *laissez-passer*, not an Israeli passport. Zakaria al-Quq sums up the anomaly of their situation: "The lack of reference for Palestinian residents of Jerusalem is one of the most difficult aspects of our lives. We are neither fully Israeli, nor are we allowed to be fully Palestinian, and so we live in a sort of no man's land. It is intolerable."[28]

3. *This process has resulted in the disruption of geographic and demographic continuity inside East Jerusalem.* Palestinians are therefore faced with a choice: they must *either* build within the municipality boundary without permits and risk demolition; or they must buy cheaper land *outside* the municipality, but in so doing lose their status as citizens of Jerusalem. "Thus the Israeli 'unified' Jerusalem pushes out its original local inhabitants from their land to an alternative site that is on the other side of a seam line that isolates them from their nearby Jerusalem birth place and the core of their economic, political, social and cultural life—the Old City."[29]

4. *Palestinians from the south and north of Jerusalem are unable to travel freely to Jerusalem* and require special permits from the Israeli authorities to do so. Jerusalem is thus effectively cut off from the rest of the Palestinian areas.

5. *"The 'eternally unified capital' of the state of Israel is the most deeply divided capital in the world."*[30] Israeli annexation of East Jerusalem can therefore hardly be called a success.

The Report *Jerusalem on the Map* sums up the process as it has developed since 1967 as follows:

> "The policy of imposing a physical reality through building settlements and seizing and controlling lands has been applied by Israel since the first day of its occupation of Jerusalem. Later, this policy has expanded to include vast areas of the surroundings of the city in the occupied Palestinian territories. During the past two years, Israel has doubled its efforts to define the final shape of the borders and areas of the Jewish Jerusalem with the aim of creating a reality that serves realization of its interests and goals to determine the status of the city before the start of the talks about a political settlement concerning the future of Jerusalem... The reality imposed by Israel today puts a lot of obstacles on the road of reaching a political settlement regarding the future of the city."[31]

If this is what has been happening in and around Jerusalem since 1967, what kind of negotiations have taken place between the two sides in an attempt to bring about a lasting peace? In the following chapter we explore the place of Jerusalem in the different negotiations between Israel and the Palestinians since 1967.

9
Jerusalem in recent negotiations

Jewish sovereignty becomes "non-negotiable"

"Jerusalem today is at the core of continuing negotiations between Israel and the Palestinian Arabs and of the larger Arab–Israeli relationship."
Bernard Wasserstein [1]

"It [Jerusalem] has… become the spinal chord of Palestinian identity."
Geries Khoury [2]

"Jerusalem and the Temple Mount are… where God and country meet, where nationalism is rewritten as millennialism."
Gershom Gorenberg [3]

"Israeli statesmen had always considered leaving Jerusalem for last to be an extremely important tactical objective, since postponement of the debate would enable Israel to continue establishing faits accomplis in the city, thereby reinforcing its status."
Meron Benvenisti [4]

"The explosive Temple Mount issue bears within it the potential to ignite a worldwide conflagration, and it is, therefore, a conflict of international importance… A bomb is waiting to go off in the heart of Jerusalem, its fuse burning with the fire of the religious fanaticism of Jew, Muslim and Christian."
Meron Benvenisti [5]

Why has it been so hard to find a peaceful solution? We need now to trace how the question of Jerusalem has been dealt with in a number of different negotiations in recent years. First we consider Israel's response to the UN resolution after the Six Day War in 1967. We then try to understand why, when official negotiations have taken place, the question of Jerusalem has so seldom been discussed. This leads on to a review of some of the main proposals that have been put forward, the most significant negotiations that have taken place and other developments which have affected the position of Jerusalem. We should then be in a position to understand what are the crucial issues and what are the main options for the future of Jerusalem.

Israel's response to Resolution 242

We have already seen (Chapter 8) that this resolution, passed in November 1967, required Arab countries to recognize the existence and sovereignty of Israel and cease hostilities against it, and required Israel to withdraw "from territories of recent conflict." The main Israeli arguments for refusing to withdraw from the occupied territories can be summarized as follows:

—Since Resolution 242 didn't say "*all* territories of recent conflict," there was never any obligation for Israel to withdraw to the 1949 or the 1967 borders.

—The assumption behind the Resolution was that agreement over final borders would be part of the final status negotiations. The Arabs have consistently refused or been reluctant to accept the existence of Israel or to negotiate peace. We have made peace with Egypt and Jordan, but not with Syria or Lebanon—or the Palestinians themselves. We will only withdraw in the context of final negotiations when Arab hostility comes to an end.

—We have already withdrawn from Sinai, and we have no further obligation to withdraw from any territory—certainly not from all the West Bank.

—Jerusalem was taken in 1967 from Jordan, which had effectively annexed it in 1967, and whose jurisdiction over it was
not recognized by the international community and therefore
had no legal status.

—You cannot blame us for winning a war that we did not start;
the Arabs have only themselves to blame for being so stupid
as to provoke the war.

—There is no legal obstacle to settling in areas of the West Bank
not inhabited by Palestinians. As long as there is no Palestinian
state, these cannot be regarded as Palestinian territory.

—We cannot give up the West Bank since it is all we have as a
bargaining chip in any final status negotiations.

—The 1948 borders were indefensible; how could we defend
a country that is only twelve miles wide at its narrowest
point?

—We need more land for immigrants; where else can we put
the immigrants from places like Russia except on the West
Bank?

The European Union and many other countries have generally
supported peace processes on the basis laid down in the UN
resolution. The USA has claimed to play the role of honest broker,
but has in recent years tended to support Israeli interpretations of
the situation.

Postponement of the Jerusalem question

Since the early 1990s the Palestinian side has constantly sought
to place the Jerusalem issue on the negotiation table. For several
years, however, Israel not only refused to allow it to be on the
agenda, but also refused to allow the Palestinian delegation to include
representatives from East Jerusalem. The issue here can be illustrated
by noting the tension that has existed at the United Nations since
the early 1970s. Lord Caradon, the British ambassador at the UN,
put forward his own personal plan in 1974 in which he spoke of
Jerusalem as a "gateway to peace," urging that it should be tackled

as the first, rather than the last, of the issues negotiated between the two sides. Israel has consistently rejected this approach at the UN. Its position has always been that, in the words of Teddy Kollek, Jerusalem "should be left to the very end."[6]

A resolution passed by the World Council of Churches in December 1998 entitled "Together on the Way" draws attention to some of the consequences of the postponement of the Jerusalem question:

> "Jerusalem has been at the heart of the Israeli–Palestinian conflict since the time of the League of Nations Mandate and Partition, yet the issue of Jerusalem has consistently been postponed to 'future generations' due to the complexities of the issues involved. The inability of the parties and of the international community to settle this question has left Jerusalem vulnerable to a series of unilateral actions which have radically altered its geography and demography in a way which violates especially the rights of Palestinians and poses a continuing threat to the peace and security of all the inhabitants of the city and the region."[7]

Avi Shlaim offers an explanation for the thinking behind Israel's approach by drawing attention to two very significant articles entitled "The Iron Wall," written by Vladimir Jabotinsky, the leader of the Revisionist movement, in 1923. These were Jabotinsky's reflections at that time on the problems involved in making peace with the Palestinian Arabs:

> "I do not mean to assert that no agreement whatever is possible with the Arabs of the Land of Israel. But a voluntary agreement is just not possible. As long as the Arabs preserve a gleam of hope that they will succeed in getting rid of us, nothing in the world can cause them to relinquish this hope, precisely because they are not a rabble but a living people. And a living people will be ready to yield on such fateful issues only when they have given up all hope of getting rid of the alien settlers. Only then will extremist groups with their slogans 'No, never' lose their influence, and only then will their influence be transferred to more moderate groups. And only then will the moderates offer suggestions for compromise. Then only will they begin bargaining with us on practical matters, such as guarantees against pushing them out, and equality of civil and national rights."

Jabotinsky's basic philosophy for dealing with the Palestinian Arabs is summed up in the concept of the "iron wall." He remains hopeful that peace will one day be established, but only on the basis of overwhelming strength and only by avoiding any premature settlement in the immediate future:

> "It is my hope and belief that we will then offer them guarantees that will satisfy them and that both peoples will live in peace as good neighbours. But the sole way to such an agreement is through the iron wall, that is to say, the establishment in Palestine of a force that will in no way be influenced by Arab pressure. In other words, the only way to achieve a settlement in the future is total avoidance of all attempts to arrive at a settlement in the present."[8]

The concept of the "iron wall" is so significant for Shlaim that he adopts it as the title for his book *The Iron Wall: Israel and the Arab World*. It is not hard to conclude that, especially over the question of Jerusalem, most Israeli governments and especially the more recent right-wing governments in Israel have in practice adopted Jabotinsky's approach and worked on his assumptions about the need to avoid—or at least postpone— peace agreements.

The Khalidi proposals, 1978

By the mid-1970s the Palestinians were becoming more vocal in their claims to Jerusalem. Then, after Sadat's visit to Jerusalem in November 1977, Palestinian leaders felt the need to state more clearly their hopes regarding the future of Jerusalem. The first specific proposals that deserve to be noticed in this context are those of Walid Khalidi, a Palestinian intellectual originally from Jerusalem. In an article in the American journal *Foreign Affairs*, he put forward his own personal solution for the Israeli–Palestinian conflict which involved the creation of a Palestinian state including the West Bank, Gaza and East Jerusalem. In a summary of this proposal, Bernard Wasserstein says that Khalidi

> "admitted that this was a reversion to the old concept of partition and that 'in some Palestinian and Arab quarters' it might be seen

as treason. But he maintained that a new generation of Palestinian and Arab leaders now accepted the concept. East Jerusalem, which he called the 'navel' of the West Bank, was 'the natural capital of Arab Palestine'. There should be no re-building of the wall there. West Jerusalem should remain the capital of Israel. There should be freedom of movement and residence. The city should be administered by a joint inter-state municipal council. And there should be a 'grand inter-faith council' for the holy places. Jews should have an 'irreversible right of access' to the Western Wall. And, while Khalidi rejected demilitarization of the Palestinian state as a whole, he urged that it would be 'supremely fitting' if Jerusalem (both east and west) were demilitarized."[9]

While there are several features of this proposal which would not have been accepted by most Israelis, Khalidi's proposals were creative and significant at the time because Palestinians until then had tended to speak from a very fixed position, demanding the return of full sovereignty to Arabs in Jerusalem, and had not often taken the initiative to put forward considered, detailed proposals of their own.

Camp David, 1978

This thirteen-day conference, convened by Jimmy Carter in September 1978, led to a peace agreement between Egypt and Israel and the eventual return of Sinai, which had been conquered by Israel in the war of 1967. Jerusalem was discussed in some detail and strong disagreement almost led to the failure of the whole conference. Sadat believed or hoped that the agreement over Sinai was somehow linked with a process that would lead to autonomy for the Palestinians and a solution to the Jerusalem problem. But for a variety of reasons, his hopes were never realized. This is how Wasserstein sums up the significance of these negotiations:

"While Egypt agreed to sign a peace treaty in return for a staged Israeli withdrawal from Sinai, discussion of the Palestinian problem and of Jerusalem became bogged down. The Egyptians' basic negotiating document called for the restoration of east Jerusalem to 'Arab sovereignty and administration', though they were prepared to agree to a 'joint municipal council'. Sadat insisted that a 'Muslim flag' must fly over the Dome of the Rock immediately—that is, in advance of any Palestinian autonomy agreement. American officials, who tried to avoid involvement in the Jerusalem question, debated half-amusedly the design of the proposed flag. But Sadat's demand was rejected out of hand by Menachem Begin, who saw such a concession as the thin end of a wedge that would dilute Israeli sovereignty over the whole city. Disagreement over Jerusalem on the last day of the summit very nearly scuttled the entire agreement. A formula was finally conjured up... They proposed that the agreement, which contained no reference to Jerusalem, be accompanied by side-letters in which President Carter and Sadat and Prime Minister Begin would each state his country's unchanged position on Jerusalem...".[10]

The consequences of the Camp David agreement as they related to the Palestinian issue are described by Benny Morris in this way:

"Begin was probably the most satisfied. He had successfully warded off all efforts to pin him down on the Palestinian problem; and he had avoided a commitment to withdraw from any part of the West Bank and Gaza. Sadat (and Carter) had gained nothing tangible for the Palestinians and Sadat ended up with a thinly veiled separate peace, something he had always tried to avoid... Begin had never seriously contemplated giving the West Bank and Gaza Arabs any substantial measure of self-rule.

"... the Egyptians maintained that Israel had almost completely failed to deliver the goods promised in Camp David regarding the Palestinians—had never taken the autonomy plan and the negotiations seriously, and continued to oppress the Palestinians in the territories. Indeed, the very neutralization of Egypt through the bilateral peace treaty enabled Begin to avoid making any concessions on the Palestinian issue, assuring the demise of the autonomy talks and the continuation of the occupation. Moreover, having safeguarded its southern flank through peace, Israel felt free in 1981 to bomb the Iraqi nuclear reactor outside Baghdad and in 1982 to invade Lebanon."[11]

Camp David in 1978, therefore, while it helped Egypt by restoring Sinai, did nothing to alter the situation in Jerusalem.

The Basic Law of 1980

After the Islamic Revolution of 1979 Iran was governed by Muslims who wanted to see Islamic solutions applied not only to Iran but also to the rest of the region. The question of Jerusalem therefore now acquired a new prominence. It was partly in response to developments of this kind that the Israeli Knesset enacted the Basic Law in July 1980 in which it affirmed that "Jerusalem, complete and united, is the capital of Israel... the seat of the President of the State, the Knesset, the Government, and the supreme Court."[12] The purpose of this legislation was, in Wasserstein's words, "to foreclose any negotiations about Jerusalem by ring-fencing it with a basic (i.e. entrenched, quasi-constitutional) law."[13] This meant that as far as Israel was concerned, Jerusalem was no longer negotiable.

All the foreign powers with representatives in Israel refused to accept Jerusalem as the capital of the state, and in order to make the point continued to keep their embassies in Tel Aviv. The position of the USA was that Israel's annexation was still illegal. But from the 1980s it began to soften its position, inclining to the view that the question of Jerusalem should be resolved through negotiation. By the 1990s they were saying that the annexed areas of Jerusalem occupied by Jews were in the same position as the settlements, and by April 2004 President Bush seemed to be questioning the accepted interpretation that Israel's occupation of the West Bank was still illegal.

The 1982 invasion of Lebanon needs to be understood not only in the context of Israel's struggle with Palestinians attacking Israel from outside, but also of Israel's intentions or hopes concerning the West Bank and Jerusalem. This is how Benny Morris relates the invasion of Lebanon to the question of the West Bank:

> "Sharon and Begin had a broader objective: the destruction of the PLO and its ejection from Lebanon. Once the organization was crushed, they reasoned, Israel would have a freer hand to determine the fate of the West Bank and Gaza Strip. Indeed, the Palestinians might give up their national political aspirations altogether or look to their fulfilment in Jordan. To further this 'Jordan is Palestine' solution, Israel might be willing to help overthrow the Hashemites,

Sharon told a group of his associates at the end of June 1982. Palestinian historian Rashid Khalidi later wrote: 'Operation Peace for Galilee' was in a very real sense a war for the future dispossession of Palestine...

"But the PLO was not destroyed or mortally wounded, as Sharon and Begin had hoped and planned. Indeed, it could well be argued that the drubbing the organization received drove it, in the end, to moderate its position, a process that culminated in Arafat's 1988 declaration recognizing Israel and repudiating terrorism. Thus, instead of demolishing the PLO and preparing the ground for Israeli annexation of the West Bank and Gaza, it can be argued that the invasion of Lebanon had, albeit very violently, groomed the PLO for participation in the diplomacy and peace process that was to characterize the 1990s and was to pave the way for its assumption of authority in parts of the West Bank and Gaza. In sum, Begin and Sharon, by invading Lebanon, can be said to have made a major contribution to the establishment of a Palestinian state."[14]

The protests that erupted in the first Intifada in December 1987 with young men throwing stones at Israeli tanks in the West Bank and Gaza were a desperate and almost certainly spontaneous response to twenty years of occupation. Benny Morris quotes these words of Rashad a-Shawa, former mayor of Gaza, to explain the background to these protests:

"One can expect such events after 20 years of harsh occupation. People have lost all hope. They are completely frustrated. They don't know what to do. They have adopted a line of religious fundamentalism, which for them is the last resort. They have lost hope that Israel will ever give them rights. They feel that the Arab states are incapable of achieving anything [for them]. They feel that the PLO, which they regard as their representative, failed to achieve anything... What has happened is an expression of the frustration and the pain over the continuing Israeli occupation."[15]

Morris also sees the resurgence of Islamic fundamentalism as part of the Palestinian response to this depressing situation:

"The PLO's demise in Lebanon had left many Palestinians bereft of hope of national salvation. Islam seemed to provide an answer. The

Likud's rise to power, the ascendancy of Jewish fundamentalism, and the threat these posed to the Palestinian patrimony and the Islamic holy sites on the Temple Mount—all helped pave the way for many Palestinians to Islamic fundamentalism..."[16]

The Palestine National Congress, 1988

"Ultimately, the result of the Intifada," says Benny Morris, "was a basic restructuring of geopolitical realities in the region, one of which was the start of the emergence of a Palestinian state."[17] Then, almost a year after the start of the Intifada, the Palestinian National Congress, meeting in Tunis in December 1988, took the very significant step of declaring a state of Palestine with Jerusalem as its capital: "The Palestinian National Council hereby declares, in the Name of God and on behalf of the Palestinian Arab people, the establishment of the State of Palestine in the land of Palestine with its capital at Jerusalem."[18] It was understood that in referring to Jerusalem the PNC was speaking of East Jerusalem (*al-Quds al-Sharqiyya*). Arafat then went on to make public statements in which he accepted Israel's right "to exist in peace and security" and renounced the use of terrorism.

Decisions taken by King Hussein of Jordan around this time also proved to be significant for Palestinian thinking about Jerusalem. From 1948 Jordan had controlled East Jerusalem and the West Bank, but these ties were cut after the Israeli conquest in 1967, although Jordan was able to retain a limited role as guardian of the Islamic holy places. From the late 1980s on, therefore, Hussein abandoned his hostility towards the PLO and accepted the principle of an independent Palestinian state on the West Bank and Gaza. According to Wasserstein, "This cutting of the umbilical cord that bound many members of the Palestinian elite in the West Bank and East Jerusalem to Amman accelerated the political and psychological movement amongst the Palestinians towards autonomy."[19] The Palestinians were now gaining more and more control of their own destiny.

Madrid, 1991 and Oslo, 1993

It was largely the fall of the Soviet Union and the Gulf War in 1991 that paved the way for the meetings held in Madrid in October 1991 under the auspices of the USA. In the negotiations leading up to the conference, Israel would not allow a separate delegation of Palestinians to take part, and only allowed them to be present as part of the Jordanian delegation. Israel also insisted that Jerusalem should not be on the agenda of the conference itself. Although the conference set up a process for continuing discussion and negotiations between Israel and the Palestinians, this slow process was eventually overtaken by the secret negotiations which culminated in the Oslo Accord.

The Declaration of Principles, signed by Rabin and Arafat on the White House lawn in the presence of Bill Clinton in September 1993, known as the Oslo Accord, stated that Jerusalem would be discussed during the "final status negotiations." It was understood that these would begin "as soon as possible but not later than the beginning of the third year of the interim period." Although the newly created "Palestinian Interim Self-Government Authority" would have no jurisdiction over East Jerusalem, Jerusalem residents would be able to take part in elections for the Self-Governing Authority in the West Bank and Gaza. While Arafat was optimistic that the agreement would lead to Israeli withdrawal from Jerusalem, Israel insisted that "Jerusalem is not part of the deal and there has been no weakening on that."[20]

Both Israel and the Palestinians agreed not to retreat from their obligations or to put obstacles in the way of implementation of the Accord. It was not long, however, before Israel was accusing the Palestinians of failing to honour their commitments. On the other hand, the Palestinian perception of Israel's failure is summed up by Ghada Karmi in this way: "It seems that the Israeli intention has been to use the interim period for consolidating its hold on Jerusalem and transforming it as far as possible into a Jewish city, so as to pre-empt any possibility of its reverting either to being a mixed city or to being a shared capital for a future Palestinian state."[21]

In October 1993, a month after the signing of the Accord, Shimon Peres as Foreign Minister wrote a private letter to Clinton and Arafat in which he made the following declaration:

> "I wish to confirm that the Palestinian institutions of East Jerusalem and the interests and well-being of the Palestinians of East Jerusalem are of great importance and will be preserved. Therefore, all the Palestinian institutions of East Jerusalem, including the economic, social, educational, and cultural, and the holy Christian and Muslim places are performing an essential task for the Palestinian population. Needless to say, we will not hamper their activity; on the contrary, the fulfilment of this important mission is to be encouraged."[22]

Later publication of this letter by the Palestinian leadership caused embarrassment to Peres, who at first denied its existence. But it has been used by the Palestinian leadership as evidence of at least a private commitment on the part of the Israeli leadership to support Palestinian institutions in East Jerusalem.

The Beilin–Abu Mazen Proposal, 1995

Between 1993 and 1995 Yossi Beilin, who was the Israeli Deputy Foreign Minister and closely linked with Shimon Peres, held a series of about twenty secret meetings with Mahmoud Abbas, known as Abu Mazen, an advisor to Arafat who later became Prime Minister in Palestine. Both sides were therefore in close contact with their respective leaders. They and their teams worked on a document in which they proposed ways of resolving all the major issues between Israel and the Palestinians. The two men agreed that Jerusalem should "remain an open and undivided city with free and unimpeded access for people of all faiths and nationalities." To the surprise and consternation of many Palestinians, however, they assumed that Israel would retain sovereignty over the whole city, although the Temple Mount would have extraterritorial status and be under Palestinian control. They proposed that Jewish Jerusalem would form an "Israeli borough" (including the Maale Adumin settlement), and that East Jerusalem would form a "Palestinian borough," al-Quds (including Abu-Dis). These two boroughs would operate under a unified umbrella municipality, the super-municipality of Jerusalem. They failed to agree on the question of sovereignty over the Old City, and therefore left it open.

When Yitzhak Rabin was murdered four days after the agreement became public, the document became a victim of the power struggles between Labour and Likud and was not discussed further. In spite of this, the proposals proved to be highly significant, since in Wasserstein's words, "No such agreed statement between responsible Israeli and Palestinian leaders had ever been achieved before during the previous century of conflict. The Beilin–Abu Mazen draft also came close to providing a blue-print for a solution of the Jerusalem problem."[23] The proposals were no doubt in the background of the next important negotiations at Camp David.

Camp David, July 2000

A commonly held perception of these talks is that Israeli Prime Minister Ehud Barak made an extremely generous and unprecedented offer to the Palestinians which Yasser Arafat flatly rejected. The truth, however, is probably much more complex than this. Since Barak's offers were made orally and never written down, there are bound to be different interpretations of what exactly was said and why Arafat turned him down. At the same time, it is generally agreed that Barak did offer to give the Palestinians responsibility for Palestinian neighbourhoods, especially in the north of Jerusalem, and to allow them to be annexed as the capital of the Palestinian state to be called "Al-Quds." In return for offers of this kind he wanted four concessions from the Palestinians:

1. that they would recognize Israel's annexation of settlements within the municipality of Jerusalem;
2. that they would recognize Israeli annexation of at least three settlements outside the municipality on the West Bank;
3. that they would recognize the historic and religious relationship of Jews to the Haram al-Sharif and accept shared sovereignty over it; and

4. that the new agreement would replace Resolution 242 as the basis for future negotiation between Israel and the Palestinians.

While it is true to say that Barak went further than the Israelis had ever gone in attempting to satisfy Palestinian demands, from the Palestinian perspective Barak's offer was not nearly as generous as Israel and the USA have tried to present it. Israeli settlements would have remained in most of the West Bank, leaving it dissected into a series of Bantustans—small, enclosed areas separate from each other. Jerusalem proved to be the final stumbling block, however, and it was disagreement over the question of sovereignty over Jerusalem—and especially the Temple Mount—that ultimately led to the failure of Camp David.

Avi Shlaim's account of what took place rejects some of the more extreme Israeli interpretations and insists that some genuine progress was made which amounted to a significant breakthrough:

"On all these issues considerable progress was made at Camp David in narrowing the gap between the two sides. It was agreed, in broad outlines, that the Palestinian state would include all of the Gaza Strip and 95 per cent of the West Bank; that the large settlement blocs along the 1967 border would be annexed to Israel but with the offer of some Israeli territory as a swap; and that the Jordan Valley, long cherished as Israel's security border, would be under exclusive Palestinian sovereignty. Barak also pledged to absorb 'tens of thousands' of Palestinian refugees into Israel under the rubric of family reunification and to contribute to an international fund for compensating the rest. On Jerusalem, Barak abruptly reversed Israel's previous position by conceding Palestinian sovereignty over the city's outer and inner suburbs and a large measure of control over the Muslim holy sites. It was on the rock of sovereignty over Jerusalem that the talks eventually foundered. But the taboo was broken. The mere fact that this and the other core issues of the Israeli–Palestinian conflict were discussed at all is significant. Jerusalem is no longer a sacred symbol but the subject of hard bargaining."[24]

A different interpretation of Camp David, however, is offered by Tanya Reinhart, a professor of linguistics at Tel Aviv University:

"Coverage of the conflicts that emerged during and after the Camp David negotiations focused primarily on symbolic issues—the holy sites in Jerusalem and the right of return. But the debates surrounding these issues only mask the real problem: that in concrete matters of land and resources, Barak offered nothing at Camp David, except preservation of the existing state of affairs... However, it is not East Jerusalem that Israel offered as the Palestinian capital... It is in fact this neighbouring village of Abu-Dis that is designed in the Beilin-Abu Mazen plan to serve as the capital of the Palestinian state. The verbal trick was that Abu-Dis would be named Al-Quds—the Arab name of Jerusalem, meaning 'the holy city'. It is only through this deceptive use of definitions that Israel can claim that it proposes that the city be divided into the Jewish part, 'Jerusalem', and the Palestinian part, 'Al-Quds'.

"... the big 'historical concession' behind Barak's willingness to 'divide Jerusalem' is nothing but willingness to consider implementation of the long-standing Israeli commitment regarding Abu-Dis using the verbal trick offered in the Beilin–Abu Mazen plan... As for the real issue of East Jerusalem, Barak had not moved an inch since he pledged that Jerusalem would remain 'the united capital of Israel for ever'. East Jerusalem was annexed by Israel shortly after its occupation in 1967 (reaffirmed in a Knesset resolution in 1980), and ever since then Israel has been appropriating land and building new settlements there. All Israel governments have declared that this is not negotiable, and that East Jerusalem will remain Israeli. Over the years, various plans commissioned by the different governments have been prepared for future arrangements for the Palestinian residents of East Jerusalem. Though they differ in some details, they are all based on the assumption that the sovereignty in Jerusalem will remain Israeli, but the Palestinian neighbourhoods will retain some sort of municipal control—what Beilin called 'an arrangement which is less than a municipality level'.

"It is hard to understand how so many have swallowed the story about Barak's willingness to divide Jerusalem... The myth of generous Israeli offers at Camp David... is nothing but a fraud perpetuated by propaganda. The Palestinian negotiators contributed to the smoke screen around Israel's offers, as they always have. They do their best to hide from their people how little they have managed to gain after years of negotiation."[25]

On 28 September 2000, Ariel Sharon made what can only be described as a highly provocative visit to the Temple Mount, protected by 1000 policemen, and no doubt with the support of Prime Minister Barak. Echoing what Motta Gur said when the Temple Mount was taken by the Israeli Defence Forces in 1967, he said, "The Temple Mount is in our hands." When asked why he was making this gesture he said, "because as a Jew I have a right to be here, and because we want to clearly exert our sovereignty over the Temple Mount."[26] It was this visit of Sharon's to the Temple Mount that sparked off the second Intifada, known as the al-Aqsa Intifada.

The Clinton proposals, 2000 and Taba, 2001

After the failure of the Camp David talks, the next move came from President Clinton who in December 2000 proposed the principle of "everything that is Arab to the Palestinians and everything that is Jewish to the Israelis." This would mean that Arab areas (including the Muslim and Christian quarters of the Old City) would be within the Palestinian state, and Jewish areas (including the Jewish quarter) would be within Israel. The Palestinians would control the Haram al-Sharif and show respect for Jewish people's historic and religious links to it. In January 2001 a further meeting between the three sides held at Taba in Sinai brought Israel and the Palestinians closer together, with a joint declaration that they were near to reaching a settlement. Those who accuse Arafat of spurning Barak's "generous" offer at Camp David are slow to recognize that at this stage at Taba some kind of final agreement seemed to be in sight.

When Barak lost the election the following month, however, Ariel Sharon became Prime Minister and refused to accept the principles that had been agreed at Taba. The al-Aqsa Intifada, which began in September 2000, took the question of Jerusalem off the agenda, and allowed Israel to accelerate its extension of settlements and the building of new settlements on the West Bank.

The Geneva Accord, 2003

The latest unofficial attempt to reach some kind of agreement came in the Geneva Accord in December 2003, which had been worked out between moderates on both sides in secret negotiations over a period of three years. The crucial points concerning Jerusalem were as follows:

—Jerusalem would be divided in sovereignty. East Jerusalem would be the capital of the Palestinian state and West Jerusalem would be acknowledged as the capital of Israel. Some settlements in East Jerusalem would remain under Israeli sovereignty.

—The Temple Mount, or the Haram al-Sharif, would be under Palestinian sovereignty.

—Much of Jerusalem's Old City would be under Palestinian sovereignty, but the Western Wall and the Jewish quarter would remain under Israeli sovereignty.[27]

The Beilin–Abu Mazen document and the Geneva Accord have at least demonstrated some of the possibilities for a peaceful, negotiated settlement over Jerusalem. If moderates on both sides are willing to make compromises, they need much greater support from the international community to enable them to persuade the extremists on both sides. They then need to put forward programmes that can win enough support to win elections even through the vagaries of the Israeli, Palestinian and American democratic processes.

The crucial issues

At the end of this survey we are now in a position to outline some of the key issues which have emerged, noting where there is at least some agreement and where opinions are still sharply divided.

Does there have to be a return to the 1967 borders in Jerusalem?

Israel insists of course that there is no question of returning to the borders of divided Jerusalem before 1967. While many Palestinians still insist on a return to the 1967 borders in Jerusalem, many others are prepared to accept *some* changes that have taken place since then.

How important is demography?

In spite of the series of declarations by the Israeli government affirming the unity of the city and Israel's sovereignty, no one can ignore the fact that Palestinians still make up at least 30 per cent of the population of Jerusalem. Menachem Klein speaks of the "irreversible geographic and demographic reality,"[28] and says that "it is people, more than anything else, that determine the identity of the land on which they live."[29] This would suggest that the actual composition of the city's inhabitants ought to have a significant bearing on the question of sovereignty.

What does the principle of self-determination mean? Do the people in any place have the right to determine their status?

If the inhabitants of the Old City, for example, were asked whether they would prefer to be under Israeli or Palestinian rule, the Jews in the Jewish Quarter and those who have settled elsewhere in the Old City would insist on remaining under Israeli rule. All the rest, however, which is the vast majority of the population of the Old City, both Muslims and Christians, would without hesitation vote to be part of the Palestinian state. The Israeli argument would be that these opinions are irrelevant because of Israel's historic claims to Jerusalem and its need to control a unified city.

Can Jerusalem remain an open city?

Almost all agree that it *can* and *must* remain an open city. Few contemplate a return to the division of pre-1967. Even if there is some sharing or division of sovereignty, there is no suggestion on either side that there should be a permanent barrier of any kind between East and West Jerusalem. Provided there can be adequate security guarantees, the general desire is that people on both sides should be free to travel to the other.

How important are the religious issues?

Israel insists that its sovereignty over the whole of Jerusalem is a purely political matter and that religious issues are irrelevant, since it guarantees complete religious freedom and access to holy sites for all the three faiths. Most Palestinians respond, however, that because of what Jerusalem is, the questions relating to religion *do* and *should* have a profound influence on the question of sovereignty. The Muslims and Christians of East Jerusalem and especially in the Old City feel it is inappropriate that they should be governed by a Jewish state. Furthermore, they point out that access to holy places in Jerusalem is at present routinely denied to Christians and Muslims from the rest of the Occupied Territories.

How important is the question of sovereignty and is it purely symbolic?

"There will be no peace," says Menachem Klein, "unless the conflict is dealt with on the level of politics and symbols."[30] It seems that while there was considerable agreement at Camp David about how Jerusalem might be administered as a unified city, it was the question of *sovereignty* over East Jerusalem, and especially the Temple Mount, which proved to be the final sticking point. While Israel seeks to minimize the issue of sovereignty as being purely symbolic and therefore of little significance, most Palestinians insist that the nature of the Old City—as well as the whole of East Jerusalem—is such that it has to be reflected in the recognition of Palestinian sovereignty over part of the city. Israeli Jews tend to act as if the question of Jerusalem has already been fixed and is not negotiable. They are only willing to discuss practical arrangements that do not challenge their sovereignty.

The options

One recent study speaks of no less than fifty-seven proposals concerning Jerusalem that were put forward between 1916 and 1994[31], and as we have seen, several proposals have been put forward since then. At the risk of oversimplification, it would seem that all the different proposals ultimately turn out to be variations on four basic models:

1. Jerusalem or part of it (i.e. the Old City) is internationalized

This was the original proposal of the UN Partition Plan of 1947. While it was favoured for a time by many foreign powers and reluctantly accepted by Israel, it was never implemented because Israel assumed control of West Jerusalem and Jordan took over East Jerusalem. Although there are some who still favour some form of internationalization, most recognize that it is not a real option at present. Both sides feel the need for sovereignty so strongly that they are unwilling to let sovereignty be surrendered to others—even to an international body like the UN.

2. Jerusalem remains under exclusive Israeli sovereignty

This option involves acceptance of Israeli annexation, while recognizing the claims of non-Jews to holy sites. Jerusalem would remain under exclusive Israeli sovereignty, but with the following provisos:

i) Special provisions should be made for the holy places (e.g., that they be placed under an inter-religious committee or some form of international control).
ii) There should be some some form of autonomy for Palestinian areas in education, health and social services through boroughs or sub-districts.

Having staked its claim to Jerusalem so strongly since 1967, Israel obviously favours this option. It wants the world to recognize the facts that have been created on the ground.

The Palestinians reject this option because it is in violation of international law concerning occupied territory, it ignores Palestinian claims to sovereignty which are based on continuous occupation for centuries, and it does not take into account either the demographic realities or the principle of self-determination.

3. Sovereignty over Jerusalem is shared

In this model, Jerusalem becomes the joint undivided capital of the two states, a "condominium of Israel and Palestine." Israel would have sovereignty over Jewish West Jerusalem and the Palestinian state would have sovereignty over Arab East Jerusalem. A special formula for shared sovereignty would cover the Old City, which would be open to all but governed by a council with representatives of the three major religions. Jewish holy places would have "extra-territorial status'—with freedom of access for all who wished to visit them.

4. Sovereignty over Jerusalem is shared by being divided between Israel and the Palestinian state.

Israel has sovereignty over Jewish West Jerusalem and the Palestinian state has sovereignty over Arab East Jerusalem.

Israel has consistently rejected this option because it wants to maintain the status quo. This, however, is the option that is preferred by the majority of the moderate Palestinians.

Clarifying the issues and reducing the number of options in this way simply underlines the need for creative thinking—and sometimes radical rethinking—on all sides. Any resolution of the conflict demands much more than merely cosmetic changes. The problem has dragged on for so long, and attitudes on all sides have become so thoroughly fixed, that if there is to be any peaceful resolution, fundamental assumptions need to be re-examined and where necessary challenged. Chapter 10 explores some of the main areas where this might be necessary.

10
"The things that make for peace"

A peaceful solution has pre-conditions

"We and they want the same thing: We both want Palestine. And that is the fundamental conflict."
David Ben-Gurion, 19 May 1936 [1]

"At its heart, a time bomb with a destructive force of apocalyptic dimensions is ticking, in the form of the Temple Mount."
Meron Benvenisti [2]

"The struggle for Jerusalem can be resolved only when there dawns some genuine recognition of the reality and legitimacy of its plural character, spiritually, demographically and—all claims to sole possession not withstanding—politically."
Bernard Wasserstein [3]

"As he came near and saw the city, he wept over it, saying, 'If you, even you, had only recognized on this day the things that make for peace...'"
Luke 19:41–42 NRSV

Having attempted in the previous chapter to survey some of the schemes that have been put forward and to address the issues and the major options, we turn now to explore basic pre-conditions for any kind of peaceful resolution of the conflict over Jerusalem and the broader conflict between Israel and the Palestinians.

If we are realistic about the worst of human nature, and if we have faced up to the worst possible scenarios, reflections of this kind need not sound like the easy and superficial reassurances of the false prophets about whom Jeremiah complained: "They dress the wound of my people as though it were not serious. 'Peace, peace,' they say, when there is no peace" (Jeremiah 6:14).

Inevitably these are the reflections of an outsider who does not live with the daily fear of a suicide bombing, the humiliation of being searched at a road block or the confiscation of his house or olive trees. But they are based on a serious attempt to understand the history and politics, to listen to both (or all) sides and to observe what has been happening on the ground in recent years.

Here are ten themes that suggest fundamental changes of attitude and approach which may be needed on *all* sides. None of them is easy. They all involve pain, a willingness to admit mistakes, to try new ways of thinking and to swim against the stream. At every stage there may be the fear of losing face, or admitting that we may have been wrong. Changing our minds or changing our approach will sometimes invite accusations of treachery from family and friends, because we seem to be questioning or even rejecting inherited assumptions about what it means to stand firm and fight for our cause.

1. Acceptance of the other

One of the fundamental problems since the end of the nineteenth century has been the difficulty that *both* sides have felt in accepting the existence of the other and accepting all that is involved in their presence as neighbours. Golda Meir's famous saying about the Palestinians is an example of an unwillingness among some Israeli Jews to recognize how the Palestinians feel about themselves: "It was not as though there was a Palestinian people in Palestine considering itself as a Palestinian people and we came and threw them out and took their country away from them. They did not exist."[4]

Attitudes of this kind have been there since the beginning of the Zionist movement. Theodore Herzl's famous saying "a people without a land for a land without a people" is an early example of *either* wishful thinking *or* culpable ignorance *or* deliberate twisting of the facts for political purposes. He must have known that Palestine was populated—even if it was not thickly populated all over—but probably assumed in his European arrogance that their numbers were insignificant, that they had no sense at all of being a people or a nation, and that they would welcome the newcomers who would bring civilization and progress. He must have been aware of the fact-finding mission of two rabbis sent out by the rabbis of Vienna to explore Herzl's ideas immediately after the Basel Congress in 1898. Their first response was summed up in a brief cable sent from Palestine: "The bride is beautiful, but she is married to another man."[5]

Simha Flapan's *Zionism and the Palestinians* gives numerous examples of Zionists from the earliest period up to the present time who have found it difficult, if not impossible, to accept the existence of the Palestinians:

> "Weizmann's attitude towards the Palestinians was the gravest error of his political leadership, more serious than any other because Weizmann did not deviate from his attitude for even a brief period. His disdain for the Palestinians originated not only in the fact that lacking previous contact with them, he was influenced by his British advisers. From the very beginning, he approached the Palestinians with a prejudice that blinded him to the most obvious facts... Weizmann was sincere in his desire for a just solution to the conflict with the Palestinians. But his non-recognition of the Palestinians as a national entity could not but lead to a policy of injustice...

> "Unfortunately, Weizmann's legacy in this most vital aspect of Jewish–Arab relations has had a more lasting impact than any other... The Palestinians were never regarded as an *integral* part of the country for whom long-term plans had to be made, either in the Mandatory period or since the establishment of the state. This explains why the Palestinian problem has remained at the heart of the Israel–Arab

conflict until the present day... Non-recognition of the Palestinians
remains until the present the basic tenet of Israel's policy-makers who,
like the Zionist leadership before 1948, nurture the illusion that the
Palestinian national problem disappeared with the creation of the
state of Jordan, leaving only the residual humanitarian problem of
the refugees to be solved."[6]

Benny Morris recognizes that Palestinians also have found it hard to
accept Jews. He says that the Zionist leaders and settlers were only
vaguely aware of the effect that their movement was having on the
Arabs and that "to a very large degree they managed to avoid 'seeing'
the Arabs..." The problem on the Arab side was that:

> "While taking note of the Jewish settlers, the Arabs proved unwill-
> ing or unable to understand them. This mutual lack of empathy, to
> be sure, has characterized the conflict ever since. The Palestinians,
> from the start, never really understood the Zionist claim to the land.
> They were not aware of or didn't care about the Jews" roots in the
> country, and took no interest in their current suffering, the main
> propellant of Zionism."[7]

It is not hard to find examples of statements made by Arab leaders
that are extremely dismissive of Jewish claims. King Faisal has said,
for example, "Only Muslims and Christians have holy places and
rights in Jerusalem." Claiming that Jews have no rights, he brushes
aside their claims to the Western Wall, saying that "Another Wall
can be built for them. They can pray against that."[8] According to
Benny Morris, Arafat "refuses to recognise the history and reality
of the 3,000-year-old Jewish connection to the land of Israel."[9] It is
reported that Arafat and his chief negotiator at Camp David refused
even to accept the idea that the Temple Mount existed on the site of
the Dome of the Rock. Maps of the Middle East in the Arab world
often either leave the area of Israel completely blank or call it "the
Zionist entity," as if giving it the name of "Israel" somehow accepts
the legitimacy of the state. Because they see the state either as a
transplant, an implant that is rejected by the body as incompatible,
or as a cancerous growth at the heart of the Arab world, they find
it hard to accept the existence of the state as an entity established
by the UN and protected by international law.

In this context, accepting the other means accepting that they exist and that they are there as neighbours on our doorstep. Even if we question their right to live where they live, there has to be a willingness to accept that either *many* or *most* or *all* of them are likely to remain there. Accepting the other therefore means refusing to pretend that they do not exist or to wish that they would disappear. Accepting the other might also mean allowing them to claim for themselves what we have claimed for ourselves. This would include accepting that they feel the same attachment to this piece of land and this city as we do—even though for slightly different reasons. "It would be odd," says Kenneth Cragg, "to imagine that Palestinians would forget in three decades what Jews remembered for eighteen centuries."[10]

Amos Oz, the Israeli novelist, was a soldier in the Israeli army during the Six Day War in 1967. This is how his experience of entering East Jerusalem and seeing Palestinians is described by Amos Elon:

"He remembered wandering through East Jerusalem one day after the war, in uniform and armed with an automatic rifle, wishing very much to feel like a man who had vanquished his foes and regained the city of his forefathers. He very much wanted to share and be part of the general celebration. 'But people are living there. They are at home and I am the intruder.' If only there had not been all those Palestinians. 'I saw enmity and resentment, hypocrisy, fear and degradation and new evil being plotted.' He felt like a man who had broken into a forbidden place. 'A stranger in a foreign city.'"[11]

Clare Amos suggests that the story of Jacob's encounter with his brother Esau contains a profound message about the need to accept the other. It is a specially poignant story because it was in this encounter that Jacob was given his name "Israel":

"It is only as long as Israel is prepared to continue to struggle in relationship with God that it can justifiably claim the name or title of 'Israel', literally the one who 'struggles with God'. However as the author of Genesis makes clear that is not the whole of the story. For there is a profound link made between this nightmare encounter and the meeting that takes place next morning between Jacob and his long-estranged brother Esau. In the one encounter Jacob sees God 'face to face' and so names the place 'Penuel'. In the other encounter which takes place after the long night is ended and dawn has broken there is at last enough light for Jacob to see Esau 'face to face' and make the amazing statement 'truly to see your face is like seeing the face of God, with such favour have you received me' (Genesis 33:4–10). Picking up on this clear hint in the biblical narrative, rabbinic tradition drew a link between Esau and the divine figure with whom Jacob had wrestled the night before. It was, some suggested, the guardian angel of Edom, the future nation of which Esau was the ancestor. But significantly in rabbinic interpretation the names 'Esau' and 'Edom' had also come to symbolize the foreign nations that were regarded with suspicion or hostility and this adds yet another dimension to the story.

"Perhaps therefore the relationship of Jacob become Israel must be triangular, between Jacob/Israel... the divine wrestler... and Esau/ Edom, so that the vocation of Israel is to wrestle both with God and with the world of national and political realities in which God's people found themselves. Daringly this would also suggest that the blessing that Jacob is offered at the end of the struggle is contingent upon the goodwill of those such as Esau's descendants. And so if Israel turns its back on either a relationship with God or a relationship with the 'foreign nations' (symbolized by Esau/Edom) then it becomes less than Israel."[12]

Accepting the other probably also means acknowledging and attempting to understand their suffering. "The political architecture of peace," says Anton La Guardia, a British journalist, in his *Holy Land, Unholy War,* "no matter how carefully the future borders are laid out, no matter how craftily the leaders finesse the question of settlements and Jerusalem, no matter how much money the world pledges to support the 'peace process', cannot be complete without each side recognizing the other's agony, and abandoning the notion that it alone is the victim of history."[13]

Marc Ellis, an American Jewish rabbi, has the same emphasis on the acceptance of suffering in his *Israel and Palestine: Out of the Ashes:* "If Jerusalem is seen as the 'broken middle' of Israel/Palestine—to be fully shared among Jews and Palestinians—and if citizenship rather than religion or ethnic identity is the path of a shared life and responsibility, then Jerusalem can indeed become a beacon of hope for Jews and Palestinians in the twenty-first century... the place that Jews and Palestinians can meet in their suffering and brokenness."[14] Can we draw any comfort from the fact that a Jew is speaking here not about power and sovereignty, but about Jews and Palestinians accepting each other and meeting in their suffering and brokenness?

2. Refusal to make exclusive claims

No one can object to exclusive claims when there is only one party involved. The problem comes when there are *others* who believe they have legitimate claims to the very same thing that we want for ourselves. If we refuse to surrender our claims completely, we either deny the claims of the other party, claiming it exclusively for ourselves, or we find some way to share it.

Ben-Gurion knew in 1936 what was the root of the conflict between the Jews and the Arabs: "We and they want the same thing: We both want Palestine. And that is the fundamental conflict."[15] Since 1967 the vast majority of Israelis would say the same thing about Jerusalem. Meron Benvenisti recognizes the same problem when he says, "One cannot escape the irony of the fact that history has decreed that the places held sacred by the Jews are the same ones that are sacred to the Arabs of Palestine."[16]

Many Israelis would no doubt argue that it is Arab hostility to Israel's existence that has forced them to take a strong stand: "Either we are in complete control or we'll be destroyed; there's no possibility that there could ever be a balance of power between us." The three crucial stages in the development of Israeli claims to Jerusalem were in 1949, 1967 and 1980. In 1949 Ben-Gurion claimed Jerusalem as the capital of Israel as a way of defying the UN Resolution which would have put the city under international rule, and as a way of continuing the collusion with Jordan at the expense of the Palestinians. In 1967, flushed with success in the Six Day War and the unexpected prize of the West Bank, Sinai and the Golan Heights, Israel asserted its exclusive claims to Jerusalem as a way of serving notice to the Arabs that they could never again challenge the supremacy of Israel. In 1980 the *Basic Law* established in constitutional law that "Jerusalem, complete and united, is the capital of Israel."

The world needs to recognize Israel's reasons for making these exclusive claims. Here is a country that owes it existence to the will of the international community as expressed in the UN, but does not feel beholden to it and reserves the right to defy the UN when it feels that its interests are threatened. And here are people who have some idea of what the Zionist project had done to the Palestinians and who know that they will always have to rely on force to keep the upper hand. With memories of the Holocaust and much Arab and Muslim rhetoric directed against "the Zionist entity," they have good reason to fear for their lives and the security of their state. So while Israel's exclusive claims are often justified in terms of history and religion, they also need to be understood as arising out of deep fear and insecurity. Self-defence, defiance and assertiveness join hands with scripture and history to make a case which the international community has not until now been able to challenge.

Exclusive claims to Jerusalem put forward by Muslims have been associated with two major challenges from the outside world. We have seen that it was the Crusaders' challenge which forced Muslims to assert their claims to Jerusalem and insist on exercising sovereignty over it. Then it was the capture of the Old City in 1967 which intensified the claims based on Islamic belief and history. In both cases it has been a serious *political* threat from outside which has called forth a heightened *religious* and *theological* response. The argument from scripture, tradition and history convinces many Muslims that only people of their faith are qualified to be in control and keep the peace between warring religious factions. At the present time, however, exclusive claims put forward on the basis of Islamic beliefs and history carry little weight because of the extreme political weakness of the Palestinians.

If we can understand the motivation behind these exclusive claims made by both Jews and Muslims, we may be in a better position to challenge the claims themselves. If we understand *why* people feel compelled to make this kind of stand, we may be better able to question *what* it is that they are demanding. The heart of the challenge to all exclusive claims made by Jews or Arabs is that Jerusalem is no ordinary city. Its very nature as a city that is holy to *three* faiths and that contains people of two main ethnic groups militates against the idea that any *one* of them should exercise exclusive sovereignty over it.

The following quotations from different writers—three Jewish and three Christian—all register a deeply-felt protest against any kind of exclusive claims that are made by one side concerning Jerusalem:

Meron Benvenisti: "'Sovereignty' being an expression of national aspirations, the assertion that exclusive Israeli sovereignty will prevail in Jerusalem is tantamount to claiming that the Palestinians do not have legitimate national aspirations with regard to the city or, if they do, they must sacrifice them in the face of stronger or more just Israeli claims. Religious or communal autonomy is perceived as being sufficient to fulfil the Palestinians" collective longings."[17]

Amos Elon: "There was an unexpected irony in the fact that Jews, who owed their present prominence in Jerusalem to their extraordinary memory of their own past, were now counting on the Arabs to forget theirs. That the Arabs would do so was very unlikely."[18]

Bernard Wasserstein: "The struggle for Jerusalem can be resolved only when there dawns some genuine recognition of the reality and legitimacy of its plural character, spiritually, demographically and—all claims to sole possession notwithstanding—politically."[19]

Elias Chacour: "Jerusalem will suffocate if it is not liberated from exclusiveness, religious or political. Jerusalem will only prosper and flourish when it opens its gates and its arms to become inclusive."[20]

Kenneth Cragg speaks of "the arrogance of exclusivism" and writes: "An inalienable, eternal, exclusified, Israeli Jerusalem would betray the fullness of Jerusalem."[21]

"Jerusalem—by irreducible historical factors—has to have a plural, that is a triple, 'ownership' of love and may not be unilaterally annexed."[22]

John Esposito: "Any equitable resolution of the future status of Jerusalem will require all its major religious communities to affirm a pluralistic theology of inclusiveness and religious tolerance in which there are no masters and servants but rather a society in which all citizens recognise their equal status and rights before God as children of Abraham."[23]

Because of what Jerusalem is, it must be shared!

3. A vision of a truly shared, open city

When exclusive claims are resisted, the way is open for catching the vision of what the city *could* be like if it were genuinely shared and open to all. There cannot be anyone who wants to go back to the divided Jerusalem as it was between 1948 and 1967 with a no man's land between the two sides. Many observers believe that although the Camp David meetings in 2000 failed to produce a full agreement, considerable progress *was* made. Menachem Klein insists that both sides agreed, for example, that "this enlarged Jerusalem was seen to be a single metropolitan unit with common characteristics and needs and would remain open."[24]

But it is not just a case of having open borders and allowing unrestricted access to the holy places of all three faiths. The Palestinian attachment to the city, which is based on both continuous occupation over centuries and (in the case of Muslims) on Islamic history and belief, demands to be expressed in terms of some kind of shared sovereignty. At its best, this is not a claim to exclusive sovereignty but simply a claim that while the Jewish state has sovereignty over *part* of the city, the Palestinian state should have equal and meaningful sovereignty over *another part* of the city.

In the present situation very few Palestinian Christians and Muslims have access to their holy sites in Jerusalem, and Christians and Muslims from the rest of the world either have little or no desire to visit the city or are prevented from doing so. Tourism is almost completely dead, and it is not just the fear of suicide bombers that keeps people away. It is inconceivable that Muslim pilgrims from other countries of the world should want in any numbers to visit Jerusalem in its present state. But in a Jerusalem that is shared and open, many thousands of Muslims would undoubtedly want to visit what they regard as their third most sacred site after Mecca and Medina. Michael Dumper in *The Politics of Sacred Space* imagines a scenario in which "there is a permanent status agreement and comprehensive peace settlement with all parties."[25]

> "Probably," he writes, "the most important challenge facing the City following a permanent status agreement is dealing with the huge projected increase of pilgrims... the increase is most likely to be from Muslim countries of Southeast and Central Asia and West Africa because most of the Jewish and Christian increase has already taken place. But even in the latter case, there is likely to be an increase as the region stabilizes and more pilgrims finally make their pilgrimage. Preparing and organizing for this increase will require interreligious coordination and intergovernment cooperation on a scale hitherto lacking."[26]

A city that is totally dominated and controlled *by one side* can hardly function as a "holy city" *for all*. A solution that is imposed will never be accepted, while a solution that is agreed by all the parties and which shares the sovereignty has some chance of being accepted. Instead of being a place that divides and separates people, Jerusalem ought to be a city that enables people of different faiths to meet each other and enter into each other's world. It presents an unparalleled opportunity for people to experience traditions of their own faith that are different from their own and to develop a sympathetic understanding of a faith other than their own.

If there is anything distinctive about the *Christian* contribution to the debate in recent years, it is probably this insistence on openness and shared sovereignty that has been expressed powerfully by church bodies and by individuals. The World Council of Churches, for example, meeting in 1998, passed very specific resolutions about Jerusalem: "... that Jerusalem be a city open to the adherents of all three religions, a place where they can meet and live together" (1.1). "Jerusalem must remain an open and inclusive city" (8.5). "Jerusalem must be a shared city in terms of sovereignty and citizenship" (8.6). Similarly a resolution of the Anglican Communion at the Lambeth Conference in 1988 spelled out the political implications of Jerusalem being a shared and open city: "The status of Jerusalem is fundamental to any just lasting peace settlement and therefore it should serve as the capital of two sovereign states, Israel and Palestine, with free access to the adherents of all three faiths."[27]

Naim Ateek, the Director of Sabeel, the Palestinian Liberation Theology Center in Jerusalem, argues against exclusive claims, suggesting that "the political must bow to the religious." The nature of Jerusalem as a holy city for three faiths has to be reflected in shared sovereignty:

> "Jerusalem itself, I believe, will ultimately withstand and defy any attempts to exclusivity. Jerusalem cannot be only Jewish. The sooner Israel recognises that this holy space called Jerusalem must be shared equally, the better it would be for the peace and security of all. In other words, although the religious significance is not totally dependent on the political, the political cannot ignore the religious. Therefore, the best requirement for a just peace would demand the sharing of the political sovereignty. The political must bow down to the demands of the religious. The political sharing of sovereignty must be our human response to the holiness of this space. The arrogance of an exclusive sovereign claim must be resisted vehemently. The world community must approach the issues of Jerusalem from its religious significance rather than from its political. It is essential to comprehend deeply that what makes Jerusalem great is not its political character. Rather, it is its religious character which is equally important to Jews, Muslims, and Christians. This is why it is mandatory for the political sovereignty to be shared. An exclusive Israeli political claim will drastically diminish the equal religious significance of the city for the three religions, therefore giving an unjust edge to one. The political should, therefore, serve the needs of maintaining the religious in the best possible way, guaranteeing the equal rights, privileges, duties, and responsibilities of the three faiths. This can best be achieved through a shared sovereignty of the city...

> "We should insist that political sovereignty over Jerusalem should begin with the acknowledgment of the overall sovereignty of God. As Daniel told King Nebuchadnessar, we need to learn '... that the Most High has sovereignty over the kingdom of mortals...' For the sake of justice, lasting security, and peace, we need a shared political sovereignty over the city, under God who is ultimately the only supreme sovereign."[28]

Kenneth Cragg challenges the argument of a rabbi who accuses Palestinians of playing the role of the mother in the presence of King Solomon who falsely claims that the baby is hers:

> "The Arab, it is said, wants to divide again the sacred city, to return it to the tragic condition of pre-1967. Chief Rabbi Goren finds a telling analogy to hand for this situation. The Arab is like the false mother in Solomon's famous episode over the twice-claimed newborn infant. The very notion of division, as Solomon proposed it in judging between the two mothers, served to identify at once the true one, namely the one who beyond all else wanted the child to live safe and whole.

> "A little reflection leads one to see how the parallel does not fit, and how the choice of it could be said to be deceptive. The modern situation about the city is of one mother and two children. It is not a case of dividing her but of her possessing them together. Had he had the mind for it, Chief Rabbi Goren might have drawn a different analogy from the Star of David itself as set on the flag of Israel. For there two equal triangles make a single six-pointed star. Could this not be a symbol for a federal, non-exclusive Jerusalem, where the centre holds for both triangles while the angles belong to themselves?"[29]

4. The main parties meeting face to face and negotiating as equals

Part of the tragedy of the present situation is that in the search for peace Israel and the Palestinians do not meet or negotiate in any sense as equals. Israel has won every war since 1948 and has the backing of the only superpower in the world. Since the Palestinians have lost every war and made many strategic and tactical mistakes, they inevitably approach any negotiating table in a position of extreme weakness and vulnerability. In some situations they have tended to be passive and reactive; instead of putting forward their own proposals, they have often found themselves simply reacting to what Israelis or other parties have offered.

It is not hard to understand why the Palestinians find themselves in this position. The Zionist movement realized from the beginning that it could only survive by being assertive and using force. "Diplomacy by declaratory gesture" is Wasserstein's description of Israel's style of diplomacy at certain stages.[30] And Avi Shlaim quotes as the background to this approach a paragraph written by an American Zionist leader, Nahum Goldman, concerning the psychological effect of the victory of 1948:

> "It seemed to show the advantages of direct action over negotiation and diplomacy... The victory offered such a glorious contrast to the centuries of persecution and humiliation, of adaptation and compromise, that it seemed to indicate the only direction that could possibly be taken from then on. To brook nothing, tolerate no attack, cut through Gordian knots, and shape history by creating facts seemed so simple, so compelling, so satisfying that it became Israel's policy in its conflict with the Arab world."[31]

If successive Israeli governments since 1948 have adopted this approach, recent Likud governments have taken it even further. And there have been many times when American support for Israel's policies has had the effect of totally overriding the process of face-to-face negotiation between Israelis and Palestinians.

There are four reasons in particular why this style of diplomacy needs to be questioned and abandoned. In the first place, quite apart from issues concerning human rights, the very size of the Palestinian community (3 million on the West Bank, 1 million in Gaza and 1 million Israeli Arabs—making a total of around 5 million Arabs—alongside 6 million Israeli Jews) demands that they should be able to negotiate as equals. Secondly, a basic understanding of psychology should tell us that a settlement that is imposed by the powerful on the weak—what Shlaim calls "the peace of the bully'[32]—if accepted at all, would be accepted with a degree of bitterness and resentment which would create further problems in the future. A settlement that is reached by direct negotiation between equals is far more likely to be accepted—enthusiastically at least by the majority—and then perhaps reluctantly by the rejectionist minority.

Thirdly, many Israeli Jews have protested publicly, sometimes at great personal cost, against what occupation has been doing to Israeli Jews. "In 1983," says Ishai Menuchin, "I refused to serve in acts of occupation, and I spent thirty-five days in military prison for my refusal. Today, as a major in the reserves of the Israeli Defense Forces, I still defend my country, but I will not participate in a military occupation that has over the decades made Israel less secure and less humane."[33] A fourth reason is that both the Beilin–Abu Mazen proposals of 1995 and the Geneva Accord of 2003 model an alternative style of diplomacy in which both sides negotiate face to face over a long period of time.

Towards the end of a recent book about Christians in Israel/Palestine, Michael Sennott, an American journalist, writes about one distinctive contribution that Christians might be able to make that is based on an understanding of the teaching of Jesus in the Sermon on the Mount. He explains the difficult concept of "turning the other cheek" in the light of the cultural context at the time of Jesus:

> "To hit someone on the right cheek assumes that the aggressor has hit the person with the back of his right hand. In the ancient customs of the land, this was considered a deep insult; this was how the powerful struck the powerless, the way a master struck his slave, or a Roman struck a Jew. But a blow administered with an open hand on the left side of the face was a blow struck at an equal. The difference between the two types of blows was actually codified in Jerusalem's local law at the time according to some historians. A backhanded slap to the right cheek of a man's peer was grounds to sue for punitive damages. The fine for a backhanded blow to a peer was 100 times the fine for a blow with the forehand. If a backhand was delivered to an underling, however, there was no fine. So when Jesus said to offer the left cheek, by this historical interpretation he wasn't prescribing a blind, masochistic pacifism. He was telling his followers, effectively, 'Confront the person offending you, forcing him to face you as an equal, but do not respond with violence in return.' That, in the context of Jesus' time and the social and legal codes that existed then, was a radical act of defiance. It turned the tables, forcing the striker to accept the humanity and the equality of the one he was striking, even if he was not legally (or militarily, or politically, or economically) recognized as an equal."[34]

The present challenge to Palestinians, therefore, is to find ways of responding to the humiliation of occupation that do not resort to the weapons that are used against them. The question for Israelis is whether they are willing to recognize the humanity and rights of their neighbours as equals. The challenge to the outside world is to find ways of using its power not to undermine either side in the conflict, but as gently or as firmly as is required, to create the context in which both sides can feel secure enough to meet and negotiate together face to face.

5. Respect for international law

The role of international law is summed up by Richard Harries in *After Evil* in a way that emphasizes the obligations on *both* Israel *and* the Arabs:

> "The recent Vatican document... has said that 'The existence of the state of Israel and its options should be envisaged not in a perspective which is itself religious, but in their reference to the common principles of international law.' This is also an approach which has been taken by the Anglican Communion. Professor Wistrich welcomes this way of approaching Israel in that it disposes of what he terms unacceptable theological baggage 'at a stroke' and leaves Christians, especially Catholics, free to adopt realistic and 'normal attitudes to Israel'... Politically, of course, international law cuts all ways. By it, the existence of the state of Israel is justified. By it, the state of Israel is called to acknowledge certain standards in relation both to its internal life and its relationship to the surrounding territories, including Palestinian areas."[35]

There are three principles in particular which are relevant to this particular conflict:

1. Israel has a right to exist as a state.
2. The inadmissibility of the acquisition of territory by force.
3. An occupying power does not have the right to make permanent changes in occupied territory.

The first two principles are clearly spelled out in Resolution 242 (see Chapter 8). They have provided the legal basis for all negotiations and have been incorporated into almost every UN resolution on the conflict. The third is clearly articulated in the Geneva conventions of 1949.

There is a widespread consensus, therefore, that on the basis of international law, the West Bank and Gaza still have the status of "occupied territories'; that the annexation of East Jerusalem by Israel is illegal; and that since Israel has no right to build settlements on the West Bank and Gaza, all these settlements are in fact technically illegal. What seems to have happened, however, is that the passage of so many years since the original resolution and the creation of so many facts on the ground have made it hard for many to believe that this is in fact the position in international law or to believe that the situation can or should be changed.

We have already noted Israel's response to the UN Resolution 242 (see Chapter 9). Many would feel that what is happening here is that Israel, because it has been the victor in every war and enjoys almost unquestioning support from the USA, seems to be putting itself above the law and setting itself up as the interpreter of international law. It argues that there are special circumstances which require it to act in a certain way in order to safeguard its own interests and guarantee its survival in a hostile world.

It would seem therefore that what is needed in this situation is for *a third party which is genuinely impartial to apply international law in an even-handed way*, proposing solutions that will involve concessions and compromises for both parties. In an ideal world this is the role that the UN should be able to play. In practice at the present time it is hardly able to play this role because of the power of the USA. The so-called Quartet, made up of the USA, the UN, the European Union and Russia, has attempted to take on this task with its "Roadmap for Peace," although until now with little success. The continuing failure to apply international law over this conflict is creating a dangerous precedent.

6. A willingness to compromise

Life would be so much simpler if every dispute could be settled on the basis of law. But of course things do not always work out this way, sometimes because the law itself is not very clear, sometimes because there are rights and wrongs on both sides, and sometimes because the law is quietly put to one side, and money, power or other interests win the day.

It also has to be recognized that some people are better than others in dealing with conflict, and certain kinds of personality find it easier than others to handle all the tension involved in negotiation. Some cultures find it harder than others to make any compromise, because it is likely to be seen as a sign of weakness, surrender or abandonment of principle. As long as it is a matter of honour, obtaining anything less than one's full rights involves shame and loss of face.

At almost every stage of the conflict Jews have been willing to settle for something less than what they wanted as their final goal, believing that time was on their side and that they would ultimately be able to achieve something nearer to their goal. Kenneth Cragg calls this "the 'ratchet' nature of Zionist achievement."[36] One of the clearest examples of this was in the Jewish response to the UN Partition Plan in 1947. While many Jews were dissatisfied with the amount of territory that was allocated to the Jewish area, they were willing to accept something less than ideal in the knowledge that in the course of time they might be able to obtain more land. Palestinians, on the other hand, have often adopted an "all or nothing" approach which sticks rigidly to what they perceive to be just demands. Writing about the response of the Palestinian leadership to proposals about partition after the Arab Revolt in 1936, Benny Morris describes their inability to compromise:

"Offered two reasonable solutions to the conflict—by Peel in 1937 and by the White Paper of 1939—the Palestinian leadership, against the advice of much of the outside Arab world, rejected both. It consistently rejected all thought of partition. Amin al-Husseini forever underestimated Zionist strength and overrated the Arabs." This underlay his unwillingness (or inability) to compromise, and proved to be his people's undoing. By the time a new leadership had learned the art of compromise and grudgingly agreed to the principle of partition, in the 1980s and 1990s, and had begun to reap the rewards of moderation (de facto sovereignty over most of the Gaza Strip and the cities of the West Bank), it was almost too late."[37]

Amos Elon reveals how difficult it is for Israel to make compromises over Jerusalem, and is hardly optimistic even about any of the compromises that might seem most reasonable:

> "Compromise in Jerusalem means more than merely moving a border here or there a little bit. For most Israelis, the struggle in the city is not over a part, but over the whole. Primarily, it is over the historic core, within the ancient walls, that includes the three major holy places. One 'reasonable' compromise could be the blurring of hard sovereign lines by recognizing two national rights within a united, jointly run municipal area. Even if the protagonists could mutually agree to such a plan (which remains doubtful), it must be noted that nowhere until now have two national capitals coexisted within the same city. There is reason to doubt that two nationalisms as raw as the Palestinian and the Israeli would be the first in known history to do so successfully. Another reasonable compromise might be the establishment of new capitals elsewhere by the two nationalities, within their respective sovereign territories. This seems equally unlikely in view of the strong religious component that shapes political attitudes toward Jerusalem."[38]

Accepting compromise often presents special problems for fundamentalists of all kinds. They tend to operate within a closed system with a fixed world view, and argue totally within the rules determined by that world view. They therefore find it hard to enter into genuine dialogue or negotiate with those who have a different stand-point. In arguments over Jerusalem, Jewish fundamentalists (often with the support of some Christian fundamentalists) present claims that are based entirely on their own scripture, tradition and history. Muslim fundamentalists similarly make great claims to Jerusalem based on their reading of the Qur'an, tradition and history, almost totally disregarding Jewish claims. Since it is almost impossible for others outside their community to challenge their case on theological grounds, it may be that outsiders can only challenge fundamentalists and encourage them to make compromises with very pragmatic approaches of this kind:

1. If you adopt an "all or nothing" approach, you may end up—literally—with nothing. Wouldn't you rather have *something*—even if it isn't everything that you want—than *nothing*?

2. Your ideal solution would probably involve ten times more suffering for a greater number of people than the situation that exists today, which you perceive to be so unjust. Even if you have been deeply wronged and suffered terrible injustice, do you really want to inflict so much suffering on others?

3. If you find that *your* kind of fundamentalism is up against *someone else's* fundamentalism, what kind of dialogue is possible? Can you have any meaningful communication with someone who operates within a different kind of system?"

4. Can't you find some way of balancing your idealism with pragmatism? We all have to live in the real world, the world as it is and not as we would like it to be. Are there not some occasions when we may have to put our ideals to one side in order to find practical solutions that simply enable us and others to live with as much security and dignity as possible?

Yitzak Frankenthal has some relevant words about realism and "a wise peace" that suggest the need for compromise: "I am not here for forgiveness or revenge but to stop the hatred and stop the bloodshed... I am a realist. I think Palestinians and Israelis may never agree on what is justice. So what we need is not necessarily a just peace but a wise peace. We all have to be realists."[39]

7. Pragmatism and concern for detail

Alongside the statesmen, diplomats and negotiators who work on the bigger picture and the broader principles, there need to be those who work behind the scenes with an eye for detail and who know what is actually involved in running a modern city. There comes a time when the politicians need to stand aside and ask the technocrats on the ground—both Jewish and Arab—to get to work with a commission like this: "Given the physical and demographic realities as they are today—in West Jerusalem, East Jerusalem and the Old City—how can we make this city function for the well-being of all its inhabitants? How could we make the different communities in this city feel that they have a sense of belonging and are genuinely proud of it? How can we feed people, look after their health, educate them and equip them for life?"

This is precisely the challenge that is taken up by a Palestinian NGO in a 432-page book entitled *The Jerusalem Urban Fabric*. The book begins with this sentence: "Jerusalem may be the key to achieving a just and comprehensive peace in the Middle East..."[40] With dozens of maps, charts and statistics, it covers issues like housing, town planning, water, electricity, sewage, agriculture, industry, medical services, trade, education, finances and the environment. A later project of the same group, the International Peace and Co-operation Centre—Jerusalem, has the title *Envisioning Jerusalem*, and starting from the situation that exists at the present time, seeks to present a vision of the kind of city that Jerusalem *could be*. Projects of this kind demonstrate that there are plenty of dedicated people who have the specialist expertise to work at the details and produce plans that could actually work.

Amos Elon's book *Jerusalem, Battleground of Memory* describes the present realities of Jerusalem with great insight and feeling in the light of its history. It ends with a vivid account of Elon's reflections in 1967 at the narrow gate of David's Citadel in Jerusalem, in which he longs that people should attach greater importance to real people and their needs at the present time than to history or monuments:

"Surely, I thought... this city has raised far more vexed ghosts of history than can safely be stomached locally. In the high noon of the ghosts, the human dimension is lost.

"On the steps by that same gate, Yehuda Amichai, the great poet of the modern city, once sat with two loaded baskets of fruit and overheard a tourist guide saying: 'You see that man with the baskets? Just right of his head there is an arch from the Roman period. Just right of his head.'

"'I said to myself,' Amichai writes, 'redemption will come only if their guide tells them: "You see that arch from the Roman period? It's not important; but next to it, left and down a bit, there sits a man who's bought fruit and vegetables for his family."'"[41]

Having been deputy mayor of Jerusalem, Meron Benvenisti speaks with some authority on the subject of the development of the city. In this passage he calls for a completely new kind of planning which is truly egalitarian in caring for the needs of *all* communities and is "process oriented":

> "After a whole generation of political planning that has fuelled the fires of intercommunal hatred, what is needed is an entirely different brand of community planning: planning that will organize the urban space in an egalitarian manner, for the benefit of all the citizens and not just one ethnic group. Jerusalem has enough space to accommodate the needs and aspirations of all its inhabitants...

> "What is needed is a 'process-oriented' approach, which requires a constant effort to grapple with the exigencies of a changing reality, with no shortcuts via once-and-for-all solutions... The process-oriented approach is solidly planted in the 'mud' of reality; there is no previously determined final and definitive goal. On the contrary, the assumption is that the two parties have conflicting final goals, and that it is pointless to exert oneself in the pursuit of a common goal, except for the purpose of conducting dialogue. Progress is measured not in terms of approaching some predetermined objective but by the mere fact of agreement, even on the pettiest of issues. Such agreement has value not only when it leads to a positive end, but also when it relates to objectives that either cannot be achieved within a given time frame, are impossible to achieve at all, or are achievable but impossible to implement. Does this analysis mean that, in the absence of a solution to the problem of Jerusalem the city is doomed to be the site of continuing violent conflicts? Is there no value in the attempt to envision a more positive political future?

> "The process-oriented approach may indeed inspire a cautious optimism. Its being grounded in reality means that the debate will address various aspects of the actual situation such as those enumerated here."[42]

Michael Dumper's *The Politics of Sacred Space* is a detailed study of the three main communities in the Old City, describing how they actually function and what developments have taken place since 1967. It is on the basis of such detailed analysis that, in the final two paragraphs, he summarizes his conclusion about the future of the city:

> "Due to the complexity of the intercommunal and political dynamics of the Old City, the negotiations over the future of Jerusalem will be equally complex. The changes that have taken place since 1967 have led to a completely new city so that a return to the status quo ante is neither likely or possible. To some extent the Oslo Accords are an indication of a softening of the Israeli position on Jerusalem as 'the eternal, undivided capital' of Israel. This does not mean that the Jewish presence has weakened. This book has illustrated many ways in which it has become much stronger in the Old City. Nevertheless, the Palestinian Muslim community, although much diminished from its heyday in the nineteenth-century period, has begun to show signs of revival and self-assertion. Similarly the church leadership has passed through a long period of torn loyalties and fragmentation and has more recently made clear its disaffection with the Israeli vision of Jerusalem.

> "There is no doubt that peace will occur only when tough decisions concerning military security and issues of resource control are resolved. Yet as the Camp David summit in July 2000 showed, even when most of these were almost in place, the passions aroused by the issue of sovereignty over the Old City led to the collapse of the totality of all the agreements. A negotiated Israel–Palestinian peace will need to involve the religious and historical concerns surrounding the holy sites. This, in turn, will mean involving the religious leadership of all the communities. Although it has been tried and failed in the past, an interreligious council of some kind that can have input into the negotiating process may be the sine qua non for peace in Jerusalem."[43]

The testimony of Benvenisti and Dumper suggests that it is vital to listen to those who know what is actually there in the city and who understand how things function best.

8. Outside pressure and support

"Why doesn't the world just stand back and let the Jews and Arabs fight it out among themselves?" There are at least two reasons why

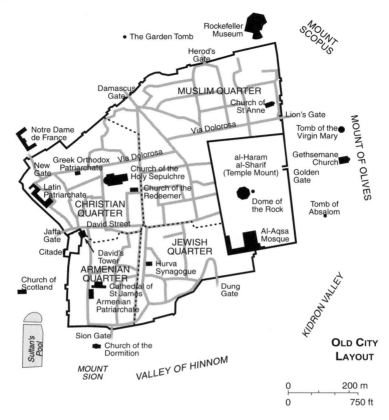

• The Garden Tomb
Rockefeller Museum
MOUNT SCOPUS
Herod's Gate
Damascus Gate
MUSLIM QUARTER
Church of St Anne
Lion's Gate
Via Dolorosa
Tomb of the Virgin Mary
Notre Dame de France
MOUNT OF OLIVES
New Gate
Greek Orthodox Patriarchate
Via Dolorosa
al-Haram al-Sharif (Temple Mount)
Gethsemane Church
Church of the Holy Sepulchre
Golden Gate
Latin Patriarchate
Church of the Redeemer
Dome of the Rock
Tomb of Absalom
CHRISTIAN QUARTER
David Street
Jaffa Gate
JEWISH QUARTER
Citadel
David's Tower
Hurva Synagogue
Al-Aqsa Mosque
ARMENIAN QUARTER
Church of Scotland
Cathedral of St James
Dung Gate
Armenian Patriarchate
KIDRON VALLEY
Sion Gate
Sultan's Pool
Church of the Dormition
OLD CITY LAYOUT
MOUNT SION
VALLEY OF HINNOM
0   200 m
0   750 ft

the wisdom of the street is totally inappropriate in this particular situation. The first is that this is to some extent what is happening at the moment—with disastrous results and with the minimum of restraint coming from outside. The conflict is spiralling out of control and has the potential to create further international conflict. It was in this kind of situation that David Grossman, a well-known Israeli novelist, writing in 2001, pointed out the desperate need for outside involvement and pressure: "Only a miracle or a catastrophe will change the situation. If you don't believe in the first and fear the latter, you realize that the only practical hope for saving Israel and the Palestinians from mutual slaughter is heavy international pressure on both of them."[44]

The second reason is that the outside world has for centuries been involved—or interfering—in Jerusalem and the rest of the region and has a great responsibility for resolving the conflict. The Middle East as it is today is largely the creation of Western powers on the ruins of the Ottoman empire which had lasted for four hundred years.[45] Thus "Ever since Herzl lobbied the chanceries of Europe to secure a charter for the Jewish colonization of Palestine," writes Anton La Guardia, "the Jewish and Palestinian questions have been in large part in the hands of the nations of the world."[46] Avi Shlaim explains the extent of Western involvement in the region in these terms:

"The key to the international politics of the Middle East lies in the relations between outside powers and local forces, whether governments, rulers, tribal chiefs, or warlords. In the nineteenth and early twentieth centuries, the club of great powers included the Ottoman empire, the Austro-Hungarian Empire, czarist Russia, Germany, France, and Great Britain. Until the 1991 Gulf War, no one great power had controlled the Middle East in modern times. There had always been at least two great powers, and usually more than two, competing for control and influence...

"The involvement of the great powers is not a unique feature of the Middle East but one that affects, in varying degrees, all regions of the world. What distinguishes the Middle East is the intensity, pervasiveness, and profound impact of this involvement. No other part of the non-Western world has been so thoroughly and ceaselessly caught up in great-power politics. In his book International Politics and the Middle East, Princeton professor L. Carl Brown aptly describes the Middle East as 'the most penetrated international relations subsystem in today's world'."[47]

It was only strong pressure from the USA in the aftermath of the Gulf War in 1991 that led to the convening of the talks at Madrid. Without a very firm hand from outside, neither Israel nor the Palestinians would have had the will to come together to make peace. Avi Shlaim has some pointed comments, however, about the way the role of the USA has changed in recent years. Writing about the talks at Madrid in 1991 he says:

"The official American position toward the Arab–Israeli conflict had remained unchanged since 1967. America supported the exchange of land for peace, refused to acknowledge the Israeli annexation of East Jerusalem, and considered the building of Jewish settlements in the occupied territories illegal and an obstacle to peace…

"In his concluding remarks Baker repeated the polite fiction that America would not impose its ideas but would act as the honest broker in furthering the peace process. But Baker knew, as did everyone else, that resolution of the Arab–Israeli conflict required more than an honest broker. The gulf between the two sides was extremely wide, and America was the only power with the resources and authority to bridge this gulf. In Madrid, America demonstrated that it also has the commitment and determination to pursue its vision of Middle East peace… Subsequent developments soon dashed many of the hopes that the Madrid encounter had raised. Just as the Gulf War was a neat war followed by a messy peace, so Madrid was a neat peace conference with a messy sequel…"[48]

He goes on to explain how changes in the US position had an adverse effect on the peace process. The statements of government officials under Clinton's administration reflected

"… a shift in American policy, away from the evenhanded approach of the Bush administration and back to the Reagan administration's Israel-first approach. As a result, America in effect abdicated its role as mediator in the peace talks and took the side of one of the protagonists. But the extent of the Clinton administration's one-sidedness was revealed only during the tenth round of talks which opened in mid-June 1993… After twenty months and ten rounds, the American-sponsored talks reached a dead-end."[49]

Writing about the Bush administration's handling of the conflict at the time of the Gulf War in 1991, Shlaim writes: "The chief flaw in the approach of previous administrations was that, while offering to act as an honest-broker, they provided Israel with open-ended economic, diplomatic, and military assistance, enabling it to defy the will of the international community."[50]

We could hardly ask for a clearer statement of the need for outside pressure and support that are genuinely neutral. It ought to be possible to use the experience of arbitration in personal and industrial disputes and apply it at the international level. But perhaps the cynics have good reason to complain that the biggest problem still seems to lie in the overwhelming and unchallenged power of the one superpower. What should have been part of the solution has become part of the problem.

9. A willingness to face up to the past

South Africa's Truth and Reconciliation Commission has provided a model of what it can mean for a country to face the ghosts of its past as it strives for a better future. Michael Sennott in *The Body and the Blood: Middle Eastern Christians at the Beginning of a New Millennium* writes of the way Bishop Desmond Tutu "presided over a bold attempt at national healing by creating a forum in which victims of apartheid heard their former oppressors confess to torture and other injustices." This is how he explains the South African approach:

> "The perpetrators were inclined to honesty because of the commission's extensive research and documentation, and because they could be granted amnesty if they told the truth. Tutu proposed what he defined as 'restorative justice' versus 'retributive justice'. 'Restorative justice' would have to embrace a way for both sides, the powerless and the powerful, the majority and the minority, to regain their dignity and to be given an opportunity for redemption. 'Retributive justice' would do little to heal the old wounds, and might even open fresh ones. This had been proven after World War I, many historians would contend, when a retributive peace agreement only fostered the divisions that fomented World War II."

Sennott goes on to describe a speech given by Desmond Tutu to an Israeli audience in 1999:

> "His speech was punctuated by disarming humour; but his passionate and somber message about forgiveness as a precondition for peace was riveting. Tutu was sensitive enough to point out that South Africa, during its struggle, did not appreciate efforts from outsiders telling them how to reach justice. But he was also courageous enough to

pose a question: 'Look, we were able to do it. Why can't it happen here?'"[51]

If the South African experience has any relevance to the Israeli–Palestinian conflict, it may be that this example could only be followed—as it was in South Africa—*after and not before* a significant breakthrough. But it still points to one basic pre-condition for reconciliation that needs to be fulfilled at some stage.

It is very evident, however, that soul-searching of this kind is already going on, if not to any great extent on the Palestinian side, at least on the Israeli side. One of the clearest examples of this process in recent months has been in the writings of Benny Morris, one of the Israeli "new historians" who has often been quoted in this book. His first book, *The Birth of the Palestinian Refugee Problem, 1947–1949* was published in 1988. He acknowledged later that his conclusion in this book "angered many Israelis and undermined Zionist historiography." Then on 21 February 2002 he wrote an article in the *Guardian* in which he spoke about his earlier optimism about the peace process and his gradual "conversion" to a much more pessimistic view about the possibilities of peace. He attacked Arafat as an "implacable nationalist and inveterate liar," and argued that whereas Israel had given up its dream of a "Greater Israel" and agreed to divide Palestine with the Arabs, the Palestinian national movement has "denied the Zionist movement any legitimacy and stuck fast to the vision of a 'Greater Palestine'." In 2003 a revised edition of the 1988 book about the refugee problem was published in which Morris produced more evidence both about the violence carried out by Israeli forces and about Arab involvement in persuading Palestinians to leave.

The following extracts from an interview with Morris carried out by Ari Shavit, which appeared in the *Ha'aretz* magazine on 9 February 2004, are a poignant example of what is involved in Israelis reflecting today on the events surrounding the birth of the state and the different conclusions they can reach:

Shavit: What you are telling me here, as though by the way, is that in Operation Hiram there was a comprehensive and explicit expulsion order. Is that right?

Morris: Yes. One of the revelations in the book is that on October 13, 1948, the commander of the Northern Front, Moshe Carmel, issued an order in writing to his units to expedite the removal of the Arab population. Carmel took this action immediately after a visit by Ben-Gurion to the Northern Command in Nazareth. There is no doubt in my mind that this order originated with Ben-Gurion. Just as the expulsion order for the City of Lod, which was signed by Yitzhak Rabin, was issued immediately after Ben-Gurion visited the headquarter of Operation Dani (July 1948).

Shavit: Are you saying that Ben-Gurion was personally responsible for a deliberate and systematic policy of mass expulsion?

Morris: From April 1948, Ben-Gurion is projecting a message of transfer. There is no explicit order of his in writing, there is no orderly comprehensive policy, but there is an atmosphere of [population] transfer. The transfer idea is in the air. The entire leadership understands that this is the idea. The officer corps understands what is required of them. Under Ben-Gurion, a consensus of transfer is created.

Shavit: Ben-Gurion was a "transferist'?

Morris: Of course. Ben-Gurion was a transferist. He understood that there could be no Jewish state with a large and hostile Arab minority in its midst. There could be no such state. It would not be able to exist.

Shavit: I don't hear you condemning him.

Morris: Ben-Gurion was right. If he had not done what he did, a state would not have come into being. That has to be clear. It is impossible to evade it. Without the uprooting of the Palestinians, a Jewish state would not have arisen here.

Shavit: Benny Morris, for decades you have been researching the dark side of Zionism. You are an expert on the atrocities of 1948. In the end, do you in effect justify all this? Are you an advocate of the transfer of 1948?

Morris: There is no justification for acts of rape. There is no justification for acts of massacre. Those are war crimes. But in certain conditions, expulsion is not a war crime. I don't think that the expulsions of 1948 were war crimes. You can't make an omelette without breaking eggs. You have to dirty your hands.

Shavit: We are talking about the killing of thousands of people, the destruction of an entire society.

Morris: A society that aims to kill you forces you to destroy it. When the choice is between destroying or being destroyed, it's better to destroy.

Shavit: There is something chilling about the quiet way in which you say that.

Morris: If you expect me to burst into tears, I'm sorry to disappoint you. I will not do that.

Shavit: So when the commanders of Operation Dani are standing there and observing the long and terrible column of the 50,000 people expelled from Lod walking eastward, you stand there with them? You justify them?

Morris: I definitely understand them. I understand their motives. I don't think they felt any pangs of conscience, and in their place I wouldn't have felt pangs of conscience. Without that act, they would not have won the war and the state would not have come into being.

Shavit: You do not condemn them morally?

Morris: No.

Shavit: They perpetrated ethnic cleansing.

Morris: There are circumstances in history that justify ethnic cleansing. I know that this term is completely negative in the discourse of the twenty-first century, but when the choice is between ethnic cleansing and genocide—the annihilation of your people—I prefer ethnic cleansing.

Shavit: And that was the situation in 1948?

Morris: That was the situation. That was what Zionism faced. A Jewish state would not have come into being without the uprooting of 700,000 Palestinians. Therefore it was necessary to uproot them. There was no choice but to expel that population. It was necessary to cleanse the hinterland and cleanse the border areas and cleanse the main roads. It was necessary to cleanse the villages from which our convoys and our settlements were fired on.

Shavit: The term "cleanse" is terrible.

Morris: I know it doesn't sound nice but that's the term they used at the time. I adopted it from all the 1948 documents in which I am immersed.

Shavit: What you are saying is hard to listen to and hard to digest. You sound hard-hearted.

Morris: I feel sympathy for the Palestinian people, which truly underwent a hard tragedy. I feel sympathy for the refugees themselves. But if the desire to establish a Jewish state here is legitimate, there was no other choice. It was impossible to leave a large fifth column in the country. From the moment the Yishuv [pre-1948 Jewish community in Palestine] was attacked by the Palestinians and afterward by the Arab states, there was no choice but to expel the Palestinian population. To uproot it in the course of war... In the end the Arabs have 22 states. The Jewish people did not have even one state. There was no reason in the world why it should not have one state. Therefore, from my point of view, the need to establish this state in this place overcame the injustice that was done to the Palestinians by uprooting them...

Shavit: I'm not sure I understand. Are you saying that Ben-Gurion erred in expelling too few Arabs?

Morris: If he was already engaged in expulsion, maybe he should have done a complete job. I know that this stuns the Arabs and the liberals and the politically correct types. But my feeling is that this place would be quieter and know less suffering if the matter had been resolved once and for all. If Ben-Gurion had carried out a large expulsion and cleansed the whole country—the whole Land of Israel, as far as the Jordan River. It may turn out that this was his fatal mistake. If he had carried out a full expulsion—rather than a partial one—he would have stabilized the State of Israel for generations.

Shavit: I find it hard to believe what I am hearing.

Morris: If in the end the story turns out to be a gloomy one for the Jews, it will be because Ben-Gurion did not complete the transfer in 1948. Because he left a large and volatile demographic reserve in the West Bank and Gaza and within Israel itself.

Shavit: In his place, would you have expelled them all? All the Arabs in the country?

Morris: But I am not a statesman. I do not put myself in his place. But as a historian, I assert that a mistake was made here. Yes. The non-completion of the transfer was a mistake...[52]

10. Hope

Israelis are reminded of the theme of hope every time they sing their national anthem, *Hatikvah* (The Hope). Their ancestors knew how to keep their hopes alive, and now that they have achieved at least one of these hopes, they go on longing for peace and security as a reward for their hard work, sacrifice and determination. Arabic-speaking Muslims and Christians use the word *amal* to speak of hope and expectation. But a much more powerful word for them is *sabr*, patience, endurance, firmness and perseverance. There is also the word *sumud*, which speaks of steadfastness in the face of adversity. When there is no hope and people sink into despair, there is always the danger of the Samson syndrome where they know that they are doomed, but in meeting their fate, want to bring the whole house down with them, inflicting the maximum casualties on their enemies.

If hope rests only on a shallow optimism that believes that things cannot get any worse and are bound to get better, it is not likely to be able to withstand constant set-backs, disappointment and even failure. For Jews, Christians and Muslims, however, hope can be based on the conviction that we live in a created universe and that striving for justice is one expression of our fear and reverence for God. Whether we like it or not, there is a process of judgment that is at work not only in the lives of individuals, but in families, communities and nations. The principle that we reap what we sow is ingrained in the moral fabric of the universe. Israelis and the Palestinians, together with all the nations involved in the conflict, are reaping, and will continue to reap, what they have sown. We do not have to wait for the Day of Judgment, because judgment of a kind is already being worked out in history here and now before our eyes.

Jews, Christians and Muslims can be confident of this because they believe in a creator God who is utterly holy and just, and who longs for his creatures to express something of that holiness and justice in their relations with each other. They can commit themselves to work for a just society and a just world, because all three faiths affirm the role of prophets who are prepared to speak the truth and confront every falsehood, wherever it is found. Ultimately there has to be a day of reckoning when every tyrant comes face to face with his/her maker, when wrongs are righted and justice is seen to be done. If there is very inadequate and imperfect justice in this life, justice and love will ultimately triumph in eternity.

If these are convictions that can be shared by believing Jews, Christians and Muslims, they can play a part in sustaining hope.

If Christians have a unique contribution to make to this process, it could be through their witness to the mystery of suffering. Kenneth Cragg suggests that what may be distinctive about the Christian world view is an understanding of the place of suffering in the divine economy—suffering that is expressed supremely in the one who suffered *in Jerusalem*.

"For the Christian is perpetually in debt to the Messianic theme in Jewish story—the theme that is the treasured matrix of the distinctively Christian conviction that the Messianic measure of the divine sovereignty wears a crown of thorns and is identified in the reach of the love that suffers to redeem—a love credibly enacted in human history in the drama of Jesus crucified and so perceived as the making of the Christian Church.

"There, in that drama and by dint of all its antecedents is, for Christians, 'the Place of the Name'. It is the clue they comprehend as the final measure of Jerusalem. To interpret Jerusalem in these terms must mean a lively participation in the Jewish rationale for Zionism, arising as this does from the anguish of Jewish experience at the hands of the European world. It we are drawing the final significance of Jerusalem from a perception of divine suffering, then 'suffering' must be the clue concerning all parties in contemporary history."[53]

For Michel Sabbah, the Roman Catholic Patriarch of Jerusalem, hope remains even when it is not vindicated by success and obvious vindication. He is content to live with a certain mystery which does not know all the answers:

"There is a mystery here. Jesus and his disciples were always a small minority. It is a mystery we live as Palestinian Christians today. I think the Christian community here will always be a small church, reflecting the life of Jesus, one that is small and one that is refused and rejected even in its homeland. There are mysteries in history. You can have much analysis, but ultimately you have to rely on mystery."[54]

Speaking at the Pontifical Council for Interreligious Dialogue at the Vatican on 19 May 2004, he said, "Humanly speaking, for the time being there is no perspective of peace. In the meantime, we live by bearing the cross, but with the cross we also bear in our hearts all the hope of the Resurrection."

The phrase "the things that make for peace" comes from the words of Jesus as he wept over Jerusalem. He knew that there was a way forward for the city that would avoid the terrible suffering which he could foresee. And he wept over Jerusalem because he knew that the time had run out, and that the city had set its face towards its final confrontation with Rome.

Is it too much to hope that in our situation today there is still time for change, still time to avert the disaster to which Jerusalem seems to be heading at the moment? If "the things that make for peace" are not "hidden from our eyes," there is still hope that Jerusalem could become a city of peace—not just for the people of three faiths, but for the whole world.

Epilogue

"If we will it, it is not a dream"

These ten chapters tracing the history of Jerusalem turn out to be like the layers of an onion. Those who have had the patience to take one layer at a time, persevering with all the conquests and changes of ownership, and who have had the imagination and empathy to enter into all the different religious ideas associated with the city may be left wondering if all this history and "mythology" can offer any clues that might help to resolve the actual conflict that is intensifying before our eyes by the day.

The story that unfolds in the Old Testament is of how an insignificant fortress with its pagan shrine becomes part of a larger story in which the creator of the universe works out a grand design that will eventually have very positive implications for every human being in every place and at any time. The God whose presence is located in the Temple in a special way is gradually revealing his character and showing his concern for every aspect of the well-being of his people. But the ultimate goal is that the Temple in Jerusalem should be "a house of prayer for all nations" and point to the hope of a renewed and restored creation, "a new heaven and a new earth" (Chapter 1).

The coming of Jesus of Nazareth adds a new twist to the tale—with its idea that a *person* can take the place of the *building*. The creator becomes a creature, a human being, in the universe he has made, and through his life, death and resurrection *in Jerusalem* fulfils in a deeper way all that the city and the Temple had symbolized before. Here is a message that his disciples want to take to the ends of the earth, allowing it to become rooted among people of diverse races and cultures (Chapter 2).

For the first 300 years Christianity is a minority religion in the Mediterranean world, often persecuted. Then, when it becomes the religion of the Roman Empire, the authorities feel the need to make Jerusalem into a thoroughly Christian city. The Church of the Resurrection (the Church of the Holy Sepulchre) becomes a focus for pilgrimage, where Christians come in order to celebrate and relive all that happened to Jesus. But triumphant Christianity cannot bring itself to be generous and inclusive, and excludes the Jews who had known Jerusalem for centuries as their holy city (Chapter 3).

The destruction of the Temple in CE 70 and the ban excluding them from the city in CE 135 are very traumatic events which live on in the imagination and the prayers of the Jewish people who remain in the land or are scattered all over the world. But they adapt positively to the loss of the Temple, while at the same time holding on to the hope of one day returning to the city and seeing the Temple rebuilt—either literally or metaphorically. Creating the Jewish state in 1948, however, and gaining control of the whole of Jerusalem in 1967 transform the world view of the Jewish people, presenting a cruel dilemma over what to do with the present inhabitants of the city and with all the stones that have been used by others to build on the site of the Temple since the time of their own ancient exile (Chapter 4).

Jerusalem is co-opted by Islam and becomes a powerful symbol of its triumph in the whole region. For reasons that are related both to religion and politics, Jerusalem becomes the third most sacred city for Muslims, and the Dome of the Rock and the Al-Aqsa Mosque provide a new place for pilgrimage. Since they are located over the ruins of the Jewish Temple and within sight of the Church of the Resurrection, these holy sites send a clear message that Islam has superseded both Judaism and Christianity. The authorities in the Islamic Empire can be reasonably tolerant of their Jewish and Christian subjects for many centuries. But then the loss of Jerusalem to Western "Christian" powers in 1917 opens the door both for new power games between the nations and for the growth of the Jewish community. These movements, working together, culminate in the creation of a Jewish state in the heartlands of Islam (Chapter 5).

Christians are forced to abandon any exclusive claims to Jerusalem because of the disaster of the Crusades. But a new phenomenon develops in the nineteenth century in which some Christians read their scriptures in a very literal way. So instead of believing that many ideas and dreams in the Old Testament have been fulfilled in the kingdom of God which comes through Jesus the Messiah, they genuinely believe that these dreams have to be fulfilled in an actual, historical return of Jews to Palestine. This world view leads these Christians to support passionately the vision of Zionism, believing that it is part of the divine plan for history which is going to reach its climax in and around Jerusalem in the very near future. The strange theological alliance between Christian Zionism and Zionism has far-reaching political implications, providing Israel with a highly powerful lobby within the one superpower in the world today (Chapter 6).

Herzl's dream of a Jewish state becomes a reality in 1948 with the creation of the state of Israel. But for many years the geography and demography of Jerusalem are such that the Jews do not attach a great deal of significance to the city. They want to have access to the Western Wall, from which they are excluded during the nineteen years that it is under Jordanian rule, but they do not actually want or need to control the Old City and the rest of East Jerusalem which are predominantly Arab. Then, however, the sudden and unexpected conquest of the whole city in the Six Day War of 1967 not only gives them access to their most sacred site, but engenders the determination and the defiance to assert that they will never surrender control of Jerusalem. It has become "one city, indivisible, the Capital of the State of Israel" (Chapter 7).

Having unilaterally asserted its claims to sovereignty over the city, Israel annexes the whole of East Jerusalem and the surrounding areas, making them effectively part of the Jewish state. Driven by a mixture of fear, insecurity and greed, it then begins an ambitious building programme to surround the city with rings of settlements in order to consolidate its grip on the city and ensure that its population is as Jewish as possible. But at this moment in time (mid-2004) the "eternally unified capital" is the most divided city in the world.

Judging simply by the facts that Israel has created on the ground in and around Jerusalem—even as far as the river Jordan—it looks as if Israel's intention is to ensure that any Palestinian entity/state that may one day emerge is as small, divided, impotent and meaningless as possible. The balance of power between a dominant Israel and the defeated, resentful Palestinians has turned the city of peace into the site where a cocktail of nationalism and religious extremism (in all three faiths) could easily ignite a global conflict (Chapter 8).

It is not as if there have not been any attempts to make peace. But the ambitions of both sides and the inequalities between them, the power equation in the rest of the world, the vagaries of Israeli and American politics and the successive explosions of violent anger and despair among the Palestinians over a continuing, illegal occupation have so far frustrated the negotiation process and prevented any peaceful resolution. Everything seems to depend on whether Israel is allowed by the rest of the world to insist on its exclusive sovereignty over the whole city or whether a formula can be found that leaves the city open and undivided but allows for some kind of shared sovereignty (Chapter 9).

When attitudes have hardened so much and we seem to be looking into the abyss, perhaps it is time to go on reflecting on areas where there may have to be a radical rethinking—not only among Israeli Jews and Palestinian Arabs but also among all three faith communities and in the corridors of power throughout the world. Provided there is sufficient change of heart and mind to make such a breakthrough possible, perhaps it is *not* too late to go back to the drawing board in order to find realistic solutions that can bring a wise peace—if not a perfect peace—to the city of peace (Chapter 10).

Theodore Herzl said of the Zionist dream "If we will it, it is not a dream." Those who still share the Zionist vision may want to reflect again on the gradual process by which Jerusalem has come to occupy such an essential place in the thinking of Israeli Jews today. They may also need to ask themselves if they can be secure enough to allow *others* to have *their* dreams, and if they are aware of the price that *others* have had to pay for the kind of success and victory that they have achieved so far—and will continue to pay if they themselves hold on to their vision of "the Greater Israel."

The particular version of the Zionist dream that is dominant at the moment is not the only one on the market. *There is an alternative dream*—a dream which is bigger and broader than either this version of the Zionist dream or the current Islamist dream. It ought to be humanly possible to find ways of acknowledging the best of both these dreams and allowing them to live side by side. What is needed is for both sides—and the rest of the world—to enter into this alternative dream of *an open Jerusalem with shared sovereignty,* and then, together, to move heaven and earth to work at all the details that could make it a reality. "If we will it, it is not a dream."

Notes

Introduction

1. See David Fromkin, *A Peace to End All Peace: The Fall of the Ottoman Empire and the Creation of the Modern Middle East*, London: Phoenix, 2000, p. 313.

2. Meron Benvenisti, *City of Stone: The Hidden History of Jerusalem*, London: University of California Press, 1996, pp. 89 and 105.

3. Amos Elon, p. 20.

4. Naim Ateek, p. xv.

5. Amos Elon, pp. 57 and 247–48.

6. Karen Armstrong, *A History of Jerusalem: One City, Three Faiths*, London: Harper Collins, 1997, p. xiii.

7. Colin Chapman, *Whose Promised Land?* Oxford: Lion Hudson, 2002, and Grand Rapids: Baker Books, 2002.

8. Kenneth Cragg, *This Year in Jerusalem: Israel in Experience*, London: Darton, Longman and Todd, 1982, p. 94.

Chapter 1

1. Naim Ateek, p. 95.

2. Karen Armstrong, p. 30.

3. Naim Ateek, *Jerusalem: What Makes for Peace!*, p. 95.

4. Meron Benvenisti, p. 144.

5. Zaki Badawi, "Jerusalem and Islam" in Ghada Karmi, *Jerusalem Today: What Future for the Peace Process?*, Reading: Ithaca, 1996, p. 137.

6. Quoted in Elon, pp. 94–95.

7. Gershom Gorenberg, p. 61.

8. Amos Elon, pp. 200 and 21.

9. Peter Walker, "Jerusalem" in eds., T.D. Alexander and Brian S. Rosner, *New Dictionary of Biblical Theology*, Intervarsity Press, 2000, p. 589.

10. Naim Ateek, p. 99.

11. F.E. Peters, *Jerusalem: The Holy City in the Eyes of Chroniclers, Visitors, Pilgrims, and Prophets from the Days of Abraham to the Beginnings of Modern Times*, Princeton: Princeton University Press, 1985, p. 53.

12. Mike Butterworth, *The Lion Handbook to the Bible*, Oxford: Lion, 2002, p. 473.

13. F.E. Peters, p. 79.

Chapter 2

1. Peter Walker, "Jesus and Jerusalem: New Testament Perspectives" in Naim Ateek, ed., *Jerusalem: What Makes for Peace!*, pp. 62, 66 and 67.

2. W.D. Davies, *The Gospel and the Land: Early Christianity and Jewish Territorial Doc-*

trine, Berkeley: University of California Press, 1974, p. 375.

3. Peter Walker, "Jerusalem" in T.D. Alexander and Brian S. Rosner, eds, *New Dictionary of Biblical Theology*, Intervarsity Press, 2000, p. 592.

4. N.T. Wright, *Jesus and the Victory of God*, quoted in Peter Walker, "Jesus and Jerusalem: New Testament Perspectives" in Naim Ateek, ed., *Jerusalem: What Makes for Peace!*, p. 64.

5. See further Colin Chapman, "God's Covenant—God's Land?" paper at Tyndale Fellowship Triennial Conference, 2003, to be published with conference papers by Intervarsity Press, 2005.

6. Peter Walker, *Jesus and The Holy City*, p. 279.

7. Peter Walker, *New Dictionary of Biblical Theology*, p. 592.

8. N.T. Wright, quoted in Peter Walker, "Jesus and Jerusalem: New Testament Perspectives" in Naim Ateek, ed., *Jerusalem: What Makes for Peace!*, p. 67.

9. Clare Amos, "Serving at the Table of Jesus Servant of Others" in *A Faithful Presence: Essays for Kenneth Cragg*, London: Melisende, 2003, pp. 118–19.

10. N.T. Wright, quoted in Peter Walker, *Jerusalem: What Makes for Peace!*, pp. 65–66.

11. Peter Walker, "Jesus and Jerusalem: New Testament Perspectives," p. 70.

12. See further Colin Chapman, *Whose Promised Land?*, pp. 185–90 and 274–84.

13. N.T. Wright, quoted in Peter Walker, p. 69.

14. D. Wenham, quoted in Peter Walker, *Jesus and the Holy City*, p. 126.

15. J.C. De Young, quoted in Peter Walker, p. 131.

16. Chris Wright, "A Christian Approach to Old Testament Prophecy Concerning Israel" in Peter Walker, ed., *Jerusalem Past and Present in the Purposes of God*, Carlisle: Paternoster, 1994, p. 18.

17. Peter Walker, *Jesus and the Holy City*, pp. 319–20.

18. Peter Walker, "Jesus and Jerusalem: New Testament Perspectives" in Naim Ateek, ed., *Jerusalem: What Makes for Peace!*, p. 62.

Chapter 3

1. Eusebius, quoted in F.E. Peters, p. 131.

2. Paulinus of Nola, quoted in Karen Armstrong, p. 202.

3. John Chrysostom, quoted in Richard Harries, p. 157.

4. Sabas, quoted in Karen Armstrong, p. 212.

5. Anba Abraham, "The Spirituality of Pilgrimage" in *Jerusalem: What Makes for Peace!*, p. 110.

6. Peter Walker, *Holy City, Holy Places? Christian Attitudes to Jerusalem and the Holy Land in the Fourth Century*, Oxford University Press, 1990; quoted in Peter Walker, "Jerusalem and the Early Christian Centuries," Carlisle: Paternoster, 1984, p. 90.

7. F.E. Peters, pp. 133–34.

8. F.E. Peters, p. 190.

9. F.E. Peters, pp. 190–91.

10. F.E. Peters, pp. 281–82.

11. F.E. Peters, p. 285.

12. F.E. Peters, p. 287.

13. F.E. Peters, p. 286.

14. Amos Elon, pp. 35–36.

15. Amos Elon, p. 166.

16. T. Mitchell, *The Society of the Muslim Brothers*, London, 1969, pp. 229–30, quoted in Antonie Wessels, "The Significance of Jerusalem for Muslims" in Naim Ateek, ed., *Jerusalem: What Makes for Peace!*, p. 59.

17. David Fromkin, p. 313.

18. Quoted in Ray Barraclough, "Land Rights in Israel and Palestine: An Australian Perspective" in Michael Prior, ed., *They Came and They Saw*, p. 182.

19. James Reston, *Warriors of God: Richard the Lionheart and Saladin in the Third Crusade*, New York: Anchor, 2002, p. xviii.

20. James Reston, p. xvii.

21. Memorandum. See full text in Appendix.

22. Karen Armstrong, p. 171.

23. Karen Armstrong, p. 173.

24. Peter Walker, "Jerusalem in the Early Christian Centuries," p. 83.

25. Karen Armstrong, p. 172.

26. Peter Walker, *Jesus and the Holy City*, p. 321.

27. Peter Walker, "Jerusalem in the Early Christian Centuries," pp. 85–87.

28. Peter Walker, "Jerusalem in the Early Christian Centuries," p. 85.

29. Karen Armstrong, p. 202.

30. James Reston, p. 215.

31. James Reston, p. 215, 256–57.

32. Kenneth Cragg, "The Excellence of Jerusalem," *Journal of Islamic Jerusalem Studies* (Winter 1998), 2:1.

33. See Colin Chapman, "Living Through the 900th Anniversary of the First Crusade: To Apologise or Not to Apologise?," *Faith to Faith Newsletter*, Number 1, November 1998.

34. See Kenneth Cragg, *The Arab Christian: A History in the Middle East*, London: Mowbray, 1992.

35. Anthony O'Mahoney, ed., *Palestinian Christians: Religion, Politics and Society in the Holy Land*, London: Melisende, 1991, p. 47.

36. Naim Ateek, ed., *Jerusalem: What Makes for Peace!*, p. xvi.

37. Naim Ateek, p. xviii.

38. Geries Khoury, "A Vision for Christian–Muslim Relations" in Naim Ateek, ed., *Jerusalem: What Makes for Peace!*, p. 39.

39. O'Mahoney, pp. 48–50.

40. O'Mahoney, pp. 52–53.

41. Charles M. Sennott, *The Body and the Blood: The Holy Land's Christians at the Turn of a New Millennium*, New York: Public Affairs.

Chapter 4

1. Mayer Gruber, "Jerusalem" in William Scott Green, Jacob Nevsner, Alan J. Avery-Peck, eds, *The Encyclopedia of Judaism*, Leiden: Brill, 2000, p. 531.

2. Zwi Werblowsky, quoted in Meron Benvenisti, p. 53.

3. Midrash Tanhuma Vayikra (Leviticus) 18, 23: Kedoshim 10.

4. Pirkei Avot (*Ethics of the Fathers*), 5.8 and Avot de Rabbi Natan; Avot de Rabbi Natan B48.

5. Rabbi Avraham Yitzhak Hacohen Kook, quoted in Meron Benvenisti, p. 78.

6. F.E. Peters, pp. 117–21.

7. F.E. Peters, p. 111.

8. F.E. Peters, p. 122.

9. Karen Armstrong, p. 154.

10. Karen Armstrong, p. 153.

11. Amos Elon, p. 154.

12. F.E. Peters, pp. 126–27.

13. Donald Wagner, *Dying in the Land of Promise: Palestine and Palestinian Christianity from Pentecost to 2000*, London: Melisende, 2003, p. 45.

14. F.E. Peters, p. 128.

15. F.E. Peters, p. 130.

16. *Authorised Daily Prayer Book* of the United Hebrew Congregations of the Commonwealth, S. Singer (trans.) London, 1998, p. 170.

17. F.E. Peters, p. 229.

18. Mayer Gruber, *Encyclopedia of Judaism*, p. 525.

19. Mayer Gruber, p. 530.

20. Mayer Gruber, p. 529.

21. F.E. Peters, p. 226.

22. Mayer Gruber, p. 528.

23. F.E. Peters, p. 279.

24. Mayer Gruber, p. 529.

25. Mayer Gruber, p. 532.

26. Mayer Gruber, p. 530.

27. Amos Elon, p. 127.

28. Israel Shahak and Norton Mezvinsky, *Jewish Fundamentalism in Israel*, London: Pluto, 1999, p. 4.

29. Amos Elon, p. 36.

30. *The Authorised Daily Prayer Book*, p. 730.

31. *The Authorised Daily Prayer Book*, pp. 772–74.

32. F.E. Peters, pp. 121–22.

33. Amos Elon, p. 60.

34. Mayer Gruber, p. 525.

35. Meron Benvenisti, pp. 83 and 85.

36. Meron Benvenisti, p. 73.

37. Mayer Gruber, pp. 532–33.

38. Israel Shahak and Norton Mezvinsky, p. 7.

39. Shahak and Mezvinsky, p. 7.

40. Shahak and Mezvinsky, p. 7.

41. Mayer Gruber, p. 532.

42. Amos Elon, p. 186.

43. Mordechai Eliahu, quoted in Amos Elon, p. 96.

44. Meir Yehuda Getz, quoted in Amos Elon, pp. 96–97.

45. Quoted in Amos Elon, pp. 108–109.

46. Yehuda Etzion, quoted in Sennott, p. 322.

47. Harry Goodman, quoted in Amos Elon, p. 100.

48. Amos Elon, p. 104.

49. Shahak and Mezvinsky, p. 6.

Chapter 5

1. H.S. Karmi, *How Holy is Palestine to Muslims?*, Islamic Cultural Press (undated), p. 5.

2. Al-Muqaddasi, quoted in Amos Elon, p. 116.

3. Amos Elon, p. 59.

4. Zaki Badawi, "Jerusalem and Islam" in Ghad Karmi, ed., *Jerusalem Today: What Future for the Peace Process?*, 1996, p. 137.

5. H.S. Karmi, *How Holy is Palestine to Muslims?*, Islamic Cultural Press, p. 26.

6. H.S. Karmi, p. 23.

7. *The Life of Muhammad: A Translation of Ibn Ishaq's Sirat Rasul Allah*, translated by A. Guillaume, Karachi: Oxford University Press, 1996, pp. 181–82.

8. Amos Elon, p. 83.

9. Mohammed Abdul Hameed Al-Khateeb, *Al-Quds: The Place of Jerusalem in Classical Judaic and Islamic Traditions*, Ta-Ha Publishers, 1998, p. 108.

10. Sami Aoun, "The Muslim Perspective in Jerusalem: A Shared Trust," Middle East Council of Churches Perspectives, No. 8, July 1990, p. 14.

11. Zachariah Bashier, *The Makkan Crucible*, Leicester: The Islamic Foundation, 1991, p. 216.

12. H.S. Karmi, pp. 1–28; Amos Elon, p. 58; F.E. Peters, p. 374.

13. Mohammed Marmaduke Pickthall, *The Meaning of the Glorious Koran: An explanatory translation*, New York: Mentor.

14. *The Koran*, translated with notes by N.J. Dawood, Penguin, 2000.

15. Antonie Wessels, p. 48.

16. F.E. Peters, pp. 185–86.

17. F.E. Peters, pp. 187–88.

18. Stephen Schwartz, *The Two Faces of Islam: The House of Sa"ud from Tradition to Terror*, New York: Doubleday, p. 31.

19. F.E. Peters, p. 198.

20. Kenneth Cragg, *Readings in the Qur'an*, London: Collins, 1988, p. 169.

21. Karen Armstrong, p. 239.

22. Amos Elon, p. 219.

23. F.E. Peters, p. 258.

24. F.E. Peters, p. 238.

25. F.E. Peters, p. 235.

26. Antonie Wessels, p. 53.

27. James Reston, p. 95.

28. James Reston, pp. 257–58.

29. Stephen Runciman, *The Crusades*, vol. III, p. 469.

30. Jeremy Johns, "Christianity and Islam" in John McManners, ed., *Oxford Illustrated History of Christianity*, Oxford: Oxford University Press, 1996, p. 166.

31. Antonie Wessels, p. 54.

32. Antonie Wessels, p. 53.

33. Zaki Badawi, p. 141.

34. F.E. Peters, p. 478.

35. H.S. Karmi, pp. 18–19, 25.

36. *Encyclopedia of Islam*, new edition, vol. IV, p. 84, under ISA.

37. F.E. Peters, p. 236.

38. Fadeel M. Abu-Nasr, *Hizb-Allah, Haqa'iq wa-Ab'ad (Hizbullah: Facts and Dimensions)*, Beirut: World Book Publishing, 2003, pp. 157–79.

39. Bassam Jirar quoted in Gershom Gorenberg, p. 191.

40. Gershom Gorenberg, p. vi.

41. Al-Khateeb, pp. 160–61.

42. Gershom Gorenberg, p. 185.

43. H.S. Karmi, p. 27.

44. H.S. Karmi, pp. 27–28.

45. H.S. Karmi, p. 17.

46. Zaki Badawi, pp. 141–42.

47. Al-Khateeb, p. 189.

48. Sami Aoun, p. 19.

49. Shaul Mishal and Avraham Sela, *The Palestinian Hamas Vision, Violence and Co-existence*, New York: Columbia University Press, 2000, p. 194.

50. Peter G. Riddell, "From Qur'an to Contemporary Politics: Hamas and the Role of Sacred Scripture" in Christopher H. Partridge, ed., *Fundamentalisms*, Carlisle: Paternoster, 2001, p. 70.

51. Amal Saad-Ghorayeb, *Hizbu'llah: Politics and Religion*, London: Pluto, 2002, pp. 161–62.

Chapter 6

1. John Hagee, *Final Dawn Over Jerusalem*, Nashville: Thomas Nelson, 2000, p. 131.

2. John Hagee, p. vii.

3. Tim LaHaye and Jerry B. Jenkins, *Armageddon*, Wheaton: Tyndale House Publishers, 2003, p. 282.

4. Stephen R. Sizer, "Dispensational Approaches to the Land," in *The Land of Promise: Biblical, Theological and Contemporary Perspectives*, Leicester: Apollos, p. 142.

5. Stephen R. Sizer, *Christian Zionism: Road-Map to Armageddon?* Leicester: Intervarsity Press (to be published).

6. Stephen R. Sizer.

7. LaHaye and Jenkins, p. 282.

8. See Robert C. Doyle, Chapter 3, "Heaven and History: Mediaeval Eschatology," *Eschatology and the Shape of Christian Belief*, Carlisle: Paternoster, 2000, pp. 114–53.

9. Stephen R. Sizer.

10. Donald E. Wagner, *Anxious for Armageddon*, Scottdale, Pennsylvania: Herald Press, 1995, p. 86.

11. Stephen R. Sizer, p. 55.

12. Donald E. Wagner, p. 92.

13. Donald E. Wagner, "Marching to Zion: Western Evangelicals and Jerusalem Approaching the Year 2000" in Naim Ateek, ed., *Jerusalem: What Makes for Peace!*, pp. 83–84.

14. Stephen R. Sizer, p. 352.

15. Stephen R. Sizer, p. 83.

16. John Hagee, *Final Dawn Over Jerusalem*.

17. Tim LaHaye and Jerry B. Jenkins, *Armageddon*.

18. Stephen R. Sizer, p. 106.

19. Donald Wagner, "Christians and Zion: British Stirrings" in *The Daily Star*, Beirut, 7 October 2003.

20. John Hagee, p. 19.

21. Tim LaHaye and Jerry B. Jenkins, p. 298.

22. John Hagee, p. 33.

23. John Hagee, pp. 194–95.

24. John Hagee, p. 18.

25. John Hagee, p. 133.

26. John Hagee, p. 131.

27. John Hagee, p. 148.

28. John Hagee, p. 114.

29. Tim LaHaye and Jerry B. Jenkins, p. 329.

30. Tim LaHaye and Jerry B. Jenkins, p. 251.

31. Tim LaHaye and Jerry B. Jenkins, p. 276.

32. Quoted in Stephen R. Sizer, "Dispensational Approaches to the Land," p. 159.

33. Stephen R. Sizer, "Dispensational Approaches to the Land," p. 156.

34. Stephen R. Sizer, *Christian Zionism, Road Map to Armageddon?*

35. Gershom Gorenberg, p. 29.

36. John Hagee, p. 132.

37. Tim LaHaye and Jerry B. Jenkins, pp. 247–48.

38. John Hagee, p. 144.

39. Tim LaHaye and Jerry B. Jenkins, p. 317.

40. Stephen R. Sizer, "Dispensational Approaches to the Land," p. 159.

41. Gershom Gorenberg, p. 35.

42. Grace Hasell, "Siege on Al-Masjidul Aqsa," *Al-Aqsa*, vol. 2, Issue 2, April 2000, p. 6.

43. Amos Elon, p. 97.

44. John Hagee, pp. 149–50.

45. Stephen R. Sizer, *Christian Zionism*, p. 214.

46. Tim LaHaye and Jerry B. Jenkins, p. 311.

47. Tim LaHaye and Jerry B. Jenkins, p. 350.

48. Tim LaHaye and Jerry B. Jenkins, p. 312.

49. John Hagee, p. 11.

50. John Hagee, p. 20.

51. John Hagee, p. 162.

52. Stephen R. Sizer, *Christian Zionism*.

53. John Hagee, p. 143.

54. John Hagee, p. 42.

55. Stephen R. Sizer, *Christian Zionism*.

56. Stephen R. Sizer, *Christian Zionism*.

57. Donald Wagner, "Bible and Sword: US Christian Zionists Discover Israel," *The Daily Star*, Beirut, 9 October 2003.

58. Paul Vallely, "A novel approach to the end times," *Church Times*, 17 October 2003.

59. Donald Wagner, "A heavenly match: Bush and the Christian Zionists," *The Daily Star*, Beirut, 11 October 2003.

60. Cyrus I. Schofield, quoted in Stephen R. Sizer, "Dispensational Approaches to the Land," p. 145.

61. Hal Lindsey, quoted in Gershom Gorenberg, p. 121.

62. Tim LaHaye and Jerry B. Jenkins, pp. 333–36.

63. Tim LaHaye and Jerry B. Jenkins, pp. 309 and 384.

64. John Hagee, p. 97.

65. John Hagee, p. 108.

66. Donald Wagner, "Marching to Zion: Western Evangelicals and Jerusalem Approaching the Year 2000," in *Jerusalem: What Makes for Peace!*, p. 80.

67. Paul Vallely, *Church Times*.

68. Tim LaHaye and Jerry B. Jenkins, p. 361.

69. Tim LaHaye and Jerry B. Jenkins, p. 222.

70. Tim LaHaye and Jerry B. Jenkins, p. 300.

71. Tim LaHaye and Jerry B. Jenkins, p. ix.

72. Tim LaHaye and Jerry B. Jenkins, p. 366.

73. Tim LaHaye and Jerry B. Jenkins, p. xvi.

74. Tim LaHaye and Jerry B. Jenkins, pp. 231–32.

75. Tim LaHaye and Jerry B. Jenkins, p. 203.

76. Tim LaHaye and Jerry B. Jenkins, p. 373.

77. Paul Vallely, *Church Times*.

78. John Hagee, p. 144.

79. John Hagee, pp. 144–46.

80. Stephen R. Sizer, *Christian Zionism*.

81. Tim LaHaye and Jerry B. Jenkins, p. 340.

82. Tim LaHaye and Jerry B. Jenkins, p. 312.

83. Stephen R. Sizer.

84. Tim LaHaye and Jerry B. Jenkins, p. 306.

85. Charles M. Sennott, p. 34.

86. Grace Halsell, *Prophecy and Politics: Militant Evangelists on the Road to Nuclear War*, Westport, Connecticut: Lawrence Hill and Co., 1986, p. 195.

87. Gershom Gorenberg, pp. 168–69.

88. Donald Wagner, *Dying in the Land of Promise*, p. 277.

89. Charles M. Sennott, p. 35.

90. Richard Harries, p. 150.

91. Quoted in Martin E. Marty, "Uncommon Cause," Sightings, 5 May 2003, www.sightings.listhost.uchicago.edu.

92. Peter Walker, "Jesus and Jerusalem: New Testament Perspectives," pp. 68, 71 and 72.

93. See, for example, John Stott, quoted in Donald Wagner, *Anxious for Armageddon*, Scottdale: Herald Press, 1995, p. 80.

Chapter 7

1. Donald Wagner, *Dying in the Land of Promise*, p. 98.
2. Bernard Wasserstein, *Divided Jerusalem: The Struggle for the Holy City*, London: Profile Books, 2002, p. 110.
3. Avi Shlaim, *The Iron Wall: Israel and the Arab World*, London: Penguin, 2000, p. 25.
4. Bernard Wasserstein, p. 205.
5. Bernard Wasserstein, p. 238.
6. Karen Armstrong, p. 344.
7. Karen Armstrong, p. 347.
8. Karen Armstrong, p. 352.
9. Amos Elon, p. 238.
10. Bernard Wasserstein, p. 2.
11. Amos Elon, p. 239.
12. Bernard Wasserstein, p. 87.
13. Amos Elon, p. 240.
14. Bernard Wasserstein, p. 4.
15. Bernard Wasserstein, p. 49.
16. Bernard Wasserstein, pp. 4–5.
17. Benny Morris, p. 656.
18. Tom Segev, *One Palestine, Complete: Jews and Arabs under the British Mandate*, London: Abacus, 2002, p. 5.
19. Bernard Wasserstein, p. 119.
20. Bernard Wasserstein, p. 125.
21. Benny Morris, *Righteous Victims: A History of the Zionist–Arab Conflict, 1881–1999*, London: John Murray, 2000, pp. 221–22.
22. Avi Shlaim, *War and Peace in the Middle East: A Concise History*, London: Penguin, 1995, p. 25.
23. Avi Shlaim, *War and Peace in the Middle East*, pp. 22–23.
24. Bernard Wasserstein, p. 151.
25. Bernard Wasserstein, p. 174.
26. Bernard Wasserstein, p. 142.
27. Bernard Wasserstein, p. 158.
28. Bernard Wasserstein, p. 160.
29. Bernard Wasserstein, p. 162.
30. Bernard Wasserstein, p. 163.
31. Bernard Wasserstein, p. 176.
32. Avi Shlaim, *The Iron Wall*, p. 25.
33. Avi Shlaim, *The Iron Wall*, p. 60.
34. Bernard Wasserstein, p. 177.
35. Bernard Wasserstein, p. 178.

36. Avi Shlaim, *The Iron Wall*, p. 61.
37. Avi Shlaim, *The Iron Wall*, p. 236.
38. Michael B. Oren, *Six Days of War: June 1967 and the Making of the Modern Middle East*, London: Penguin, 2002, p. 208.
39. Michael B. Oren, p. 245.
40. Michael B. Oren, p. 245.
41. Michael B. Oren, p. 246.
42. Bernard Wasserstein, p. 328, and Avi Shlaim, *The Iron Wall*, p. 245.
43. Benny Morris, p. 331.
44. Bernard Wasserstein, p. 238.
45. Avi Shlaim, *The Iron Wall*, pp. 252–53.
46. Michael B. Oren, pp. 311–12.
47. Avi Shlaim, *The Iron Wall*, p. 235.
48. Bernard Wasserstein, p. 206.
49. Benny Morris, p. 321.
50. Michael B. Oren, p. 255.
51. Meron Benvenisti, p. 35.

Chapter 8

1. Bernard Wasserstein, p. 205.
2. Bernard Wasserstein, p. 310.
3. Benny Morris, p. 659.
4. Meron Benvenisti, pp. 36–37.
5. Bernard Wasserstein, p. x.
6. Amos Elon, pp. 89–90.
7. Amos Elon, p. 89.
8. Amos Elon, p. 198.
9. Amos Elon, p. 91.
10. Michael B. Oren, p. 309; and Amos Elon, p. 90.
11. Amos Elon, p. 90.
12. Benny Morris, p. 331.
13. Meron Benvenisti, p. 131.
14. Amos Elon, p. 42.
15. Benny Morris, pp. 330–31.
16. Amos Elon, p. 242.
17. Donald E. Wagner, *Dying in the Land of Promise*, p. 226.
18. Avi Shlaim, *War and Peace in the Middle East*, pp. 116–17.
19. Rami Nasrallah, Rassem Khamaisi and Michael Younan, *Jerusalem on the Map*, Jerusalem: The International Peace and Co-operation Center, 2003, p. 31.

20. Rami Nasrallah, Rassem Khamaisi and Michael Younan, p. 15.

21. Justus R. Weiner, *Illegal Construction in Jerusalem: A Variation of an Alarming Global Phenomenon*, Jerusalem Center for Public Affairs, 2002.

22. Bernard Wasserstein, p. 218.

23. Bernard Wasserstein, p. 258.

24. U.O. Schmelz, *Modern Jerusalem's Demographic Evolution*, Jerusalem Institute of Israeli Studies.

25. Rami Nasrallah, Rassem Khamaisi and Michael Younan, p. 48.

26. Rami Nasrallah, Rassem Khamaisi and Michael Younan, p. 16.

27. Avi Shlaim, *The Iron Wall*, pp. 581–82.

28. Bernard Wasserstein, p. 310.

29. Rami Nasrallah, Rassem Khamaisi and Michael Younan, p. 34.

30. Bernard Wasserstein, p. x.

31. Rami Nasrallah, Rassem Khamaisi and Michael Younan, p. 48.

Chapter 9

1. Bernard Wasserstein, p. xv.

2. Geries Khoury, "A Vision for Christian-Muslim Relations," in Naim Ateek, ed., *Jerusalem: What Makes for Peace!*, p. 38.

3. Gershom Gorenberg, p. 84.

4. Meron Benvenisti, p. 43.

5. Meron Benvenisti, pp. 89 and 105.

6. Bernard Wasserstein, p. 232.

7. "Together on the Way: Statement on the Status of Jerusalem," General Assembly, 4 December 1998.

8. Avi Shlaim, *The Iron Wall*, p. 14.

9. Bernard Wasserstein, pp. 251–52.

10. Bernard Wasserstein, p. 236.

11. Benny Morris, pp. 486–87 and 493.

12. Menachem Klein, p. 65.

13. Bernard Wasserstein, p. 242.

14. Benny Morris, pp. 509 and 558.

15. Benny Morris, p. 562.

16. Benny Morris, p. 569.

17. Benny Morris, p. 596.

18. Bernard Wasserstein, p. 260.

19. Bernard Wasserstein, p. 260.

20. Bernard Wasserstein, p. 264.

21. Ghada Karmi, "The Future of Jerusalem," Lecture at the Royal Institute of International Affairs, London, December 1999; *Al-Aqsa*, vol 2, Issue 2, April 2000.

22. Bernard Wasserstein, p. 303.

23. Bernard Wasserstein, p. 291.

24. Avi Shlaim, *The Iron Wall*, pp. xiii–xiv.

25. Tanya Reinhart, *Israel/Palestine: How to End the War of 1948*, New York: Seven Stories Press, 2002, pp. 32–35, 38–39, 50–51.

26. Charles M. Sennott, p. 334.

27. *The Independent*, 2 December 2003.

28. Menachem Klein, p. 3.

29. Menachem Klein, pp. 4–5.

30. Menachem Klein, p. 16.

31. M. Hirsch, D. Mousen-Couriel and R. Lapidoth, *Whither Jerusalem? Proposals and positions concerning the future of Jerusalem*, The Hague: Martinus Nijhoff, 1995.

Chapter 10

1. Avi Shlaim, *The Iron Wall*, p. 18.

2. Amos Elon, pp. 244–45.

3. Bernard Wasserstein, p. xiv.

4. Golda Meir, *The Sunday Times*, 15 June 1969.

5. Avi Shlaim, *The Iron Wall*, p. 3.

6. Simha Flapan, *Zionism and the Palestinians*, London: Croom Helm, 1979, pp. 12, 78 and 83.

7. Benny Morris, pp. 654–55.

8. Bernard Wasserstein, p. 233.

9. Benny Morris, *The Guardian*, 21 February 2002.

10. Kenneth Cragg, *This Year in Jerusalem*, p. 59.

11. Amos Elon, p. 90.

12. Clare Amos, "Text, Tribulation and Testimony: The Bible in the Context of the Middle East," Peake Lecture, 2002.

13. Anton La Guardia, *Holy Land, Unholy War*, p. 157.

14. Marc Ellis, *Israel and Palestine: Out of the Ashes*, London: Pluto, 2002, pp. 12, 80–81.

15. Avi Shlaim, *The Iron Wall*, p. 18.

16. Meron Benvenisti, p. 77.

17. Meron Benvenisti, p. 217.

18. Amos Elon, p. 243.

19. Bernard Wasserstein, p. xiv.

20. Elias Chacour, "Empty Tomb and Risen Lord" in Naim Ateek, ed., *Jerusalem: What Makes for Peace!*, p. 15.

21. Kenneth Cragg, "The Will and the Dream" in Michael Prior, ed., *They Came and They Saw*, p. 253.

22. Kenneth Cragg, "The Excellences of Jerusalem" p. 15.

23. John Esposito, "Christian-Muslim Relations in Historic Perspective" in Naim Ateek, ed., *Jerusalem: What Makes for Peace!*, p. 34.

24. Menachem Klein, p. 3.

25. Michael Dumper, *The Politics of Sacred Space: The Old City of Jerusalem in the Middle East Conflict*, London: Lynne Rienner Publishers, 2002, p. 155.

26. Michael Dumper, pp. 150–51.

27. Lambeth Conference, July 1998, "Resolution on the Holy Land," v. 20.

28. Naim Ateek, "A Palestinian Theology of Jerusalem" in *Jerusalem: What Makes for Peace!*, pp. 100 and 104.

29. Kenneth Cragg, *This Year in Jerusalem*, p. 132.

30. Bernard Wasserstein, p. 240.

31. Avi Shlaim, *The Iron Wall*, p. 40.

32. Avi Shlaim, *War and Peace in the Middle East*, p. 131.

33. Roane Carey and Jonathan Shainin, *The Other Israel: Voices of Refusal and Dissent*, New York: The New Press, 2002, pp. 123–24.

34. Charles M. Sennott, pp. 417–18.

35. Richard Harries, p. 150.

36. Kenneth Cragg, *This Year in Jerusalem*, p. 28.

37. Benny Morris, p. 660.

38. Amos Elon, p. 250.

39. Charles M. Sennott, p. 430.

40. Rassem Khamaisi and Rami Nasrallah, eds, *The Jerusalem Urban Fabric: Demography, Infrastructure and Institutions*, Jerusalem: International Peace and Cooperation Center, 2003.

41. Amos Elon, p. 251.

42. Meron Benvenisti, pp. 168, 223–24.

43. Michael Dumper, p. 168.

44. David Grossman, "Where Death is a Way of Life," *Guardian Weekly*, 17–23 June 2001.

45. See David Fromkin, *A Peace to End All Peace: The Fall of the Ottoman Empire and the Creation of the Modern Middle East*; and Avi Shlaim, *War and Peace in the Middle East: A Concise History*.

46. Anton La Guardia, p. 337.

47. Avi Shlaim, *War and Peace in the Middle East*, pp. 3–4.

48. Avi Shlaim, pp. 116–17.

49. Avi Shlaim, pp. 122–23.

50. Avi Shlaim, p. 139.

51. Charles M. Sennott, p. 428.

52. Benny Morris, "On Ethnic Cleansing": Introduction and Interview by Ari Shavit, *New Left Review*, 26 March/April 2004, pp. 37–51.

53. Kenneth Cragg, "The Place of the Name: A Christian Perspective" in Ghada Karmi, ed., *Jerusalem Today: What Future for the Peace Process?*, p. 168.

54. Charles M. Sennott, p. 29.

Appendix

Significance of Jerusalem for Christians

Memorandum of the Patriarchs and Heads of the Christian Communities in Jerusalem 14 November 1994

1. Preamble

On Monday 14 November, 1994, the heads of Christian communities in Jerusalem meet in solemn conclave to discuss the status of the holy city and the situation of Christians there, at the conclusion of which they issued the following declaration:

2. Jerusalem, Holy City

Jerusalem is a city holy for the people of the three monotheistic religions: Judaism, Christianity and Islam. Its unique nature of sanctity endows it with a special vocation: calling for reconciliation and harmony among people, whether citizens, pilgrims or visitors. And because of its symbolic and emotive value, Jerusalem has been a rallying cry for different revived nationalistic and fundamentalist stirrings in the region and elsewhere. And, unfortunately, the city has become a source of conflict and disharmony. It is at the heart of the Israeli–Palestinian and Israeli–Arab disputes. While the mystical call of the city attracts believers, its present unenviable situation scandalises many.

3. The Peace Process

The current Arab–Israeli peace process is on its way towards resolution of the Middle East conflict. Some new facts have already been established, some concrete signs posted. But in the process Jerusalem has again been side-stepped, because its status, and especially sovereignty over the city, are the most difficult questions to resolve in future negotiations. Nevertheless, one must already begin to reflect on the questions and do whatever is necessary to be able to approach them in the most favourable conditions when the moment arrives.

4. Present Positions

When the different sides involved now speak of Jerusalem, they often assume exclusivist positions. Their claims are very divergent, indeed conflicting. The Israeli position is that Jerusalem should remain the unified and eternal capital of the State of Israel, under the absolute sovereignty of Israel alone. The Palestinians, on the other hand, insist that Jerusalem should become the capital of a future State of Palestine, although they do not lay claim to the entire modern city, but envisage only the Eastern, Arab part.

5. Lessons of History

Jerusalem has had a long, eventful history. It has known numerous wars and conquests, has been destroyed time and again, only to be reborn anew and rise from its ashes, like the mythical phoenix. Religious motivation has always gone hand in hand with political and cultural aspirations, and has often played a preponderant role. This motivation has often led to exclusivism or at least to the supremacy of one people over the others. But every exclusivity or every human supremacy is against the prophetic character of Jerusalem. Its universal vocation and appeal is to be a city of peace and harmony among all who dwell therein.

Jerusalem, like the entire Holy Land, has witnessed throughout its history the successive advent of numerous new peoples: they came from the desert, from the sea, from the north, from the east. Most often the newcomers were gradually integrated into the local population. This was a rather constant characteristic. But when the newcomers tried to claim exclusive possession of the city and the land, or refused to integrate themselves, then the others rejected them.

Indeed, the experience of history teaches us that in order for Jerusalem to be a city of peace, no longer lusted after from the outside and thus a bone of contention between warring sides, it cannot belong exclusively to one people or to only one religion. Jerusalem should be open to all, shared by all. Those who govern the city should make it "the capital of humankind." This universal vision of Jerusalem would help those who exercise power there to open it to others who also are fondly attached to it and to accept sharing it with them.

6. The Christian Vision of Jerusalem

Through the prayerful reading of the Bible, Christians recognise in faith that the long history of the people of God, with Jerusalem as its centre, is the history of salvation which fulfils God's design in and through Jesus of Nazareth, the Christ.

The one God has chosen Jerusalem to be the place where His name alone will dwell in the midst of His people so that they may offer to Him acceptable worship. The prophets look up to Jerusalem, especially after the purification of the exile: Jerusalem will be called "the city of justice, faithful city" (Isaiah 1:26–27) where the Lord dwells in holiness as in Sinai (cf. Psalm 68:18). The Lord will place the city in the middle of the nations (Ezekiel 5:5), where the Second Temple will become a house of prayer for all peoples (Isaiah 2:2, 56:6–7). Jerusalem, aglow with the presence of God (Isaiah 60:1), ought to be a city whose gates are always open (Isaiah 17).

In the vision of their faith, Christians believe the Jerusalem of the Prophets to be the foreseen place of the salvation in and through Jesus Christ. In the Gospels, Jerusalem rejects the Sent-One, the Saviour; and he weeps over it because this city of the prophets that is also the city of the essential salvific events—the death and resurrection of Jesus—has completely lost sight of the path to peace (cf. Luke 19:42).

In the Acts of the Apostles, Jerusalem is the place of the gift of the Spirit, of the birth of the Church (Acts 2), the community of the disciples of Jesus who are to be His witnesses not only in Jerusalem but even to the ends of the earth (Acts 1:8). In Jerusalem, the first Christian community incarnated the ecclesial ideal, and thus it remains a continuing reference point.

The book of Revelation proclaims the anticipation of the new, heavenly Jerusalem (Revelation 3:12; 21:2, cf. Galatians 4:26; Hebrews 12:22). This Holy City is the image of the new creation and the aspirations of all peoples, where God will wipe away all tears, and "there shall be no more death or mourning, crying out or pain, for the former world has passed away" (Revelation 21:4).

7. The earthly Jerusalem in the Christian tradition prefigures the heavenly Jerusalem as "the vision of peace." In the liturgy, the Church itself receives the name of Jerusalem and relives all of that city's anguish, joys and hopes. Furthermore, during the first centuries the liturgy of Jerusalem became the foundation of all liturgies everywhere, and later deeply influenced the development of diverse liturgical traditions, because of the many pilgrimages to Jerusalem and of the symbolic meaning of the Holy City.

8. The pilgrimages slowly developed an understanding of the need to unify the sanctification of space through celebrations at the Holy Places with the sanctification in time through the calendared celebrations of the holy events of salvation (Egeria, Cyril of Jerusalem). Jerusalem soon occupied a unique place in the heart of Christianity everywhere. A theology and spirituality of pilgrimage developed. It was an ascetic time of biblical refreshment at the sources, a time of testing during which Christians recalled that they are strangers and pilgrims on earth (cf. Hebrews 11:13), and that their personal and community vocation always and everywhere is to take up the cross and follow Jesus.

9. The Continuing Presence of a Christian Community

For Christianity, Jerusalem is the place of roots, ever living and nourishing. In Jerusalem is born every Christian. To be in Jerusalem is for every Christian to be at home.

For almost two thousand years, through so many hardships and the succession of so many powers, the local Church has been witnessing to the life and preaching, the death and resurrection of Jesus Christ upon the same Holy Places, and its faithful have been receiving other brothers and sisters in the faith, as pilgrims, resident or in transit, inviting them to be reimmersed into the refreshing, ever living ecclesiastical sources. That continuing presence of a living Christian community is inseparable from the historical sites. Through the "Living Stones," the holy archaeological sites take on "life."

10. The City as Holy and as Other Cities

The significance of Jerusalem for Christians thus has two inseparable fundamental dimensions:

1. a Holy City with Holy Places most precious to Christians because of their link with the history of salvation fulfilled in and through Jesus Christ;
2. a city with a community of Christians which has been living continually there since its origins.

Thus for the local Christians, as well as for local Jews and Muslims, Jerusalem is not only a Holy City, but also their native city where they live, whence their right to continue to live there freely, with all the rights which obtain from that.

11. Legitimate Demands of Christians for Jerusalem

In so far as Jerusalem is the quintessential Holy City, it above all ought to enjoy full freedom of access to its Holy Places, and freedom of worship. Those rights of property ownership, custody and worship which the different churches have acquired throughout history should continue to be retained by the same communities. These rights which are already protected in the *Status Quo* of the Holy Places according to historical *firmans* and other documents, should continue to be recognised and respected.

The Christians of the entire world, Western or Eastern, should have the right to come on pilgrimage to Jerusalem. They ought to be able to find there all that is necessary to carry out their pilgrimage in the spirit of their authentic tradition: freedom to visit and to move around, to pray at holy sites, to embark into spiritual attendance and respectful practice of their faith, to enjoy the possibility of a prolonged stay and the benefits of hospitality and dignified lodgings.

12. The local Christian communities should enjoy all those rights to enable them to continue their active presence in freedom and to fulfil their responsibilities towards both their own local members and towards the Christian pilgrims throughout the world.

Local Christians, not only in their capacity as Christians *per se*, but like all other citizens, religious or not, should enjoy the same fundamental rights for all: social, cultural, political and national. Among these rights are:

1. the human right of freedom of worship and of conscience, both as individuals and as religious communities,
2. civil and historical rights which allow them to carry out their religious, educational, medical and other duties of charity,
3. the right to have their own institutions, such as hospices for pilgrims, institutions for the study of the Bible and the traditions, centres for encounters with believers of other religions, monasteries, churches, cemeteries, and so forth, and the right to have their own personnel and run these institutions.

13. In claiming these rights for themselves, Christians recognise and respect similar and parallel rights of Jewish and Muslim believers and their communities. Christians declare themselves disposed to search with Jews and Muslims for a mutually respectful application of these rights and for a harmonious coexistence, in the perspective of the universal spiritual vocation of Jerusalem.

14. Special Statute for Jerusalem

All this presupposes a special judicial and political statute for Jerusalem which reflects the universal importance and significance of the city.

1. In order to satisfy the national aspirations of all its inhabitants, and in order that Jews, Christians and Muslims can be "at home" in Jerusalem and at peace with one another, representatives from the three monotheistic religions, in addition to local political powers, ought to be associated in the elaboration and application of such a special statute.

2. Because of the universal significance of Jerusalem, the international community ought to be engaged in the stability and permanence of this statute. Jerusalem is too precious to be dependent solely on municipal or national political authorities, whoever they may be. Experience shows that an international guarantee is necessary.

Experience shows that such local authorities, for political reasons or the claims of security, sometimes are required to violate the rights of free access to the Holy Places. Therefore it is necessary to accord Jerusalem a special statute which will allow Jerusalem not to be victimised by laws imposed as a result of hostilities or wars but to be an open city which transcends local, regional or world political troubles. This statute, established in common by local political and religious authorities, should also be guaranteed by the international community.

Conclusion

Jerusalem is a symbol and a promise of the presence of God, of fraternity and peace for humankind, in particular, the children of Abraham: Jews, Christians and Muslims. We call upon all parties concerned to comprehend and accept the nature and deep significance of Jerusalem, City of God. None can appropriate it in exclusivist ways. We invite each party to go beyond all exclusivist visions or actions, and without discrimination, to consider the religious and national aspirations of others, in order to give back to Jerusalem its true universal character and to make of the city a holy place of reconciliation for humankind.

H B Diodoros I—*Greek Orthodox Patriarch*
H G Archbishop David Sahagin for the *Armenian Patriarch*
H G Dr Anba Abraham—*Coptic Archbishop*
H G Abba Matheos—*Ethiopian Archbishop*
Archbishop Lutfi Laham—*Greek-Catholic Patriarchal Vicar*
Mgr. Augustine Harfouche—*Maronite Patriarchal Vicar*
H B Michel Sabbah—*Latin Patriarch*
Very Revd Fr Joseph Nazzaro—*Custos of the Holy Land*
H G Dionisius Jazzawi—*Syriac Archbishop*
H G Bishop Samir Kafity—*Anglican Bishop*
H G Bishop Naim Nassar—*Lutheran Bishop*
Mgr Pierre Abdel-Ahad—*Catholic Syriac Patriarchal Vicar*

Index

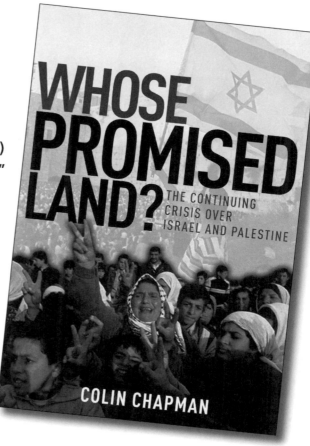